Staging Modern American Life

WHAT IS THEATRE?
Edited by Ann C. Hall

Given the changing nature of audiences, entertainment, and media, the role of theatre in twenty-first-century culture is changing. The **WHAT IS THEATRE?** series brings new and innovative work in literary, cultural, and dramatic criticism into conversation with established theatre texts and trends, in order to offer fresh interpretation and highlight new or undervalued artists, works, and trends.

ANN C. HALL has published widely in the area of theatre and film studies, is president of the Harold Pinter Society, and is an active member in the Modern Language Association. In addition to her book *A Kind of Alaska: Women in the Plays of O'Neill, Pinter, and Shepard*, she has edited a collection of essays, *Making the Stage: Essays on Theatre, Drama, and Performance* and a book on the various stage, film, print, and television versions of *Gaston Leroux's Phantom of the Opera*.

Published by Palgrave Macmillan:

Theatre, Communication, Critical Realism
   By Tobin Nellhaus

Staging Modern American Life: Popular Culture in the Experimental Theatre of Millay, Cummings, and Dos Passos
   By Thomas Fahy

Authoring Performance: The Director in Contemporary Theatre (forthcoming)
   By Avra Sidiropoulou

Staging Modern American Life

Popular Culture in the Experimental Theatre of Millay, Cummings, and Dos Passos

Thomas Fahy

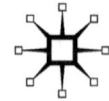

STAGING MODERN AMERICAN LIFE
Copyright © Thomas Fahy, 2011.
Softcover reprint of the hardcover 1st edition 2011 978-0-230-11595-8
All rights reserved.

First published in 2011 by
PALGRAVE MACMILLAN®
in the United States—a division of St. Martin's Press LLC,
175 Fifth Avenue, New York, NY 10010.

Where this book is distributed in the UK, Europe and the rest of the world, this is by Palgrave Macmillan, a division of Macmillan Publishers Limited, registered in England, company number 785998, of Houndmills, Basingstoke, Hampshire RG21 6XS.

Palgrave Macmillan is the global academic imprint of the above companies and has companies and representatives throughout the world.

Palgrave® and Macmillan® are registered trademarks in the United States, the United Kingdom, Europe and other countries.

ISBN 978-1-349-29709-2   ISBN 978-0-230-33959-0 (eBook)
DOI 10.1057/9780230339590

Library of Congress Cataloging-in-Publication Data

Fahy, Thomas Richard.
    Staging modern American life : popular culture in the experimental theatre of Millay, Cummings, and Dos Passos / Thomas Fahy.
       p. cm.—(What is theatre?)

    1. American drama—20th century—History and criticism.
2. Experimental drama, American—History and criticism. 3. Popular culture—United States—History—20th century. 4. Popular culture in literature. 5. Millay, Edna St. Vincent, 1892–1950—Dramatic works. 6. Cummings, E. E. (Edward Estlin), 1894–1962—Dramatic works. 7. Dos Passos, John, 1896–1970—Dramatic works. 8. Experimental theater—United States—History—20th century. I. Title.

PS351.F25 2011
812′.5209—dc22   2011010323

A catalogue record of the book is available from the British Library.

Design by Newgen Imaging Systems (P) Ltd., Chennai, India.

First edition: October 2011

For Tatyana

Contents

List of Figures ix

Acknowledgments xi

Introduction 1

1. "I Cannot *Live* without a Macaroon!": Food, Hunger, and the Dangers of Modern American Culture in Edna St. Vincent Millay's *Aria da Capo* and Other Plays 21

2. "Damn Everything But the Circus!": The Ambiguous Place of Popular Culture in E. E. Cummings' *Him* 53

3. Planes, Trains, and Automobiles: Technology and the Suburban Nightmare in the Plays of John Dos Passos 85

Conclusion 133

Notes 137

Bibliography 165

Index 175

Figures

1	Cast of Ziegfeld girls in "Midnight Frolic" (1918)	5
2	Edna St. Vincent Millay (1914)	29
3	Queens, New York in the 1920s. "Dezendorf's Delightful Dwellings"	94
4	Charles Lindbergh (1902–74) working on engine of "The Spirit of St. Louis" (1927)	123

Acknowledgments

I WANT TO THANK ANN C. HALL, SAMANTHA HASEY, and the team at Palgrave Macmillan for making this book a reality. It was a pleasure working with you every step of the way.

Over the years, I have been the beneficiary of the insightful feedback, immense generosity, unwavering support, and dear friendship of Kirstin Ringelberg, Susann Cokal, James MacDonald, and John Lutz. Thanks for the many hours you spent reading and commenting on this manuscript.

I am fortunate to have so many supportive and generous colleagues at Long Island University—including Jeanie Attie, Kay Sato, Deborah Lutz, James Bednarz, Marge Hallissy, Dennis Pahl, Katherine Hill-Miller, and the C. W. Post Campus Faculty Research Committee. I also want to express my appreciation to Michael Webster, whose E. E. Cummings expertise enhanced chapter 2, and to Meghan Finn for sharing her impressive 2008 production of *Him* with me. My thanks to *Modern Drama* (University of Toronto Press), *The Journal of American Culture* (Wiley-Blackwell), *Spring: The Journal of the E. E. Cummings Society* for permission to reprint some of the material included in this book.

Lastly, none of this work would be possible without the love and support of my family, especially my mother and father, Mike and Jen Fahy, who generously contributed to the cover design. I cannot thank Victoria Tsinberg enough for the countless hours she spent with Nicolai while I was writing this book. And Tatyana always finds ways to remind me of the truly important things in life. It is with love and gratitude that I dedicate this book to you.

Introduction

WHETHER ONE ENJOYED DINING AT UPSCALE RESTAURANTS ON FIFTH AVENUE, spending an evening in bohemian tearooms, watching films in a picture palace, or attending a show set on the Mississippi riverbank, popular culture in early twentieth-century New York offered economic and cultural fantasies that appealed to audiences of all social classes. Even though these groups desired (and had access to) different objects and experiences, popular culture tended to communicate similar messages. It celebrated materialism and upper-class living. It presented ethnic differences in terms of the exotic and the primitive. And it promoted escapist pleasure over social realism. As Slavoj Žižek has argued in *The Plague of Fantasies*, "[A] fantasy constitutes our desire, provides its co-ordinates; that is, it literally 'teaches us how to desire'" (7). Even when these economic fantasies inspired envy, for instance, they did so in the context of the American prosperity myth, which promised most people (particularly whites) access to greater wealth and a higher social status. Ultimately popular culture in the Teens and Twenties was teaching America to desire the same things.

In contrast, the Little Theater Movement began producing plays at this time that emphasized realism. These works tried to offer audiences greater insights into everyday life, not escapist fantasies. In some cases, these insights focused on the messages of mass culture itself. *Staging Modern American Life: Popular Culture in the Experimental Theatre of Millay, Cummings, and Dos Passos* examines the integration of and challenges to popular culture found in the theatrical works of these writers. Their plays, which have largely been marginalized in discussions of theatre history and literary scholarship, offer a hybrid theatre that integrates the popular with the formal, the mainstream with the experimental. As people who enjoyed mass entertainment, these writers appreciated its vitality and fun. They understood its widespread appeal because it spoke to them in similar ways. Nevertheless, they had reservations about its social influence. Edna St. Vincent Millay, E. E. Cummings, and John Dos Passos expressed these concerns through dramatic works that challenged the predominant fantasies surrounding gender, race, and class at the time. They hoped, in other words, that the presentation of fantasy in their hybrid theatre would both entertain and warn against the complacency, sociopolitical apathy, and materialism endorsed by popular culture.

Although each chapter of this book offers a detailed discussion of some aspect of popular culture in the early twentieth century, the first part of the introduction ("'Something for Everybody': Popular Entertainment in New York") gives an overview of the fantasies found in theatrical entertainment at the time. It is a snapshot of the kind of amusements that Millay, Cummings, and Dos Passos participated in and wanted to explore in their own writings for the theatre. The second part ("Popular Culture and Realism in the Little Theater Movement") discusses the Little Theater Movement with a particular emphasis on the Provincetown Players, which produced plays by Millay and Cummings. It also examines the ways this movement influenced American entertainment more broadly, highlighting the important relationship between popular and formal arts.

"Something for Everybody": Popular Entertainment in New York

Even the most cynical New Yorker must have marveled at the dizzying array of entertainment in the early twentieth century. Not long after the city renamed Longacre Square in honor of the *New York Times* in 1904 (the same year its first subway opened), "Times Square" became a hot spot for amusement culture. Upscale restaurants with cabaret-style entertainment were competing for customers by 1907, and within a few years, the first American cabaret theatre, the *Folies Bergère,* opened on Forty-Eighth Street and Broadway. Such venues as Rector's, Murray's Roman Gardens, Churchill's, and Bustanoby's (all located on Broadway between Thirty-Ninth and Forty-Ninth Streets)[1] provided live music, dancing, and liquor to customers who could interact with performers. This democratization of entertainment was a large part of its appeal—giving audiences intimate access to those onstage and each other. "In removing theatrical boundaries," Lewis A. Erenberg explains in *Steppin' Out: New York Nightlife and the Transformation of American Culture, 1890–1930,* "the cabaret modified the sacredness of the stage area and encouraged the audience to share it" (126). Singers, dancers, and musicians performed at eye level with patrons. Comedians moved among the crowd as part of the act, and the audience eagerly participated in the show by dancing with each other—trying out the latest steps of the Turkey Trot, Bunny Hug, Grizzly Bear, and Fox Trot.[2] The "dance craze" of 1912–16, fueled by public dance halls and ballrooms, appealed to young people seeking the excitement, fun, and romance of city nightlife. As the names of these dances and the nature of cabaret performances suggest, New York provided entertainment that eroded barriers between the formal and the intimate. It invited everyone to share in the city's glamour.

The revenue generated from alcohol—even in the age of Prohibition—also enabled club owners to invest in décor that enhanced the escapist fantasies of the experience. Patrons often found themselves transported to European villages, French chateaux, ancient Roman villas, bohemian tearooms, ocean liners, cowboy ranches, and pirates' dens. Nothing was too over-the-top for the Jazz Age. The main dining hall at Murray's Roman Gardens, for example, resembled the atrium and courtyard of a Roman villa. Colonnades ran along each side of the room. Trees, statues, and fountains surrounded the diners as well, and an ancient temple rose to the ceiling. This setting—with its large, open space and high ceilings—"suggested the lofty opulence and power of the diner. Diners at Murray's enjoyed the feeling that their success enabled them to be part of the best of all earlier civilizations" (Erenberg 45).

Though most speakeasies dispensed with such trappings, fantasy remained a significant part of the experience. The speakeasy,[3] a generic term for any place selling alcohol during Prohibition, typically provided a bare-bones space for men and women to drink, dance, flirt, and listen to jazz. By the mid 1920s, more than 5,000 speakeasies were operating in Manhattan, and another 10,000 could be found in Brooklyn.[4] These numbers are particularly striking given the skyrocketing cost of alcohol. The price of beer by the quart, for example, jumped 600 percent between 1916 and 1920, and a quart of gin went up 520 percent to $5.90 by 1928 (Kyvig 22). At a time when the average worker earned between two and five dollars a day, this cost was significant. Yet the expense, criminality, and dynamic (even dangerous) mixture of people contributed to the appeal of these places. As Michael A. Lerner suggests, "[T]he spectacular décor, the entertainment, and the exhilarating experience of breaking the law in a nightclub or cabaret attracted a mixture of people from all levels of society. Whether midtown clerks, Fifth Avenue socialites, Irish politicians, street toughs, plumbers, or housewives, patrons were transported by the sense of freedom and possibility brought about by dancing and drinking in an unregulated environment with unfamiliar people" (142). Speakeasies put the carefree spirit and excesses of the era within everyone's reach.

Chorus girls became another prominent feature of city entertainment and male fantasy in the early twentieth century. Sultry photographs of these women filled the pages of magazines, and newspapers dedicated columns to gossip about their romantic lives. Their popularity can largely be attributed to impresario Florenz Ziegfeld. His first *Follies* appeared in 1907, and he subsequently produced a new show every year for more than two decades[5] (figure 1). Despite the range of entertainers who appeared onstage during these productions, Ziegfeld's "girls" were the stars of the show. These young women, billed as the most beautiful in the world, danced in highly choreographed, mechanical routines—moving in long lines across the stage while kicking and gesturing in synchronized motion. Ziegfeld presented these slender, white women as both erotic and pure. Their whiteness contrasted the wild sexuality of cootch dancers (belly dancers) like "Little Egypt" and other exotic female performers who first dazzled audiences at the Chicago World's Columbian Exposition in 1893. By dressing his girls in lavish costumes and providing a backdrop that suggested Parisian sophistication,[6] Ziegfeld offered middle-class audiences an image of wholesome female sexuality. The Ziegfeld girl became the girl next door—an "active, modern [woman]," as Erenberg notes, "but not so active that she represented a threat to fragile male egos" (218–219). This erotic fantasy, in other words, helped maintain reassuring fantasies about male power at a time when women were rejecting the patriarchal mores of Victorianism.

Figure 1   Cast of Ziegfeld girls in "Midnight Frolic" (1918)
Source: Photograph by Alfred Cheney Johnston. Library of Congress.

Furthermore, the presence of these women at cabaret restaurants and upscale speakeasies enabled many men to see and flirt with them after the show. This intimate access collapsed the distance between the image onstage and real life.

The popularity of the *Follies* inspired many imitators, from Broadway shows to burlesque, that tried to capitalize on similar images of female sexuality. The Minksy brothers, for instance, frequently parodied Ziegfeld's productions at the National Winter Garden on the Lower East Side. In 1917, they built a runway into the auditorium of this burlesque theatre and introduced the "accidental" strip when one performer unbuttoned her bodice while leaving the stage. Over the next few years, as Rachel Shteir argues, Billy Minksy "took a page from cabaret and Broadway by encouraging the principals to step off the runway, sit in the audience, and flirtatiously applaud their colleagues" (101). These audiences, which were predominantly working- and lower-middle-class men, found this proximity exhilarating. It encouraged them to view the staged identity of these women as authentic, blurring the line between the fantastic and the real.

Vaudeville, on the other hand, offered a different kind of fantasy in the 1910s, toning down its signature vulgarity and ethnic humor to appeal to women and children.[7] These shows drew on existing forms of popular arts such as singing, dancing, minstrelsy, bawdy skits, acrobatics, animal acts, short plays, freak shows, female impersonation, strongman routines, and eventually short films, which were interspersed among live acts. As this variety suggests, vaudeville tried to include "something for everybody"—escapist entertainment for men, women, and children of all classes and ages. With ticket prices between ten and twenty-five cents, these theatres offered hours of amusement at affordable prices. Vaudeville's popularity also enabled many entrepreneurs to build luxurious theatres, which raised the shows' status and, as historian David Nasaw explains, helped patrons "forget that they were paying half of what it cost to attend the legitimate theater" (29). These elegant buildings allowed lower- and middle-class people to imagine themselves as part of the social elite for an evening. At times this was evidenced in the clientele. The celebrity status of many vaudeville stars attracted affluent audiences as well, making it rather common for them to attend a two-dollar Broadway show one night and vaudeville the next.

Soon after the introduction of moving pictures in 1895, this new entertainment captured the imagination of the public in its glamorous portrayal of upper-class life. "Nickelodeons" (a fabricated word combining the cost of admission with the Greek term for theatre) began appearing in storefronts nationwide in the early twentieth century. These venues, which seated between 200 and 500 people, primarily clustered in working-class areas because silent films were both affordable and accessible to immigrants. One didn't need to speak English to enjoy them. A typical fifteen- to twenty-minute program featured such spectacles as dancing, horse-drawn carriage rides, foreign lands, waves crashing against the shoreline, city life, speeding trains, and historical reenactments. Within a few years, movies shifted from a collection of random scenes to narrative, and the most popular genres were comedies with sexual innuendo, trick films using special effects like splicing, and movies based on dime novels and melodrama, such as *The Great Train Robbery* (1903).[8] Regardless of genre, most of these films "centered on men and women from upper-middle and wealthy classes: people who lived in a large spacious houses, kept servants, owned cars and earned their money from business, finance or the professions" (Sklar 89). These films not only made wealth—and the material goods it enabled one to have—desirous, but it also equated upper-class life with the glamorous lives onscreen.

Though some white, middle-class patrons attended moving pictures, too,[9] they did not embrace the cinema in large numbers until D. W. Griffith's epic fantasy *The Birth of a Nation* (1915). At two-and-a-half hours, this story of post–Civil War America presents the Ku Klux Klan as heroically saving the South from black rule and restoring white, Southern values to a fractured country. It was the longest film made at that point, and its reassuring racial fantasies—along with its grand scale, varied filming techniques, musical accompaniment, and frequent use of captions—resonated with educated white audiences. Specifically, the Klansmen, who came from families of privilege, were motivated by nostalgia for a time when white power was unchallenged. Thus through vigilantism, this film suggests that such a fantasy could be restored.

The Birth of a Nation also helped inspire the extravagance of the movie palace age. Longer features required larger venues and more projectors, which nickelodeons could not provide. Instead, many "picture palaces" with neoclassical facades, electrically lit marquees, chandeliers, and ornate interiors were designed to seat over a thousand people. Early architects for these structures believed that décor contributed to the escapist fantasies of film. Like Westerns, crime stories, melodramas, historical dramas, comedies, and love stories on the screen, movie auditoriums offered an affordable, elegant escape from everyday concerns. As Richard Butsch explains, "[T]he essence of the picture palace was luxury at moderate prices, more expensive than the nickelodeon or the neighborhood house but less than big-time vaudeville or legitimate drama theaters" (161).[10]

Cabaret, vaudeville, nickelodeons, picture palaces, and these other entertainments certainly contributed to the dazzling nightlife of New York, but it was Broadway theatre that made the city a mecca for entertainment culture. Even though talking pictures threatened the market for commercial theatre, the latter reached the zenith of its popularity in 1927—the same year the first "talkie," *The Jazz Singer* with Al Jolson, amazed audiences.[11] According to theatre historian Jack Poggi, an astonishing 263 new plays were produced on Broadway during the 1926–27 season, and 264 appeared the following year.[12] Most American plays in the nineteenth and early twentieth centuries relied heavily on the conventions of melodrama. These sentimental works typically presented human experience in polarized terms (such as good/evil, right/wrong, moral/immoral), made clear distinctions between heroes and villains, relied on predictable plot twists, and emphasized elaborate staging. Likewise, the actors in these productions tended to communicate emotion through exaggerated physical and verbal gestures. Many of these characteristics were still evident on the 1920s stage—both on Broadway and less-expensive theatres throughout the city. Two of the most popular genres at the time were domestic melodramas/dramas and comedies (including farce and sentimental comedy). These works, as Brenda Murphy explains, "[W]ere written in the mode of what is generally called bourgeois realism—they were representations of the middle class, concerned with middle-class problems, and reflected a middle-class view of the world... What distinguished [these domestic plays] was their focus on marriage, divorce, and family life" ("Plays and Playwrights," 318). Anne Nichols' domestic melodrama *Abie's Irish Rose* (1922) offers one example of this genre's popularity. It premiered at the Fulton Theatre on West 46th Street, and its unprecedented 2,327 performances spanned the next five-and-a-half years. This play about Jewish-Irish intermarriage begins with Abe "Abie" Levy's decision to introduce his new bride, Rosemary Murphy, to his father as "Rosie Murphyski." Rosie's father soon exposes the ruse, and the couple struggles to appease both sides of the family—getting married by a rabbi and then again by a Catholic priest, among other things.[13] Though critics panned the work, the popularity of the play, which was subsequently made into two films and a weekly radio program, suggests the appeal of and need for some of the comforting messages of popular entertainment. In this case, the farcical portrait of intermarriage dilutes the social complexities of this issue at a time when eugenics was convincing the majority of white Americans to preserve Anglo-Saxon purity at all costs.

Musical theatre and musical comedies also capitalized on the "exotic" appeal of cultural differences, particularly of African American life, in ways that tried to sidestep contemporary racial tensions. Because of jazz's association with black culture, speakeasies, improvisation, and sensuality (through syncopated rhythms), many people considered it a low art form responsible for corrupting the morals of young people.[14] White musicians, however, offered a more palatable version of jazz music (i.e., softer and smoother) for white audiences. With "Alexander's Ragtime Band" (1911), Irving Berlin became the first white man to incorporate ragtime and the syncopated rhythms of African American music into his songs. Although African American musician Will Marion Cook and poet Laurence Dunbar had introduced this musical style to Broadway years earlier,[15] it was Berlin's piece that influenced what young Americans wanted to hear and dance to, and his *Watch Your Step: The First All-Syncopated Musical* (1914) started a ragtime craze on Broadway. Jerome Kern's collaboration with Guy Bolton and P. G. Wodehouse, for example, incorporated similar African American musical elements in *Oh, Boy!* (1917) and *Oh, Lady! Lady!!* (1918), and in 1924, George and Ira Gershwin's *Lady, Be Good!* produced the first Broadway musical "to convey a kind of jazz style that was deemed safe enough for white audiences" (Riis 432). George Gershwin, who wanted to be taken seriously as both a classical and jazz composer, accomplished a similar feat a few months earlier with *Rhapsody in Blue,* which helped make jazz a respectable art form for white audiences.

Perhaps the most important musical of the era, though, was Jerome Kern and Oscar Hammerstein's *Show Boat* (1927), which had 570 performances in New York. The scope of the production epitomized the grandiosity of 1920s theatre—featuring a chorus of nearly one-hundred people, lavish sets, and a nuanced storyline with rich characterization. The almost three-and-a-half-hour show surprised audiences with its realistic portrait of alcoholism, miscegenation, passing, the disintegration of family, and race relations in the South. Spanning a forty-year period between the 1880s and 1920s, the music reflects these different time periods by including songs styled after operetta, show tunes, vaudeville numbers, African American spirituals, ragtime, and jazz.

Show Boat may have been the first musical (by a white composer) to depict African Americans seriously and sympathetically—as opposed to the caricatures popularized by minstrelsy—but it did so in the context of segregated and/or whites-only venues. From Lower East Side movie theatres to many Harlem vaudeville houses, American theatres of all types either excluded African Americans or relegated them to the balcony.[16] In Harlem, though, two distinct types of cabarets and nightclubs existed in the Teens and Twenties. As scholar Shane Vogel notes, the first type "staged spectacular productions of black performance primarily for white, middle-class audiences" (80) in a somewhat segregated environment. The Cotton Club, which opened in 1923, offered such a space for whites who wanted to "slum it" for the evening. The club quickly became a hot spot for the city's elite as well as bohemian artists who traveled uptown to experience these shows against the tidied up backdrop of a cotton plantation. The second type of theatre presented black performances for black audiences, offering more authentic examples of African American cultural identity.

Though the above constitutes only a sampling of commercial entertainments at the time, it highlights some of the principal trends and types of amusements that people were clamoring to see. New York's popular theatre scene, however, was not merely characterized by fantasy, spectacle, and grandeur. Small amateur theatre, starting in the East and West Villages and eventually making its way up to Broadway in the 1920s, also contributed to this kaleidoscope of entertainment offerings.[17] Unlike most of the entertainment found in the city, these intimate productions used the conventions of realism to challenge the artifice and fantasies of popular culture.

Popular Culture and Realism in the Little Theater Movement

Interestingly, the earliest examples of noncommercial theatre in America operated on the same scale as popular amusement. Working under the assumption that the public was eager to see and willing to pay for great art, a group of wealthy men formed the New York Theatre in 1909, spending $3 million to build a massive, state-of-the-art auditorium on Sixty-Second Street and Central Park West. They contracted the best actors, directors, and stage technicians of the day to be part of a repertory company. Lee Shubert, whose family was already beginning to reshape the theatre business, even served as business manager. Yet the exorbitant cost for maintaining such a facility forced the enterprise to close after two seasons. Nevertheless, the Little Theater Movement soon took hold in community, university, rural, settlement house, and municipal theatres all across the country. As Poggi explains, "The movement grew rapidly: from fifty groups in 1917, to three or four hundred by 1925, and to over a thousand by 1929" (107). The most successful and professional of these groups could be found in New York City.

Inspired by noncommercial theatre in Europe, England, Ireland, and the Soviet Union, many of these groups wanted to produce compelling, experimental drama for contemporary audiences. The most influential groups of the Little Theater Movement were the Neighborhood Players, the Washington Square Players, and the Provincetown Players. Alice and Irene Lewisohn founded the Neighborhood Players during their time as social workers on the Lower East Side. The sisters supervised a number of artistic activities that included a dramatic club. This club evolved into the Neighborhood Players and eventually garnered the attention of professional actors, directors, and technicians who assisted with production and training. By 1915, they opened a 300-seat playhouse on Grand Street and produced short plays by George Bernard Shaw, Anton Chekhov, John Galsworthy, and others. Between 1920 and 1927, when the theatre established a permanent professional company, they staged forty-three plays.

In Greenwich Village, the Liberal Club brought together neighborhood writers, painters, musicians, journalists, and activists in a space that fostered animated discussions about art, ideas, and politics—along with liberal doses of drinking, dancing, and romantic intrigue. In 1914, it staged a one-act play by member Floyd Dell, and this inspired several others, including Susan Glaspell, George Cram Cook, and Robert Edmond Jones, to form a theatre group called the Washington Square Players. They wanted to produce high-quality American and European plays that would help elevate theatre in the United States. Their first performance in 1915 was a critical success that attracted the attention of professional actors, but eventually a number of playwrights and actors left the Washington Square Players to form the Provincetown Players. The former group produced works until 1918, when financial concerns closed them down. The Theatre Guild (1919–39) emerged shortly thereafter, and as historian Mark Fearnow suggests, they can be considered a continuous organization.[18] Unlike the Provincetown Players, this group primarily produced non-American works. "Board members justified their choices by arguing that few American plays existed of the quality that the Guild required and that, moreover, the Guild's seasons of Strindberg, Tolstoy, Molnár, Shaw, Pirandello, Kaiser, Claudel, and Andreyev offered a kind of school for the degraded American authors whose only exposure had been to a crass commercial stage" (Fearnow 358). Its success enabled it to launch a theatre school, publish a magazine, produce plays that traveled around the country, and build a 900-seat theatre on Fifty-Second Street in 1924–25.

The Provincetown Players, which began informal productions in 1915, included writers, artists, actors, and social activists who lived in Greenwich Village for most of the year but vacationed in Provincetown, Massachusetts, during summers. The Players launched its first official series in the summer of 1916, featuring George Cram Cook and Susan Glaspell's *Suppressed Desires,* Eugene O'Neill's *Bound East for Cardiff,* and Susan Glaspell's *Trifles* among others. These works premiered in a small, refurbished building on a Provincetown wharf, and each play consciously rejected the theatrical conventions of the day. The amateur actors and simple sets offered, as Murphy states, "a realist aesthetic of directness and authenticity" that audiences recognized as quite original (*The Provincetown Players,* 11). The enthusiastic reception of these plays inspired the group to establish a theatre on Macdougal Street in Greenwich as well. In the fall of that year, they also articulated the artistic goals for the organization: "It is the primary object of the Provincetown Players to encourage the writing of American plays of real artistic, literary and dramatic—as opposed to Broadway—merit" (qtd. in Murphy, 12). The treatise goes on to define the group as a nonprofit theatre that encouraged the collective participation of its members. Everyone contributed to the acting, set design, costuming, and direction. Rehearsals also provided an opportunity for members to debate aesthetic, philosophical, and artistic issues.

The Players' staging of Eugene O'Neill's *The Emperor Jones* in 1920 irrevocably changed the group. Cook, who was president of the organization, crafted a highly professional production for the play, hiring the African American actor Charles Gilpin as the lead and spending over $500 for a set that included a plaster dome with a reflective surface. A few months earlier, O'Neill's *Beyond the Horizon* ran for 111 performances on Broadway and garnered the Pulitzer Prize, and not surprisingly Cook viewed *The Emperor Jones* as an opportunity to raise the profile of the Provincetown Players. In their subsequent season, for example, they focused on four-act plays (as opposed to the one-act works that had previously characterized the group) because this format suited Broadway. The group suddenly seemed eager for uptown theatrical success, but Cook could not have anticipated the full impact of *The Emperor Jones's* success. As Poggi recounts, "The next morning the box-office treasurer was greeted with an unprecedented sight of people lined up on Macdougal Street waiting to buy tickets. Over a thousand new members subscribed in the first week" (113). The play then ran for 200 performances on Broadway. Its popularity can be understood, in part, as a response to O'Neill's recent success as a playwright, Charles Gilpin's electrifying performance, and the staging effects produced by the dome.

Overnight, the Provincetown Players shed its status as a small, inconspicuous theatre group for something much bigger. Tensions immediately emerged over the artistic direction of the group. Should they move away from their origins as amateur art theatre and professionalize? Should they define success by Broadway runs? *The Emperor Jones* gave them little choice in the matter. By the time they produced O'Neill's *The Hairy Ape* in 1922, he and Cook fervently disagreed over its direction, the technical aspects of the production, and the broader political control of the Players. An infuriated Cook decided to suspend the organization's activities for the 1922–23 season, and it officially disbanded in 1923. The history of the Provincetown Players did not end there, however. The group went through a number of incarnations for the rest of the decade, and it would continue to be defined by a struggle between amateur and professional productions.[19]

The Provincetown Players and other prominent little theatre groups not only began drawing bigger audiences in their own right, but they also influenced Broadway. As Poggi explains,

> Many productions of the Provincetown, the Actors' Theatre, and especially the Guild were successful in uptown runs. Moreover, the noncommercial theater contributed some of its best directors, designers, and actors to Broadway. Finally, the best American writers, whether or not they started in the noncommercial theater, wrote either for the commercial theater or for the near-commercial Guild once they had become established. Broadway was so successful in adopting their plays and techniques that many noncommercial groups found little reason for existence. (147–148)

Poggi's assertion points to a larger truth about entertainment culture in New York at the time. All aspects of the theatre—from the Provincetown Playhouse to the Cotton Club—influenced and shaped each other, highlighting a complex and often contradictory exchange among the arts. As many scholars have noted, popular culture is not shaped from the top down.[20] It involves a web of influences that includes contributions from every social, economic, and ethnic group. From the seamstress on the Lower East Side to the debutante on Forty-Second Street, New Yorkers experienced many of the same entertainments, albeit in very different spaces. Just as successful Broadway shows were subsequently produced for the working class a season or two later in "ten-twenty-thirties" (a name referring to the ticket prices for these stock theatre companies[21]), modern experimental playwrights, along with the directors and producers who gravitated toward the Greenwich Village theatre scene, influenced the kind of work that appeared on Broadway.

These types of exchanges fascinated and appealed to Millay, Cummings, and Dos Passos—all of whom enjoyed popular entertainments and participated in the Little Theater Movement. The lives of these artists intersected in a variety of ways as well. E. E. Cummings and John Dos Passos became friends during their undergraduate years at Harvard University. They wrote poetry, joined the school's Poetry Society, which met regularly to discuss current work in the field, including Millay's verse in *Poetry* magazine, and even went to burlesque shows together. Millay and Dos Passos were arrested in front of the Boston State House while protesting the impending execution of Sacco and Vanzetti in 1927, and they sat next to each other in the paddy wagon. (Her husband, Eugene Boissevain, bailed them out the same afternoon.) Like so many modernists, Millay, Cummings, and Dos Passos were also "high lowbrows"—a phrase that Charlie Chaplin used to describe his own desire to achieve "mass acceptance and elite adulation in a single stroke" (Douglas 70). They wanted to transcend the highbrow/lowbrow divide for similar reasons. Millay and Cummings wrote poetry about conventional themes and used time-honored forms like the sonnet to appeal to readers. Dos Passos' sympathies for the working class shaped his belief that art could resonate with the masses and bring about social change. The integration of popular culture in their works, therefore, provided another way for them to speak to the widest possible audience, to comment on modern American life, and to incorporate the vitality of these entertainments into so-called high art. As Dos Passos remarked in his introduction to *Three Plays,* these popular arts may be "cheap...and tinselly, where all that glitters is gold, but [they tend] to mirror very directly every whim and change in the popular mind. This makes [them] socially more valuable than the legitimate stage, as well as infinitely less shallow" (xix). All of these playwrights tried to use popular culture to give their dramatic works a similar social value.

For a time, all of them lived in Greenwich Village, and they were greatly influenced by the city's diverse entertainment culture—from the avant-garde art and radical politics of the Village to Harlem nightclubs. They read *The Masses,* a socialist magazine, and lived alongside blue-collar immigrants as well as bohemians with family money. They attended street performances in the East Village, amateur plays at the Provincetown Playhouse, modernist art shows, vaudeville, the *Follies,* opera, and film. They sampled restaurants throughout the city and enjoyed cabaret-style entertainment at places like Roumanian Hall, one of Cummings' favorite hangouts. They found roller coasters, freaks, animal acts, acrobats, and the general atmosphere of amusement parks like Coney Island thrilling. They listened to jazz and Stravinsky—Dos Passos even helped to build the set for the premiere of *Les Noces* in Paris.

They didn't partake in all of these amusements equally, of course. It would be difficult to imagine Millay sitting alongside Cummings at his favorite burlesque theatre, for instance, but these writers did transform their passion for amusement culture, which reflected the popular tastes of the period, into powerful works for the stage. Millay, Cummings, and Dos Passos viewed the theatre as a fertile space for commenting on popular culture—a space that audiences typically associated with lighthearted entertainment, not critical engagement. They hoped that fusing popular trends with innovative drama would create a vital art form that revealed powerful truths about everyday life in America. Millay's *Aria da Capo* (1919) satirizes elite restaurant culture and Bohemia during World War I, for example, to expose both as encouraging escapism over sociopolitical engagement. Cummings' *Him* (1927) incorporates elements of vaudeville, burlesque, minstrelsy, and freak shows, in part, to raise concerns about entertainment that objectifies the body—particularly women and African Americans. The protagonist's desire to create art is impeded in large part by the messages he has internalized from popular culture. Dos Passos presents characters enamored with the suburban dream of home ownership and the technology of transportation. In *The Garbage Man* (1923), *Airways, Inc.* (1928), and *Fortune Heights* (1933), his characters view both homes and cars as important symbols of social success, but they don't question the materialist culture that drives people into debt and self-destructive behaviors.

These plays also reflected and contributed to the various innovations of modernist drama at the time. Since the early twentieth century, modernism has often been understood as antithetical to and hostile toward "low" culture, and the ensuing debates about this characterization continue to shape our understanding of this movement. Andreas Huyssen has famously remarked that "modernism constituted itself through a conscious strategy of exclusion, an anxiety of contamination by its other: an increasingly consuming and engulfing mass culture" (vii). He goes on to note the dogged persistence of this dichotomy despite the fact that it was "always challenged as soon as it arose."[22] The dramatic works of Millay, Cummings, and Dos Passos, while trying to transcend this debate, also reveal profound anxieties about mass culture. As with other modernist techniques invested in breaking apart traditional forms, such as cinematic montage, stream of consciousness, and overlapping harmonies in jazz and atonal music, these writers wanted to erode the boundary between stage and audience. The actors in Millay's two interweaving stories, for instance, continually step out of character either to question the script or to receive a prompt. Cummings and Dos Passos include similar anti-theatrical moments in *Him* and *The Garbage Man*. Cummings has the stage rotate four times throughout the play to give the audience different perspectives on the action, and Me, the central female character, explicitly points out the artifice of theatre itself: "[The audience] is pretending that this room and you and I are real" (139). Likewise, the jazz musicians in Dos Passos' drama run down the aisle to take their seats on stage, and his central protagonist jumps off the stage in the final moments.

Inspired by the works of Eugene O'Neill and John Howard Lawson, Cummings and Dos Passos also experimented with expressionism as a way to dramatize the unconscious. As Julia A. Walker has argued, American expressionism, which is significantly different from the German movement, is "a complicated artistic response to the forces of modernization. For, giving shape to these experimental plays was the vague but intensely felt anxiety that new communication technologies would displace the human artist from the act of making meaning, mechanically reproducing bodies (e.g., in film), voice (e.g., in phonograph recordings), and words (e.g., the typewriter)" (2).[23] I would add that these techniques in Cummings and Dos Passos—as well as the elements of Millay's work that prefigure absurdist drama—reflect anxieties both about technology and the ability of "highbrow" artists to create meaningful work in an age dominated by popular culture. Technology embodied in trains, cars, and planes literally destroys bodies in Dos Passos' plays, but part of its destructive power comes from the social value attributed to material possessions in America. Cummings' and Millay's plays present characters who destroy each other (physically and emotionally), and they turn to the escapist pleasures of popular culture to avoid thinking about their own greed, selfishness, and personal biases. Ultimately, these playwrights seem to fear that the comforts and pleasures of mass culture may already be too enticing to the public for either high drama or hybrid drama (combining the popular with the experimental) to challenge in meaningful ways.

Overview

The first chapter of *Staging Modern American Life* examines the role of food and popular culture in Millay's dramatic works with a particular emphasis on *Aria da Capo*. Most theatregoers in 1919 would have recognized the dual significance of the banquet in this play—as a reference to both the war effort and elite popular culture. Two years earlier, the Food Administration had launched an aggressive publicity and volunteer campaign for food conservation. Recent crop shortages in the United States threatened efforts to support the Allies, and the government hoped a campaign of food conservation and healthy substitution would prevent rationing. The decadent food being eaten in the opening scene raises questions about the effectiveness of these efforts and the propaganda used to achieve them. At the same time, this banquet offers a parody of the growing entertainment and restaurant culture in New York City. By 1913, New York was the restaurant capital of the United States. Lobster palaces and other ostentatious dining establishments were hot spots for prosperous urbanites and the uptown theatre crowd—people seeking an escape from everyday life to indulge in material pleasures and the illusions of extreme wealth. The meanings associated with food here reinforce Millay's broader message about some of the dangerous excesses of American culture—a culture that often valorizes escapism over social and political engagement and encourages audiences to forget history rather than to contemplate its consequences. Just as this play condemns the brutality of war and the coercive power of nationalistic propaganda, it warns that the escapist pleasures of entertainment and modernist art can be socially irresponsible as well. They can, as the title of the play suggests, lead people and nations into thoughtless repetition, into committing the same atrocities over and over again.

Cummings offers a similar message about popular culture in America, and chapter 2 focuses on his desire to integrate the vitality of this entertainment, as exemplified by the circus and burlesque, into formal theatre. His passion for these arts has led most critics to overlook his ambivalence about them, and in many respects, *Him* expresses Cummings' struggles to create a hybrid drama that embraces high and low culture. Some of his concern stems from the tendency of sideshows to objectify and eroticize the people on display. At its worst, popular culture reduces people—such as women and African Americans—to caricatures. It reinforces explicit or tacit prejudices on the part of audiences, instead of offering images that might encourage people to question such biases. As Him and Me's failed relationship suggests, its emphasis on the body creates real barriers between men and women that can prevent intimacy and mutual understanding. The shift in the play from circus imagery to that of the freak show (along with the ambivalent portrait of each) captures Cummings' concerns about the limitations of using popular modes in formal art. Ultimately, *Him* suggests that the artist needs to capture the vitality of popular culture in ways that demand critical thought and engagement. Art needs to invite intellectual assessment, or it risks encouraging audiences to accept spectacle as truth.

At first glance, the third chapter may not seem as clearly related to the discussions of Millay and Cummings, but "Planes, Trains, and Automobiles: Technology and the Suburban Nightmare in the Plays of John Dos Passos" argues that the technology of transportation (which brought popular amusements within reach to an increasing number of Americans)[24] and the suburban home were active parts of popular culture as well. Certainly, Dos Passos' characters listen to jazz, talk about movies, attend Broadway shows, drink, and dine at cabarets, but his plays focus on the destructive impact of suburbanization in the United States. As part of his desire to debunk the American prosperity myth, he often presented suburbia—particularly the dream of owning a home outside the city—as a corrosive force on the individual. Just as buying a new car symbolized a person's social status in the early twentieth century, so did owning a home. By the 1920s, segregated suburban communities existed for all classes and ethnic groups in the United States, and Dos Passos viewed these developments as a microcosm for the socioeconomic hierarchies that were dividing people. His portrait of the suburbs also includes a critique of the technologies enabling this growth at the time, particularly the modes of transportation that many believed would expand the possibilities of suburban development even further. For Dos Passos, the setting of the suburbs provided another way to integrate high and low culture into the theatre, to expose the dangerous racial, class, and gender hierarchies of suburbanization, and to challenge the underlying myths of home ownership.

The emphasis on popular culture in *Staging Modern American Life* is an attempt to offer new readings of these works with an eye to American cultural studies, highlighting Millay's, Cummings', and Dos Passos' insightful examination of mass entertainment and the tensions surrounding it at the time. This book also argues that these works play an important role in the development of American theatre. In many respects, these plays have been marginalized in critical discussions of theatrical history because Millay, Cummings, and Dos Passos are predominantly associated with other literary genres. Scholars, teachers, and students typically approach Millay and Cummings as poets, and the academy discusses Dos Passos as a novelist—even though his books are rarely taught. Admittedly, when compared with their work in these other genres, playwriting constitutes a fraction of their output, but these categorizations continue to limit both our understanding of their art and the development of American theatre. Recent scholarship has begun to correct this lapse. Marc Robinson's sweeping survey of American theatre, *The American Play: 1787–2000* dedicates several pages to *Him*, presenting it as one of the most important interwar plays, and Sarah Bay-Cheng and Barbara Cole's *Poets at Play: An Anthology of Modernist Drama* reprints Millay's *Aria da Capo* and act III of Cummings' *Him*. It is my hope that this book will contribute to the renewed critical interest in such works by giving drama a more central place in discussions of these writers and inviting further examinations of the intersection between popular and experimental theatre.

CHAPTER 1

"I CANNOT *LIVE* WITHOUT A MACAROON!": FOOD, HUNGER, AND THE DANGERS OF MODERN AMERICAN CULTURE IN EDNA ST. VINCENT MILLAY'S *ARIA DA CAPO* AND OTHER PLAYS[1]

EDNA ST. VINCENT MILLAY SEEMED TO HAVE AN INSATIABLE APPETITE FOR WRITING AND PERFORMANCE. From the first pages of her earliest diary in 1907, she described amateur theatrical productions, concerts, and staged readings, all of which were an integral part of her family life. As biographer Nancy Milford explains, Millay "began to perform at the same age she began to write, and her early involvement was prompted and sustained by her mother's passionate interest" (9). These dual interests intensified throughout her life, and in the years leading up to her most important play, *Aria da Capo,* she zealously pursued both—performing theatre and music in high school, editing the school paper, acting the lead in Vassar's sophomore party play, receiving the 1916 intercollegiate prize for her poem "The Suicide," writing plays for a university drama course, and publishing her first book, *Renascence and Other Poems* (1917).

Aria da Capo stands out among these early works not merely for its modernist sensibility but also for the way it satirizes the excesses of both avant-garde and popular culture in its critique of war. Specifically, the play presents two overlapping dramas about escapism and violence. The first features two characters from commedia dell'arte, Pierrot and Columbine, who are feasting on a banquet of exotic foods and musing on romantic clichés. These two lovers lampoon various aspects of modernist culture, including cubism, atonal music, socialist philosophy, and the Provincetown Players. The second drama, a pastoral dialogue between two shepherds from book VII of Virgil's *Eclogues*, interrupts their seemingly frivolous repartee. This disruption blurs the line between theatricality and reality for the audience. As Cothurnus, the "Masque of the Tragedy" and director, stops the scene to usher in the shepherds, Pierrot steps out of character in exasperation: "Wadda you think this is,—a dress-rehearsal?" (12). This new drama quickly places these Virgilian shepherds in a two-man war. First they build a wall of crepe paper; then each claims exclusive ownership of the land and resources on his side of the wall. Greed and suspicion soon lead to murderous violence. After the two shepherds kill each other, Cothurnus closes his promptbook with a loud bang, places the banquet table from the commedia dell'arte scene over the dead bodies, and calls Pierrot and Columbine back on stage. At the sight of the bodies, Pierrot protests, saying that the audiences will be outraged by these deaths, but Cothurnus persuades him to continue: "[P]lay the farce. The audience will forget" (35). Pierrot and Columbine begin their scene again, and the curtain slowly falls.

In 1919 Millay considered *Aria da Capo* "a peach,—one of the best things I've ever done" (qtd. in Milford 178), and perhaps this isn't surprising. It was the theatre, after all, that brought her into the bohemian scene of Greenwich Village. After meeting Charles Ellis in 1917, who had recently begun designing and painting sets for the Provincetown Players, Millay auditioned for a role in Floyd Dell's play *The Angel Intrudes,* and she soon became part of the troupe. Her work with the Players, which included Susan Glaspell, Eugene O'Neill, and John Reed, as well as her involvement with Dell, Max Eastman, John Sloan, and some of the other people associated with the socialist magazine *The Masses,* shaped her artistic sensibility in ways that would be evident throughout her career. She may not have been an activist like her lover Dell, but life in Greenwich Village exposed her to a new world of political engagement through art. It inspired her to incorporate a greater degree of social consciousness into her writing. Village activism, as embodied by the editorials and visual art of *The Masses*, preached revolutionary politics, condemning U.S. involvement in World War I, contemporary working conditions, capitalism, the power of the press, the inferior position of women in society, and, as John Reed explained, "[T]he whole weight of outworn thought that dead men have saddled upon us" (qtd. in Maik 21). Villagers smoked, drank, engaged in premarital sex, experimented with sexuality, and philosophized about art and politics. Women bobbed their hair and refused to wear corsets. Men wore corduroy and flannel shirts. Some Villagers claimed to have little interest in money and material success, although many of them relied on family support to live this bohemian lifestyle. Other Villagers seemed rather sanguine about renting poorly heated, shabby apartments, and some even painted their walls scandalous colors like orange and black.[2] Millay, who bobbed her hair, kept up with the most current dances, and learned to drive in 1920, was no exception to this.[3] In fact, many considered her to be the embodiment of the flapper generation, and some of her poetry ("My candle burns at both ends") seemed to give voice to the New Woman. As Anne Cheney observes in *Millay in Greenwich Village*, "[I]n the Pre-Twenties, Millay became the living symbol of the freedom and hedonism of the Village" (37).

Millay's relationship to mainstream American culture, however, tempered the influence of Greenwich Village on her work. Just as the young writer defied convention, she also participated in some of the same outlets for entertainment as corseted women and "uptown men who wore suits with vests and high starched collars" (Milford 162). Dance halls, restaurants, cabarets, vaudeville, speakeasies, automobiles, amusement parks, sports, theatre, film, and concerts were staples of everyday life in America between 1910 and 1930, and Millay enjoyed many of these. As a result, she tried as an artist to navigate both worlds, and *Aria da Capo* expresses, in part, her own ambivalence about participating in avant-garde and mainstream popular culture. She found certain aspects of modernist art, like the cubist and futurist works of the Armory Show, for example, offensive in their "eccentricities" and "willful defiance of tradition" (qtd. in Cheney 32); yet she contributed to the innovations of the Provincetown Players.[4] Millay recognized the ways in which entertainment culture encouraged audiences to forget and thus indirectly support the war and other hardships; yet she couldn't condemn this culture entirely. The difficulty for Millay stemmed from her desire to reach the widest possible audience with her work—from fellow bohemians to the crowds that attended cabarets and dined at elite restaurants uptown. This desire required Millay to craft an accessible modernist art. As Suzanne Clark demonstrates in her analysis of sentimentalism in Millay's poetry, "[H]er poetics were always founded on commonality. She may shock her audience, but she does not separate herself from them…The gestures of social revolt don't always sever ties" (69). The same could be said of Millay's dramatic fable, *Aria da Capo,* in that its incisive sociopolitical satire is directed at both the audience and herself.

Millay tries to strike a balance between her aesthetic sensibility and newfound political consciousness, in part, through her presentation of food in the play. Throughout her career, Millay used food as a powerful image for issues that were important to her. From the social and sexual freedom of women to the need for political engagement, Millay's art often captures her own sociopolitical concerns while challenging readers to question their own attitudes and behaviors. As mentioned earlier, while she certainly sympathized with America's attraction to entertainment, she also recognized that it tacitly encouraged apathy. The rise of leisure culture represented the country's prosperity, and everyone wanted to partake of this. With shorter workweeks and a greater degree of disposable income, Americans in the early twentieth century sought out new and exciting forms of amusement—amusement that often tapped into widely held fantasies about class mobility. Just as Pierrot and Columbine dine on elegant foods and discuss highbrow art in *Aria da Capo,* many American consumers (of all classes) indulged in the idea of having more. Some frequented the Waldorf Hotel for dinner. Others went to "picture palaces" (which often featured films about upper- and upper-middle-class life), bought etiquette manuals to learn more about dining rituals, and dressed in high-class fashions. Millay understood these impulses. As someone who came from a relatively poor family and who struggled financially as a young artist, she valued money and the comforts it offered. Just as these popular entertainments had become central to daily life in the Teens and Twenties, her art, she believed, could be part of mainstream American culture as well. The role of food in her work, along with her use of traditional poetic forms like the sonnet, captures this belief. Food forges community. As E. N. Anderson explains in *Everyone Eats: Understanding Food and Culture,* "[O]ne main message of food, everywhere, is *solidarity.* Eating together means sharing and participating... We evolved as food sharers and feel a natural link between sharing food and being personally close and involved" (125). Millay sought this kind of solidarity by crafting accessible works.

Most theatregoers in 1919 would have recognized the dual significance of the banquet in her play—as a reference to both the war effort and elite popular culture. Two years earlier, the Food Administration had launched an aggressive publicity and volunteer campaign for food conservation. The decadent food being eaten in the opening scene of *Aria da Capo,* however, raises questions about the effectiveness of these efforts and the propaganda used to achieve them. At the same time, this banquet offers a parody of the growing entertainment and restaurant culture in New York City. By 1913, New York was the restaurant capital of the United States. Lobster palaces and other ostentatious dining establishments were hot spots for prosperous urbanites and the uptown theatre crowd—people seeking to escape from everyday life and indulge in material pleasures and the illusions of extreme wealth. The meanings associated with food here reinforce Millay's message about some of the dangerous excesses of American culture more broadly—a culture that often valorizes escapism over social and political engagement and encourages audiences to forget history rather than to contemplate its consequences. Just as this play condemns the brutality of war and the coercive power of nationalistic propaganda, it warns that the escapist pleasures of entertainment and modernist art can be socially irresponsible as well. They can, as the title of the play suggests, lead people and nations into thoughtless repetition, into committing the same atrocities over and over again.

WINNING THE WAR ONE MEAL AT A TIME

It might be fair to say that food was on the minds of most Americans when Edna Millay first entered the Greenwich Village scene in 1917. The farmlands of Europe had been devastated by the first few years of World War I, and recent crop failures in the United States contributed to a global food shortage, threatening the Allies' efforts abroad. At home, these shortages caused food prices to soar. They jumped a staggering 19 percent in 1916 (Levenstein 109), and in February of the following year, just a few months before Millay graduated from college and moved back to the city, there were food riots in several cities including New York. According to Harvey A. Levenstein in *Revolution at the Table: The Transformation of the American Diet*, "[T]he New York rioters attacked food shops and burned pedlars' pushcarts in the lower East Side and in the Brownsville and Williamsburg sections of Brooklyn. Demonstrators marched on the Waldorf Hotel in an attempt to confront the governor. A delegation of protesters accosted the mayor in his office, demanding the seizure of all stored foods and the establishment of municipal food shops and markets" (109–110). Not only was food a crucial tool for the war effort (both to sustain Allied and American troops and to weaken the enemy by cutting off their access to foodstuffs[5]), but it could also ignite violence and panic at home. To prevent more riots, shortages, hoarding, and inflation, President Woodrow Wilson put forth legislation to create the Food Administration, and in May 1917, he appointed Herbert Hoover to run it (Levenstein 137–138).

Broadly speaking, the Food Administration was designed to galvanize American support for the war by asking people to make sacrifices through food conservation and healthy substitution. It persuaded the public to use flour, sugar, and butter more sparingly, which Millay would reference in a satirical piece for *Vanity Fair* in 1923 (discussed later). It encouraged "meatless Mondays" and "wheatless Wednesdays." And it supplied households with menus and information about nutrition to convince people to change their diets: "If Americans could be taught about the interchangeability of proteins, fats, and carbohydrates... [and] if they could learn to fill their bellies on fruits and vegetables too perishable to send to Europe," Levenstein explains, "then soldiers and civilians overseas could be supplied, pressures on domestic prices could be eased, and there would be no need for rationing" (138). This message also marked the first widespread attempt on the part of the U.S. government to educate the public about nutrition.

The Food Administration recognized, however, that explaining the health benefits of a nutritious diet wouldn't be enough to motivate the conservation efforts necessary to avoid rationing; instead it appealed to people primarily in terms of patriotism. Borrowing many of its publicity strategies from the advertising industry, the Food Administration insisted that eating differently (and less) was part of one's patriotic duty, and it confronted Americans with daily reminders of this responsibility. Newspapers and magazines published "canned" articles (propaganda masquerading as news) so frequently that some were perceived as government publications.[6] Companies such as Wesson Oil and Armour's Foods incorporated slogans like "Help Save the Nation by Helping the Nation Save" into their advertising campaigns. Libraries received newsletters with guidelines for disseminating information about the war effort, and Herbert Hoover even "wrote directly to clergymen, urging them to preach on the subject of food conservation" (Capozzola 98). There was a tendency in all of these propaganda efforts to use slogans to motivate behavior, and Millay satirizes this tactic in "'Say Shibboleth': a Dialogue between a Sentimental Citizen and An Advertising Expert." This essay ran in the April 1923 issue of *Vanity Fair* while Millay was writing regular articles for the magazine under both her real name and her pseudonym Nancy Boyd, and it echoes one of the underlying concerns of *Aria da Capo*—the ease with which Americans can be manipulated into inaction or thoughtless action by advertising. From buying household goods to supporting a war, the advertising industry has a power, according to Millay's essay, that the public needs to assess critically, not accept without question. Specifically, her advertising expert's remarks: "Now the only way to get the public to think is to tell it what to think. The public does scrupulously as it is told to do...FOOD WILL WIN THE WAR. Of course; it has won every war. Whether it was important to win the war one did not consider. One simply left off eating sugar" (40). Food conservation, the advertising expert implies, functioned as a form of misdirection. It focused the public's attention on actions like avoiding sugar, in part, to discourage people from asking broader questions about the war itself. Millay's concerns about government propaganda in "Say Shibboleth" suggest that, at the time of her work on *Aria da Capo,* she was aware of and interested in the sociopolitical meanings associated with food during the war.

Given the propaganda efforts of the Food Administration and the changing attitudes about body size in America at the time,[7] it seems fitting that Millay would explore food and bodies in her writing. Highly conscious of the ways in which her appearance could promote her career, she often capitalized on the visual spectacle of her body. Her bright red hair, shiny green eyes, delicate facial features, and slender body captivated others, as did her reputation for being sexually free (figure 2).

She also realized that her image, such as the photograph that appeared alongside her poetry in the November 1920 issue of *Vanity Fair*, helped make her a celebrity. Photographs of female dancers, Broadway actresses, vaudeville performers, and beautiful revue stars filled the magazine in the 1920s, and this context encouraged readers to view Millay in similarly sensational and erotic terms. Specifically, this picture catches Millay as she looks away from the camera with a wistful expression. The light falls on her bare neck and shoulder, and the slightly unfocused image gives her an ethereal quality that resonates with some of the poetry printed next to it:

> What lips my lips have kissed, and where, and why,
> I have forgotten, and what arms have lain
> Under my head till morning; but the rain
> Is full of ghosts tonight, that tap and sigh
> Upon the glass and listen for reply. (49)

This kind of verse about forgotten lovers and sexual passion, along with her reputation as a bohemian poet, only fueled widely held assumptions about the autobiographical nature of her writing. Her visible body was now becoming part of that appeal as well. As an actor, Millay also recognized the power of bodily performance. "Her poetry readings," as Cheryl Walker has noted, "were like dances of the seven veils, and though [Millay] grumbled about feeling like a prostitute ('If I ever felt like a prostitute it was last night,' she wrote in one letter about a reading), she was eager to exploit the power of advertising and visual solicitation for projects she approved of" (89). Her awareness of the social and artistic importance of bodies is also expressed in many of her works through speakers who are driven by bodily urges, such as eating and sex.

Figure 2 Edna St. Vincent Millay (1914)
Source: Photograph by Arnold Genthe (Library of Congress).

This aspect of Millay's writing situates her work in a time-honored literary tradition of presenting food and hunger as metaphors for sexual desire, but in the context of the early twentieth century, Millay makes this link specifically to celebrate free love and to reject social conventions that restrict women. In "Feast," for example, a poem from her Pulitzer Prize–winning collection *The Harp-Weaver and Other Poems* (1923), she presents hunger and thirst as ideal conditions: "I came upon no wine/ So wonderful as thirst... I came upon no fruit/ So wonderful as want." Desire is preferable to satisfying one's hunger—for love, for novelty, for sexual satisfaction—because it prevents complacency. It drives one to pursue new experiences and to live life fully. As a result, the speaker chooses not to eat and drink ("I will lie down lean/ With my thirst and my hunger"), preferring instead to taste from "every vine" and to gnaw at "every root." Like the Edna Millay who burned her candle at both ends, this poem celebrates the gender politics and principles of free love that characterized bohemian life in the Teens and Twenties.[8] It valorizes constant movement and novelty. And it undercuts the social imperative for marriage. Why should a woman settle for marriage, or one lover for that matter, when she can retain social and sexual freedom? In the wake of suffrage, the New Woman, who hungered for expanded political and social power, was asking such questions. Sensual hunger also drives the bohemian rejection of conventionality in Millay's "Recuerdo." Published in *A Few Figs from Thistles* (1920), this poem recounts an evening that two lovers spend going "back and forth all night on the ferry" (2), eating fruit and giving away their money and food to a poor, immigrant woman. Like the hipsters of Allen Ginsberg's *Howl* (1956), these bohemians are characterized by constant movement (a state that exhausts but exhilarates them) and a desire to break free from social conventions. Not only does the food become an image for their mutual sexual attraction, but it also captures their carefree attitude about living. They want more than they need (eating an apple and a pear "from a dozen of each we bought somewhere" [2]), consume only one of each, and discard the rest. By giving away the remaining fruit and most of their money, they reject the values of a society that privileges wealth and materialism over living in the moment. Saving food or money, in other words, implies an interest in the future. Reading a newspaper suggests engagement in the world outside of personal experiences. These things are not part of the bohemian ethos of the poem.

Some of her early work for the theatre, including *The Princess Marries the Page*,[9] uses hunger and eating as metaphors for sexual desire as well. Millay read this play, which premiered at Vassar and was subsequently produced by the Provincetown Players, at her first Greenwich Village reading in 1917. It depicts a burgeoning romance between a princess and a prince, a handsome, young man who has disguised himself as a page to infiltrate the king's retinue. This deception is not motivated by politics, though. Love compels him to spy on the court in order to be near the princess. Though she successfully hides him from the king's guards at first, the page/prince eventually surrenders and produces evidence of his innocence. The king, who already recognizes his daughter's fondness for the young man, invites him to dinner in the hopes of calling him "son" one day. Clearly, this fairy tale incorporates numerous elements from conventional tales, such as the courtly setting, a long-haired princess in a tower, a page who turns out to be a prince, an apple, a dark forest, and talk of fairies. However, Millay's princess consistently beats her father at chess, verbally spars with the prince, enjoys literature, rejects the notion of being rescued (in fact she tries to save the prince several times), manipulates language adeptly (putting on a performance in two voices to trick the soldiers and almost duping her father), and eats an apple as a sign of her sexual hunger. These characteristics not only give Millay's fairy tale a modern sensibility, casting women as independent, assertive, and creative, but also her hunger presents sexual desire in women as natural, as something that should be expressed without embarrassment or reservation.

The references to food establish a tension between hunger and satisfaction in the play that nonetheless points to some of the dangers of overindulgence. Millay's princess takes pleasure in the idealized romance of books, and she retreats to the tower in the opening scene to read. Finding a flute-playing page in this space, she immediately dismisses him, asking him to substitute food for music: "Go to the cook, who's making cakes today,/ And say I said you were to have your fill" (1). The page rejects this notion of satisfaction. He doesn't want to fill his stomach with desserts—something sweet but insubstantial. He hasn't even touched the apple in his coat pocket because he is too preoccupied with his unspoken love for her. Instead he plays a mournful, improvisatory piece on the flute, capturing both his bittersweet affections (which have made him an outcast in the eyes of his father and a criminal) and his anxiety about his impending death for supposedly spying on the king. As the passion between them intensifies, he puts aside his flute, and she stops reading. Their hunger for arts (reading and music respectively) is being replaced by a hunger for each other, and Millay presents the prince's apple as a metaphor for this mutual desire. The prince compares her with the fruit in ways that suggest his admiration for her autonomy and youthful beauty: "And such an apple?/ So ruddy and incomparable a fruit?" (14). Likewise, when the princess discovers the fruit, she pleads for it: "Oh, but please give it to me—please!—I love/ Apples! I want it so, I have to have it!" (14). Her sexual desire for him is further suggested when she eagerly takes several bites: *"[She seizes the apple and scurries with it to the seat of the window, where she begins to eat it, with both hands, like a squirrel... With a deep sigh of satisfaction.]* 'Ah-h-h!'" (15). Like her books at the outset of the play, the fruit substitutes for romance here. It offers a tantalizing taste of the pleasure and happiness they could find in each other—not unlike the impulsive kiss she gives him a moment earlier. She then offers the prince a bite, but he refuses, realizing he cannot earn her love in the context of deception. He must give himself up and disclose the truth. When the king discovers the prince's noble intentions, he invites him to dinner with one caveat: "I am told/ That lovers never eat!" (48). In the closing scene both the prince and princess admit that they are not hungry and laugh, remembering the king's pronouncement. Love replaces physical hunger, but it doesn't fill them. It leaves room for ongoing desire. Even though *The Princess Marries the Page* ultimately presents a marriage that occurs on equal terms (socially and emotionally) as the way to achieve happiness, it still promotes the kind of hunger valorized in "Recuerdo." Neither lover overindulges by eating too much. They savor their love instead.

Millay's experiences in the Village, however, would inspire a radically different treatment of hunger and satisfaction in *Aria da Capo*, which she began writing in 1918 and premiered with the Provincetown Players in December 1919.[10] Unlike hunger, which Millay tends to associate with bohemian culture, she often links images of consumption and excess with mainstream America, and as *Aria da Capo* suggests, both of these states can lead to social and political apathy. The unread newspaper in "Recuerdo" reflects some of the more carefree aspects of bohemian life, but along with the kind of alienating modernist art that thrived in the Village, these aspects of Bohemia seemed socially irresponsible to Millay in the last two years of the war. As Brenda Murphy argues in *The Provincetown Players and the Culture of Modernity, Aria da Capo* "is an exposure not only of the theatre, and perhaps specifically the Provincetown Players, which continues its self-involved, lighthearted aesthetic play in the midst of a world that has been devastated by world war and the utter disillusionment it has occasioned, but also of the pre-war Zeitgeist of Greenwich Village bohemia, which appears escapist and frivolous rather than daring and unconventional in this context" (149). Millay never offered an explicit interpretation of *Aria da Capo,* but her friends, those involved in the production, and early reviewers immediately recognized its antiwar message. Edmund Wilson, for example, felt "thrilled and troubled by this little play... There was a bitter treatment of the war, and we were all ironic about war" (qtd. in Milford 183), and *New York Times* theatre reviewer Alexander Woollcott wrote: "Very likely it would pass over the heads of the average unthinking audience, but surely no mother from a gold-starred home, who saw the war come and go like a grotesque comet and who now hears the rattlepated merriment of her neighbors all the more distinctly because of the blank silence in her own impoverished home—surely no such mother will quite miss the point of 'Aria da Capo'" (40–41). In addition to the play's message about the war, a full appreciation of its popularity[11] and significance also needs to recognize the ways in which Millay is commenting on mainstream American culture as well.

The food in *Aria da Capo*—macaroons, artichokes, caviar, peacocks' livers, mutton, persimmons, and other exotic delicacies—suggests a conflict between the wartime conservation efforts of the Food Administration and self-interest, aligning food with the other satirical targets of the work. It begins with a banquet in which Pierrot and Columbine sample elegant foods while discussing romantic clichés, modern arts, and bohemian philosophy. Like Pierrot's depiction of contemporary painting and atonal music, for example, this meal is presented as frivolous and elitist, not to mention excessive for two people. Pierrot and Columbine eat irresponsibly, and their attitude about food mocks the message of conservation and substitution that was integral to the Food Administration's efforts:

> *Columbine:* Pierrot, I'm getting tired of caviar
> And peacock's livers. Isn't there something
> else
> That people eat?—some humble vegetable,
> That grows in the ground? (10).

This is precisely what Americans were being asked to do in the last two years of the war—to consume fruits and vegetables, to substitute oats and grains for wheat, to get lard from vegetable oils, and to eat less meat. Yet Millay's characters seem oblivious to the notion of conservation. They consume to the point of excess ("I am always wanting/ A little more than what I have" [6–7]) or boredom, and they even eat meat: "'Mutton!'—now *there's* a thing you can lay/ the hands on,/ And set tooth in!...Food is my only lust" (11). Like Columbine's question about vegetables, Pierrot's lust for lamb (the very animal the warring shepherds strive to protect in the middle section of the play) reflects the kind of self-interest that tends to undermine collective action in the United States. Pierrot only cares about satisfying his appetites, and neither he nor Columbine is engaged with the world beyond personal experience. Millay doesn't condemn their failure to conserve food per se. She makes Pierrot's and Columbine's thoughtlessness the focal point of her critique. They are not protesting the war or the Food Administration's propaganda. They are merely wasteful consumers. Selfishness and satisfaction lead to political disengagement, and as the play progresses, Millay will present their unthinking behavior as morally irresponsible as well.

By choosing this moment with the mutton to introduce the story of the warring shepherds, Millay connects food with her warnings about the dangers of wartime propaganda. Specifically, she uses the grazing sheep as a metaphor for a public that passively accepts propaganda as truth. Corydon begins the scene by wondering if his sheep can think beyond immediate need and gratification: "Do they only question/ Where next to pull?—Or do their far minds draw them/ Thus vaguely north of west and south of east?" (15–16). As with her satire in "Say Shibboleth," she presents Americans as either thoughtless or content when being told what to think. Thyrsis replies:

> One cannot say... The black lamb
>   Wears its burdocks
> As if they were a garland... and drinks the bitten grass
> As if it were a wine. (16)

Sheep are easily satisfied. They graze wherever someone leads them, and their thick wool insulates them from the sharp thorns of the burdocks (the real world). All of this helps them remain content. Propaganda offers similar comforts to people. It reduces the complexity of issues or events, like war, to simple categories such as right/wrong, good/evil, and black/white. These dichotomies insulate people from moral ambiguity and uncertainty, making bitten grass taste like wine. Pierrot resists this oversimplification for a moment ("Anyway, I am tired/ Of black and white. At least I think I am" [13]), but he ultimately surrenders the scene to Cothurnus. His phrase about black and white is both a literal reference to the set design for the original production[12] and an expression of his frustration with being told to *see the world* in black and white. But Pierrot's protests are fleeting. He subsequently drifts in and out of the shepherd's drama, oblivious to their story, and at the end, he returns to the banquet as if nothing has happened.

Millay's most explicit attack on propaganda occurs through the character of Cothurnus, the director figure who interrupts the opening scene and represents the propagandistic forces that manipulate human behavior and generate support for imperialistic greed. Unlike the other characters, Cothurnus expresses no desire to eat or drink; instead, he feeds lines to the characters, telling them what to say and do. His ominous opening statement captures his tireless, watchful control over others: "I never sleep" (12). His place onstage (*"Seats himself on high place in back of stage"* [14]) and subsequent statements that he can play the scene without the actors and that "I am the scene" (14) further remind the characters and the audience that he is the driving force of the drama. He is present but visibly removed from the action, since he only needs language to coerce people into self-destructive behavior and denial. He elicits the basest emotions from the shepherds—greed, ambition, and a desire for conquest—and he reminds them that "the important thing is that you speak the lines,/ And make the gestures" (15). Words and gestures are far more important than truth. They are often consumed/accepted easily, while masking sinister motives, such as Thyrsis's plot to murder Corydon and Corydon's greed ("I could give him a necklace,/ And snatch it back" [30]).

Words can also manipulate behavior. Cothurnus's need for linguistic control is largely responsible for transforming this pastoral scene into a bloody battlefield. After the shepherds agree to begin the play, one of them suggests making up a song, but he forgets the next line. Cothurnus quickly prompts him: "I know a game worth two of that" (16). Cothurnus doesn't want the shepherds to think creatively or to express independent thought. He demands scripted language, and throughout the scene, the characters repeat the exact words he recites. In the context of a play in which specific lines need to be recited, this makes sense, but the repetition can also be understood in terms of propaganda. Cothurnus controls the message and actions of the play by insisting on a scripted text. In fact, every time the shepherds consider abandoning the game altogether, Cothurnus interrupts:

> *Corydon:* We seem to be forgetting
>   It's only a game...
> *Thyrsis:* I know it, Corydon.
> *(They reach out their arms to each other across the wall.)*
> *Cothurnus: (Prompting.)* "But how do I know—"
> *Thyrsis:* Oh yes... But how do I know this isn't a trick. (20–21)

Cothurnus's words literally come between the men here, and this embrace, a gesture of reconciliation and friendship, will eventually turn into murderous strangulation. In Millay's production notes, she describes Cothurnus's voice as spoken "without intonation, and quite without feeling, as if he had said the same words many times before" (52). There is supposed to be something familiar about Cothurnus's words, like the messages of propaganda, and the thoughtless repetition of these lines suggests a passive acceptance of this manipulation. Certainly in a drama where actors seem to step in and out of character, the script could be rejected or changed, but these players go along with it. They parrot the lines Cothurnus feeds them, just as people were meant to parrot the slogans distributed by the government. As the action of *Aria da Capo* becomes increasingly violent, Millay suggests that the tacit acceptance of propaganda has serious consequences. It can contribute to actual violence.

Throughout the shepherds' story, Millay also makes thirst part of her condemnation of imperialism and war. The game begins with the men building a wall of crepe paper and deciding "that over there belongs to me,/ And over here to you!" (16). These arbitrary walls represent territorial disputes typical of imperial powers. Even the offstage argument that we hear between Pierrot and Columbine reinforces this. As he tries to rename her Pierrette, she struggles to assert her autonomy: "My name is Columbine," she replies. "Leave me alone!" (17). Naming is an integral part of colonialism. It is an act of control as well as erasure—an attempt to impose a new identity on a place or culture. Corydon gets caught up in this desire to name when he discovers precious stones filled with gold on his side of the wall:

> I can't be bothered with a few untidy
> Brown sheep... I'm a merchant.
> ... I dare say I could be an emperor!
> ... I can't make up my mind
> Whether to buy a city, and have a thousand
> Beautiful girls to bathe me, and be happy
> Until I die, or build a bridge, and name it
> The Bridge of Corydon,—and be remembered
> After I'm dead. (25–26)

Wealth changes his relationship to land. It is no longer a place where sheep can roam freely. It is something to own and label, and Millay presents the language of conquest and empire building here to highlight the egotism motivating colonialism. The imperial fantasies that both shepherds share about ownership inspires an insatiable thirst for more, and this dynamic reflects Millay's concerns about America's growing role as a global, imperial power, which intensified with the Spanish-American War in 1898 and the acquisition of several Spanish colonies including Puerto Rico, Guam, and the Philippines. The escalating struggle between the shepherds suggests that acquiring new territory is only the beginning. After laying claim to their respective sides of the wall, each shepherd becomes increasingly invested in hoarding resources and plotting to acquire more. Thyrsis, who has all of the water on his side, threatens to withhold it from Corydon's thirsty flock. He has abandoned the notion that he once cared for the same animals. As Corydon exclaims, "*Your* sheep! You are mad, to call/ them/ Yours—mine—they are all one flock!" (19). The notion of borders changes his view of himself and others. It breeds selfishness, and it robs him of compassion. Corydon behaves the same way, and he only recognizes the artificiality of this wall (which has divided the land and alienated them from each other) after it's too late. At the end of the play, he gropes around the stage while the poison takes effect, and he says: "There isn't any wall,/ I think" (33). The hungers in this play promote greed, but unlike the hungry speakers of her poetry from this period, the desire for more in *Aria da Capo* comes at the expense of others and of the self. Millay gives voice to this when Thyrsis mocks Corydon's own thirst: "Ho, so you've changed your mind?—/ It's different,/ Isn't it, when you want a drink yourself" (29). Imperialism, with its insatiable drive for power and land, is personally and socially destructive. It corrupts the self and other. A tension also emerges between Millay's explicit critique of wartime propaganda here and the implicit, metatheatrical anxiety about the act of playwriting that provides the vehicle for the critique. At some level, the Cothurnus character is both an explicit critique of manipulative politics and an implicit working out of the tension Millay felt in doing something similar. Highly political art has the power to manipulate behaviors and beliefs, and the line between this work and propaganda, between a game and real violence, can be thin indeed. During World War II, Millay would succumb to pressure by the Writers' War Board to produce a propaganda play, *The Murder of Lidice* (1942), and the consequences on her health, her friendships, and her art would be severe.

Mind Your Manners: Fine Dining, Class, and Commedia dell'Arte

Food also played an integral role in entertainment culture by the time Millay lived in Greenwich Village. The upper classes—and those who wanted to be perceived as such—flocked to elegant restaurants throughout the city. They drank champagne and dined on the kind of the elite cuisine that Pierrot and Columbine sample in *Aria da Capo*. According to Lewis Erenberg, they sought "arenas for the consumption of fine food and the display of status and refinement" (55). This opportunity among wealthy urbanites to flaunt their social status began with the Waldorf Hotel on Fifth Avenue. Built in 1893, the Waldorf quickly became the social center of New York City nightlife. The wide-open spaces and glass walls of its main restaurant, Palm Garden, made it *the* place to showcase wealth and power. Its success inspired other hotels and restaurants to follow suit, and by 1912, numerous establishments on Broadway, including Roman Gardens, Bustanoby's, Churchill's, Murray's, and Reisenweber's, offered ostentatious settings for elegant dining. Modeled on the décor of Fifth Avenue mansions and aristocratic European houses, the crystal chandeliers, ornately carved interiors, and elaborate service transported patrons to the world of extreme wealth—as did the opportunity to hobnob with the theatre crowd, flirt with Broadway chorus girls, drink, play poker, and celebrate sporting events. One of the most popular late-night meals was lobster and champagne, and these restaurants, which were nicknamed lobster palaces, embodied this new interest in conspicuous consumption among the upper classes. Lobster palaces even thrived during the Food Administration's conservation campaign. Initially, restaurant owners were nervous about possible rationing, but the government allowed hotels and restaurants, "in the name of patriotism, to serve reduced portions without any corresponding reduction in prices" (Levenstein 141). This was a sacrifice for the war that they were more than willing to make. Needless to say, Millay couldn't afford to frequent lobster palaces, but she didn't have to leave Greenwich to come in contact with this crowd. The prosperous urban sect not only indulged in the aristocratic fantasies of uptown restaurants as well as the more illicit pleasures of cabarets and dance halls, for example, but they also traveled down to the Village to get a glimpse of bohemian life. The mystique of this artistic, intellectual community with its carefree attitudes about sex and money appealed to uptown elites as another form of escapist pleasure (Erenberg 253).

Eating also played into contemporary middle-class fantasies about wealth and privilege, particularly through social manners. Etiquette manuals provided a popular outlet to indulge in fantasies about social mobility, offering readers advice on virtually every act of social intercourse from bodily management to eating. Along with rules about the need to avoid coughing, sneezing, yawning, and picking one's teeth in public, these books dedicated page after page to eating. Using knives and forks properly, furnishing dining rooms, setting the table, and inviting guests for dinner, for example, became markers of one's civility and sophistication. In fact, most aspects of dining became highly ritualized in the second half of the nineteenth century as the middle class sought greater respectability. As John Kasson explains in *Rudeness and Civility: Manners in Nineteenth-Century Urban America*, "[B]ecause the act of dining bore such high ritual stakes among the middle classes, it needed to be performed in protected circumstances. One etiquette manual declared: 'Eating is so entirely a sensual, animal gratification, that unless it is conducted with much delicacy, it becomes unpleasant to others'" (199). On one level, this type of advice reflects the important role that food played in establishing and maintaining social hierarchies. On another level, it reveals the increasing importance the middle class placed on such rituals as they sought to transcend these barriers.

In his anthropological study of the cultural, biological, and social function of food, E. N. Anderson notes that the upper classes often use food as a form of social separation. "Elite groups *always* try to mark themselves off by consumption of special-status or prestige foods (caviar, champagne, goat cheese, etc.), and upwardly mobile people try to rise in respect by being seen eating those foods" (136). Restaurant culture in the early twentieth century and the popularity of etiquette manuals clearly demonstrate this tendency in American culture as well—a tendency that reflects a long tradition of associating food with social and class formation. Claude Lévi-Strauss's study of the Bororo Indians of central Brazil, for example, argues that food preparation is central to the development of human society. Cooked food denotes civilization in the early stages of a society. It distinguishes humans from animals: "The conjunction of a member of the social group with nature must be mediatized through the intervention of cooking fire, whose normal function is to mediatize the conjunction of the raw product and the human consumer, and whose operation thus has the effect of making sure that a natural creature is at one and the same time *cooked and socialized*" (336; emphasis in original). This process of socialization is eventually shaped by cultural practices such as table manners. As Mikhail Bakhtin points out in his history of carnival celebrations, bodies and bawdy behavior at the table are now policed and regulated in a way that would have seemed strange to an earlier era. The Renaissance marked a shift from the "popular-festive tradition" of the banquet to the "private eating or private gluttony and drunkenness" (301) of the bourgeois feast. Not only has this modern feast become a private affair, but it also lacks the social freedoms of the carnival, which celebrated excess, public community, free expression, and social justice. For Bakhtin, the ordered, restrained character of the modern feast merely solidifies class hierarchies, enforcing social convention and self-restraint. It demands the suppression of one's natural impulses and desires.

Millay also believed that etiquette rituals, like the ostentatious displays of wealth at lobster palaces and the popularity of books offering advice on social manners, discouraged sociopolitical engagement. They invited audiences to remain uncritical of surface behaviors and social practices, and she sought to lampoon this aspect of American life throughout her work. She even intended her first novel, *Hardigut*, which she never finished, to be a satire about bodily appetites: "People, otherwise perfectly sane and normal," she wrote, "do not eat in public, or discuss food except in innuendos and with ribald laughter" (qtd. in Milford 248). Her ideas for this project make the connection between eating (that sensual, animal gratification) and sex clear—a connection that etiquette manuals hinted at. Though most of these texts avoided explicit discussion of sex, some alluded to it by giving advice about nose blowing and scratching. Robert Tomes's *The Bazar* [sic] *Book of Decorum: The Care of the Person, Manners, Etiquette, and Ceremonials* (1870), for instance, cautions readers about the indecorous nose: "It should never be fondled before company, or, in fact, touched at any time, unless absolutely necessary. The nose, like all other organs, augments in size by frequent handling, so we recommend every person to keep his own fingers, as well as those of his friends or enemies away from it" (113). As this text suggests, society wanted to regulate all types of bodily management to promote self-discipline and sexual repression.

Millay recognized that this was particularly true in regard to the social and moral propriety expected of women, and she found this self-policing deleterious for women. In her poem "Macdougal Street" (1920),[13] the speaker, who is trying to fall asleep after a fleeting encounter with a man in the Village, struggles to reconcile her sexual attraction to him with the behaviors expected of a middle-class woman ("lady"). She chides herself for being "so shy" and even envies the "dirty Latin child" for speaking with and flirting openly with him: "I wish I were a ragged child with ear-rings in my ears!" Her conflicted perception of the Village and its food reflects the social values of self-restraint that have trapped her. The Village is depicted as chaotic. Fat, slovenly women squat on stoops. Babies and cats crowd the filthy, cluttered streets, and dirty children haggle with vendors. Like the lives of this working-class, Italian community, even the food, which is associated with irreverent and illicit humor, is out in the open: "The fruit-carts and clam-carts were ribald as a fair... She had haggled from the fruit-man of his rotting ware." This carnival-like atmosphere unnerves the speaker, however. It suggests sexual and social freedoms that she associates with the lower classes, and as a result, she perceives the vendor's fruit as rotting. Even though she views the handsome stranger as a king with darling hands (an attempt to distinguish him from this immigrant community in terms of class), she retreats to her middle-class identity, returning to her quiet room to weep.

In addition to an unfinished play entitled "Food,"[14] in which Millay intended to satirize eating rituals, her second theatrical piece written at Vassar, *Two Slatterns and a King* (1917), links food with social performances of gender and class. This play, which was produced by the Other Players the following year,[15] depicts a king who searches for the ideal wife by inspecting kitchens throughout his land. "I will go from house to house,/ Unheralded... And that maid whose kitchen's the neatest/ Will I have to be my sweetest" (12). The king encounters two women, Tidy and Slut, who embody neatness and "slovenly ease," respectively. Tidy completely identifies with her kitchen, taking great satisfaction in cooking, cleaning, and serving others: "Oh, full is every cupboard, sharp is every knife!—/ My bright, sunny kitchen is the pride of my life!" (11). Food is bountiful and fresh in this house. It contributes to the domestic ideal she embodies. Slut, however, is indolent and sloppy: "In clutter and filth I am quite content" (11). Her table is weighed down by "stale food" and unwashed plates. Both women are clearly types (the neat freak and the slob), but on the day of the king's visit, they reverse roles. By Chance (the narrator of the play), Tidy's kitchen is a disaster: milk has soured; her broiled duck was dragged away by the neighbor's dog; the cakes, pies, and tarts in the oven have burned; and the quince jelly has boiled over. Slut, however, has decided to clean her house for the first time—simply out of boredom. Of course, she finds the acts distasteful ("My bones ache and I find no bliss" [15]). The king decides to marry Slut and doesn't discover her true nature until the following day. Because the king so completely equates women with their domestic duties (cooking, cleaning, and caretaking), he is easily deceived by appearances, and the play announces this moral in the prologue and epilogue: "Be not o'er hasty in your decision,/ For he who heedeth not this rule/ BY CHANCE HE WILL BE CALLED A FOOL!" (18). It is foolish for society to determine a woman's worth based on her performance as a housecleaner and a cook. At the same time, women like Tidy have accepted these roles. She doesn't just *weep* because the king accuses her of deception. She is *devastated* because she uses the same superficial standards to judge herself—standards that etiquette manuals reinforced. Tomes's *The Bazar* [sic] *Book of Decorum,* for example, explicitly addresses the slattern: "No man can long endure a slattern at home, and especially if she appears the fine lady abroad, and thus shows her contemptuous preference of the opinion of others to his" (172). Social convention among the middle and upper classes demanded the regulation of a woman's public and private life, and as this text suggests, men could—and would—expect equally dazzling performances in both arenas. Not surprisingly, Tidy tacitly agrees with the king's plan to "go/ From kitchen to kitchen, that I may know/ And judge for myself what maid is worth/ To sit at my side" (14). Like etiquette advice on hosting a dinner party, the preparation and display of food here determine her social value as a potential wife—a determination that has class implications as well. Her mishandling of food not only makes her unworthy to sit at his side as queen, but it also suggests other possible social lapses that would be inexcusable among aristocratic and upper-class society. Ultimately Millay presents these kinds of performances (of gender and of class status) as inauthentic and harmful to both men and women.

This "inauthenticity" captures some of Millay's larger concerns about the excesses of American culture, particularly its investment in image over substance, fantasy over reality. In a period of wartime, these elements of popular culture take on serious consequences, and her use of commedia dell'arte in *Aria da Capo* reflects these dangers. As mentioned before, the foods of the opening banquet of the play are excessive and frivolous. Columbine—much like Nora from Henrik Ibsen's *A Doll's House*[16]—has an insatiable appetite for macaroons: "I cannot *live* without a macaroon!" (5). A few moments later, she says the same thing about vinaigrette. She is preoccupied with garnish and dainty foods (caviar, peacocks' livers, and persimmons), not the kind of meal that can satisfy real hunger, and when Pierrot suggests that she try a vegetable (mushrooms), she cannot bring herself to substitute something so common for these other delicacies: "[M]ushrooms...mushrooms...I cannot *live* with...How do you like this gown?" (10). Food, like fashion, is about appearance. It's about what people see, and Columbine takes delight in associating herself with refined cuisine and upper-class culture. There is a performative quality to this meal, as there was to the conspicuous consumption that uptown hotels and restaurants offered wealthy patrons or the rituals insisted upon in etiquette manuals. These rituals were so crucial that contemporary manuals, such as *Putnam's Handbook of Etiquette: A Cyclopedia of Social Usage, Giving Manners and Customs of the Twentieth Century* (1913), often presented their violation as criminal: "To attempt to smoke at any meal, without being cordially invited by one's entertainers to do so, is little short of a social crime in a guest of either sex" (Roberts 226). Columbine, who later criticizes Pierrot for his outfit and insists on retrieving her hat, offers a grotesque and parodic violation of such behavioral codes. When juxtaposed with the shepherds' violent deaths at the end of the play, her investment in the ethos that undergirds etiquette produces an ironic departure from these superficial norms.

Millay further reinforces the class implications of this banquet by invoking commedia dell'arte—an art form she had been familiar with since college.[17] Food was a staple of these improvisatory dramas, which started in sixteenth-century Italy. They not only included open-air banquets with singers, musicians, and copious amounts of food and wine, but they also featured characters that were driven entirely by bodily appetites. As Antonio Fava explains in *The Comic Mask in the Commedia Dell'Arte: Actor Training, Improvisation, and the Poetics of Survival,* the zanni or comic servants embody the importance of food and consumption in this art form. "For him, everything tastes good and everything is worth eating. In his vision of the world, everything goes spontaneously into his mouth" (59). Not everything is worthy of eating in Millay's drama, though. Her Pierrot and Columbine, who are servants in traditional commedia dell'arte,[18] pose as aristocrats, and to do so they need to eat the food of the wealthy to be associated with upper-class life. Arguably part of this class performance is reflected in the title of the play as well. Most scholars point out that this drama mirrors the three-part musical structure of a typical aria (ABA), but no one has commented on the fact that the title is incorrect. Millay, who studied music and was an avid opera fan,[19] certainly knew that the proper terminology was "da capo aria" ("da capo" meaning "from the beginning" or "from the head"). In part the inversion of this title, placing the adjective after instead of before the noun, reflects the difference between musical terminology (a specialized use of the language) and spoken Italian. For those without a background in music, it would be more normal to say "aria da capo," so servants like Pierrot and Columbine would probably use this phrase. Millay's title, like Pierrot's New York dialect when he steps out of character, further undercuts the highbrow association with opera that these characters crave. It exposes class as a performance or spectacle, and it mirrors the social inversion that allows Columbine and Pierrot to pose as aristocrats—as "heads" (*capos*) of society.

The food in *Aria* also operates like other aspects of popular and artistic culture that distracted Americans from serious social and political engagement. For example, Millay mocks the dilettantes who flocked to the Village to live a bohemian lifestyle by having Pierrot sample various artistic and philosophical identities as one might try on clothes (composer, painter, socialist, etc.), and this satire of bohemian life and highbrow art is interspersed with references to food. Thus, after assuming the identity of an atonal composer (à la Schoenberg) who writes *Uptown Express at Six O'clock,* for example, Pierrot impatiently asks for a drink. And, his request recalls an earlier exchange between Pierrot and Columbine when he invites her to drink with him: "Well, let us drink some wine and lose our heads / And love each other" (6). Drinking, in both instances, is about losing one's head or common sense. It privileges emotion and pleasure (love and alcohol) over thinking, a trend that Millay recognized as part of American culture more broadly. When Columbine accuses Pierrot of drinking too much, he agrees, blaming his perpetual dissatisfaction:

> Yes, I dare say I do...Or else
>   too little.
> It's hard to tell. You see, I am always wanting
> A little more than what I have,—or else
> A little less. There's something wrong. (6–7)

In fact the play suggests that there is something wrong with the endless desire that consumerism instills. Consumerism equates happiness with acquiring something new (material objects and social status) and/or becoming dissatisfied with what one has. But Millay's characters cannot recognize this failing because they are so easily distracted. When Pierrot poses a question that could lead to serious discussion, for example, Columbine redirects his attention toward food:

> *Pierrot:* Where does one go from here!
> *Columbine:* Here's a persimmon, love. You always liked them.
> *Pierrot:* I am become a critic; there is nothing
> I can enjoy...However, set it aside;
> I'll eat it between meals. (10–11)

Eating is a way to avoid serious contemplation, and critical engagement, which, as can be implied from Millay's attack on literary critics here, detract from one's pleasure. Pierrot's solution is to eat constantly in between meals, to have a constant source of entertainment and distraction.

The way that food misdirects attention has much more serious implications at the end of the play. Once the shepherds kill each other, food becomes the focal point again, offering something to distract the characters (and by extension the audience) from contemplating the significance of the shepherd's tale. When the commedia dell'arte figures see the dead bodies of Thyrsis and Corydon, Pierrot protests a return to his frivolous banquet scene: "We can't/ Sit down and eat with two dead bodies lying/ Under the table!" (35). Cothurnus rejects this idea, and once he convinces them that the audience will not care, Pierrot and Columbine hide the bodies with a tablecloth and *"merrily set their bowls back on the table"* (35). They accept (and agree with) Cothurnus's justification for inaction here, which enables them to dismiss any moral or legal qualms about their deaths. They resume eating: "I cannot *live* without a macaroon!... Is this my artichoke/ Or yours? (35–36). The rituals of dining allow them to ignore the bodies. Food provides a kind of satisfaction that makes them complacent. Of course in traditional commedia dell'arte, killing is merely an illusion. A character onstage may believe that s/he has killed someone, but murder is usually revealed to be a mistake. If death does occur, it tends to remain invisible to the action onstage. "The truly dead, in Commedia, are already dead before the curtain rises. Or if they really have to die during the show, they never appear. They die unseen" (Fava 64). Millay inverts this commedia tradition by forcing the audience to witness the murder of the shepherds and to stare at their bodies. Her antiwar critique requires us to look at these casualties, to be reminded of what her audience didn't have to witness in a war fought so far away. Her drama also demands that we listen to Pierrot and Columbine's trivial exchanges about food, romance, art, and other forms of popular culture against the backdrop of war. This juxtaposition undermines the kind of investment that all Americans (from upper-class elites to bohemians like herself, from middle-class moviegoers to blue-collar workers) have in diversion and the spectacle of entertainment. It also challenges audiences to see beyond the immediate pleasures of leisure culture. Pierrot remarks in the closing lines of the play: "Ah, Columbine, as if it mattered!" (36). These words certainly capture the play's critique of popular culture—of the things that preoccupy Americans and distract them from more meaningful political and social participation. When first seeing the stage after the shepherds' battle, Columbine complains about the clutter, but Pierrot responds: "I think it's rather diverting/ The way it is" (34). He values diversion. Even the three-part structure of the play (heralded by this return to commedia dell'arte) suggests America's readiness to embrace amusement in the aftermath of tragic events like war. The war can be swept under the table amidst this display of entertainment and food. It can be forgotten.

Millay raises these concerns explicitly in her later dramatic work *The Murder of Lidice* (1942), and she does so, in part, through food. Images of hunger and eating can be found throughout Millay's later works. As Jo Ellen Green Kaiser explains in "Feeding the Hungry

Heart: Gender, Food, and War in the Poetry of Edna St. Vincent Millay," Millay's poetry between 1940 to 1944 "constructs food, and particularly eating, as a means of crossing over from [a] private aesthetic sensibility to the world of war" (89). In the 1920s, Kaiser argues, "Millay used metaphors of hunger to mediate aesthetic sensibility and worldly engagement. Perpetual hunger represents, in her early work, the body's need to sound its own desire in order to transcend itself" (82). The problem with eating is that it "returns the body to its particular history, enabling it to enter the world, and particularly the world at war" (82). Kaiser concludes that this return to history comes at a price. It requires "discarding the aesthetic sensibility, moving the poet from the world of poetry proper to the realm of propaganda" (82). When considering Millay's early plays, however, her use of hunger does not suggest such a stark dividing line. There isn't a clear shift from the personal to the political, as Kaiser suggests, but a return to the latter. When comparing the images of food in *Aria da Capo* with her propaganda play, *The Murder of Lidice* (1942), her later work demonstrates a return to political issues that first emerged during her time in the Village.

The Writers War Board, which asked Millay to contribute to the propaganda efforts of the U.S. government, wrote the preface to the first print edition for *The Murder of Lidice,* describing it as a dramatic verse narrative about the destruction of the small village of Lidice, Czechoslovakia. On June 10, 1942, the Nazis burned the village church and houses, executed the priest, shot 173 men and boys, transported 203 women to a concentration camp in northern Germany, and gassed most of the 104 children.[20] The play was broadcast by NBC on the radio in October of that year, and as one might expect from propaganda, it depicts the village in idealized terms. This strong, religiously devout community "worked as one" (3), lived off the land, and marked the change of seasons by planting and harvesting. Food embodies industry and community here; it is produced collectively, as the villagers rely on each other and the land for sustenance. The play's central character, a beautiful, young woman named Byeta, has recently gotten engaged to Karel, another boy from the village, but talk of "Heydrich the Hangman" (SS-Obergruppenführer Reinhard Heydrich) soon casts a shadow over their courtship. Eventually, the Nazis slaughter the men, women, and children and set all of Lidice afire. The most vividly described murder is that of a bleeding baby whose head is smashed against a wall. The child also becomes a metaphor for the village itself, which is compared to "the murdered body of a little child,/ Innocent, happy, surprised at play,—/ The murdered body, stained and defiled,/ Tortured and mangled, of a helpless child!" (31).

This shift from a child at play to this lifeless, mangled body parallels the changing significance of food in *The Murder of Lidice*. By the end of the play, food is no longer a source of sustenance; it is a weapon in the hands of Hitler: "The maniac killer who still runs wild—/ Where he sits, with his long and cruel thumbs,/ Eating pastries, moulding the crumbs/ Into bullets (for the day is always near/ For another threat, another fear/ Another killing of the gentle and mild)" (31). Pastries are not harvested or cultivated. They signify leisure and pleasure, suggesting that Hitler takes joy in the suffering he causes. The desserts are also an image for imperialism. Hitler is insatiable, consuming one pastry (country) after another, and he leaves nothing behind. Even the crumbs can be transformed into weapons that destroy people and places in order to acquire more land. Millay concludes with a sentiment that captures some of her conflicted feelings about mainstream American culture, a sentiment that she could have made while writing *Aria da Capo:*

> Careless America, crooning a tune:
> Catch him! Catch him and stop him soon!
> Never let him come here!...
> Oh, my country, so foolish and dear,
> Careless America, crooning a tune,
> Please think!—are we immune? (32)

Millay recognizes that mainstream, commercial American culture tends to promote entertainment over serious engagement, escapism over activism. Americans would rather sing sentimental love songs than think about Hitler's threat. As with *Aria da Capo,* this drama warns of the dangerous consequences of such an attitude. Perhaps her lifelong association with popular culture, as a successful writer, celebrity, and actress, made her message resonate with listeners. The fan mail that she received after the first broadcast of *The Murder of Lidice* suggests as much. But the fact that many close friends were highly critical of this work again highlights Millay's predicament as she tried to straddle the worlds of popular culture and modern art.[21]

Conclusion: Food, Love, and War

In many ways, Millay's passionate bohemian lifestyle laid waste to the hearts and bodies in her life. Floyd Dell continued to worry about Millay's fidelity long after their relationship ended; Edmund Wilson struggled to get over her refusal to marry him, and journalist George Slocombe seemed unable to accept his own decision to break things off with her in 1920. Of course, Millay suffered as well. She felt heartbroken and dazed when James Lawyer stopped their affair because of his suicidal wife and his newfound interest in Millay's younger sister, Kathleen. Millay also suffered from a "'botched abortion' which left her bleeding and weakened" that year (Milford 197). Love often seemed to be a battle of sorts for Millay, and she depicted these struggles in her writing. Love as a kind of war game—with physical and psychological casualties—provides another connection between the two narratives of *Aria da Capo*. Pierrot and Columbine's romance seems rooted in nothing more than physical attraction. They don't appear to understand or listen to each other. They mask biting comments with humor and avoid any topic that might lead to a serious discussion about their relationship or life more broadly. In this way, the play not only portrays the relationship between shepherds as corrupted by greed and selfishness, but it also suggests that the commedia lovers will fall victim to similar impulses. They greedily consume food and care more about themselves than each other. Eating and drinking seem to have replaced their genuine desire for each other—behavior that the speakers of "Recuerdo" and the characters of *The Princess Marries the Page* reject.

Given the combative relationships depicted in *Aria da Capo*, it isn't entirely surprising that some of the power of Millay's antiwar critique in *Aria da Capo* comes from her presentation of food. Millay's lifelong, artistic interest in food and eating rituals found perfect expression in this work. While the banquet, along with Pierrot's and Columbine's posturing, dramatizes this contemporary obsession with class mobility, Millay began, as World War I continued, to perceive such forms of escapist entertainment as reckless. When Woodrow Wilson launched the Food Administration (alongside the Committee on Public Information), food became part of the government's propaganda efforts to manipulate people into action and/or inaction. Millay weaves this aspect of government coercion into both narratives of the play. Not only does Cothurnus force all of the players into increasingly dangerous and callous behavior, but the food that Pierrot lusts for, lamb, comes from the same animal that the shepherds should be protecting, the same animal that becomes a metaphor for a public that desires at some level to be directed and led. Both Pierrot's wasteful posturing and the shepherd's increasing greed are ultimately destructive. By juxtaposing the commedia dell'arte material with the shepherd's story, Millay's critique of the brutality of war, forces the audience to consider its relationship to popular culture as potentially irresponsible. Perhaps this is why Millay chose to write *Aria da Capo* as a fable instead of a realist work. She recognized the problems in American culture but was ambivalent about judging them too harshly. Millay had a great affection for America in spite of its often careless passion for entertainment. She didn't see herself as standing apart from this desire for amusement. She enjoyed the same pastimes and shared some of the same wants and dreams. This is part of the genius of the play. She reaches her audience in the exact way they expect from entertainment culture—in a humorous, accessible manner—but with a message that suggests the dangerous frivolity of placing so much importance on something as inconsequential as a macaroon.

CHAPTER 2

"DAMN EVERYTHING BUT THE CIRCUS!": THE AMBIGUOUS PLACE OF POPULAR CULTURE IN E. E. CUMMINGS' *HIM*

AT THE AGE OF SIX, Edward Estlin Cummings went to the circus for the first time. "Saw jaguars, hyena, bear, elephants, baby lion, and a father lion, baby monkeys climbing a tree," he wrote excitedly in his diary that night.[1] This experience left an indelible mark on Cummings, beginning a lifelong passion for the big top, sideshows, and wide range of popular amusements. As biographer Richard S. Kennedy notes, the young Cummings relished family outings to the circus: "His father or his Uncle George took him to Forepaugh and Sells Brothers Circus (where he once rode an elephant), to Ringling Brothers, and on one glorious occasion to Barnum and Bailey where he saw sideshows for the first time—the freaks and sword-swallowers" (23). These moments inspired some of Cummings' earliest poems and sketches, which feature various circus acts and Buffalo Bill Cody.[2] As he worked to develop his own aesthetics and artistic philosophy in the Teens and Twenties, Cummings balanced his passion for popular culture with a growing interest in modernism. He read experimental prose and poetry along with the Krazy Kat comic strip. He attended the Armory Show as well as vaudeville, picture palaces, and sideshows. He listened to atonal music and ragtime. And he admired the Provincetown Players while frequenting burlesque and striptease acts. For Cummings, these amusements had a vitality that was often missing from high art—a vitality he was trying to capture in his own work.

In the early twentieth century, there was no better place to indulge in these passions than New York, and Cummings moved to Greenwich Village in 1917 to write, paint, and partake in city nightlife. For the next decade his stylistic experimentation as a poet would link him with the modernist movement. He produced several controversial volumes of verse, *Tulips and Chimneys* (1923), *XLI Poems* (1925), *&* (1925),[3] and *Is 5* (1926), as well as a prose narrative about being in a French detention center during World War I, *The Enormous Room* (1922).[4] He also began exhibiting his paintings in 1919. Some of his art appeared in the *Dial* alongside the works of Picasso, Braque, and Lachaise, and his 1931 book *CIOPW* (an acronym for Charcoal, Ink, Oil, Pencil, and Watercolor) assembled black and white reproductions of his visual art from the 1920s. Throughout these innovative works, Cummings often featured popular subjects, such as the circus and burlesque. In the poem "Buffalo Bill's," for example, he depicts both the breathtaking speed of Buffalo Bill's famous pigeon-shooting act[5] and the speaker's admiration for it by compressing two groups of words: "and break onetwothreefourfive pigeonsjustlikethat" (*Complete Poems* 90). The space between these clusters represents the momentary gap between watching Bill fire the gun and seeing the clay pigeons explode. Such techniques and subject matter reflect Cummings' attempts to capture the rhythms of modern life and popular culture in his art.

He would arguably achieve his greatest synthesis of popular and formal arts in *Him*. This play, Cummings only major dramatic work,[6] was published in 1927 and first performed by the Provincetown Players the following year.[7] It depicts the gradual disintegration of the romantic relationship between Him (a struggling playwright) and Me (his lover). Him wants to create an original, dynamic work of art that contains lowbrow elements, but he cannot reconcile this goal with his identity as a highbrow artist who lives in the world of ideas, the imagination, and wordplay.[8] His conception of the artist as an isolated figure on a tightrope high above humanity is part of the problem. He hasn't found a way to integrate his artistic life with the real world around him—the world of popular culture, relationships, and parenthood. When Me proposes that he write something profitable, something that "people would like" (18), Him mocks the idea, but his alter-ego, O. Him (or Other Him), does exactly this. O. Him's unfinished play, which makes up act II, incorporates a range of theatrical styles to satirize 1920s life, particularly the theatre, psychoanalysis, the advertising industry, science, fascism, and American ignorance about postwar Europe.[9] The nine scenes of this play within the play parallel the nine months of Me's pregnancy, a fact she has kept hidden from Him. Although Me clings to the hope that Him can break free from the insular world of high art and love her and their child, she ultimately realizes that he loves only his idea of her (as opposed to her true self), and she ends their relationship. Him subsequently tries to forge a connection with the real world by traveling to Europe and participating in popular culture. He even attends a freak show in the penultimate scene, yet his horror when Me appears as a mother figure in place of the final freak and his inability to finish his play suggest that he cannot reconcile high and low, that he still prefers the illusions offered by art over the social and emotional demands of everyday life.

Cummings' use of numerous theatrical forms here is a testament to the profound impact of popular culture on modernist artists like himself. He often found the most exhilarating examples of dramatic art in circus and burlesque shows, not contemporary theatre,[10] and his work as a theatre critic in the 1920s celebrated popular culture as high art. Throughout these writings, he argues that the circus and "burlesk" (which he spells with a "k" to distinguish it from the contrived performances of stock burlesque companies) capture a "supreme alive-ness which is known as 'beauty'" (114).[11] This quality comes from the dynamism and spontaneity of the performers as well as the multidimensional perspective offered by these shows. Specifically, Cummings considers the three-ring circus "a gigantic spectacle; *which is surrounded by an audience,*—in contrast to our modern theatres, where an audience and a spectacle merely confront each other" ("The Adult," 112). Likewise, "[B]urlesk enables us to (so to speak) *know around* a thing, character, or situation" ("You Aren't Mad," 127). Presenting audiences with a broader perspective on the performance makes these art forms interactive and energetic, not static. They offer the possibility of experiencing the whole performance simultaneously in ways that Cummings might have equated with the cubist works of Picasso[12] or the fragmented scenes of Eliot's *The Waste Land.*

His personal investment in these entertainments, however, has led most critics to overlook the ambivalence about popular culture in *Him.* Cummings certainly tried to infuse the energy and excitement of urban life and modern entertainment into *Him.* But this play is also about the problems of integrating formal and popular arts. Some of his concern stems from the tendency of sideshows to objectify and eroticize the people on display. At its worst, popular culture reduces people—such as women and African Americans—to caricatures. It reinforces explicit or tacit prejudices on the part of audiences, instead of offering images that might encourage people to question such biases. As Him and Me's failed relationship suggests, its emphasis on the body creates real barriers between men and women that can prevent intimacy and mutual understanding. The shift in the play from circus imagery to that of the freak show (along with the ambivalent portrait of each) captures Cummings' concerns about the limitations of using popular modes in formal art. Ultimately, *Him* suggests that the artist needs to capture the vitality of popular culture in ways that demand critical thought and engagement. Art needs to invite intellectual assessment, or it risks encouraging audiences to accept spectacle as truth.

"THE GREATEST SHOW ON EARTH": CIRCUSES, ART, AND AMERICAN LIFE

The dynamic movement and aliveness of big top performances, which Cummings admired so greatly, were emblematic of the circus's historical development in America. The circus expanded with the country, reflecting its cultural and ethnic diversity, its social hierarchies and prejudices, and its growing appetite for spectacle. Prior to the nineteenth century, circuses didn't travel much. Showmen built wooden arenas near major cities, in part, to give horseback riders enough room to perform, and these permanent structures made the circus a predominately urban pastime. The introduction of canvas tents in 1825, however, transformed the scope of this entertainment. The circus became mobile, and with the help of the steam-powered engine, one of the most important technological developments of the era,[13] circuses soon reached a national audience. Trains moved heavy equipment, animals, and hundreds of performers, stagehands, and managers with efficiency and speed. As a result, rural communities and small towns throughout the country had access to this art for the first time. "Circus Day," as it was often called in advertising and journalistic accounts, soon became a significant cultural event for Americans. When the circus came to town, shops and schools closed down. Factories and farms stopped production. And people from surrounding communities traveled great distances to be part of the event.[14] The growing popularity of the circus affected its staging in the second half of the century as well. With an increase in the number of midsections in the tent, the original circular big top stretched like a rubber band, acquiring a rectangular shape with curved ends. An interior "Hippodrome" track also circled the periphery of the arena, and this addition enabled clowns, freaks, jugglers, charioteers, elephants, ostriches, monkeys, and other exotic animals to parade in front of seated viewers. This parade happened, of course, while trapeze artists, acrobats, and horseback riders performed at center stage.

By 1870, the tireless entrepreneur P. T. Barnum turned his attention back to the circus that had given him his start,[15] and his efforts further sensationalized this entertainment. Even though several successful circuses were traveling the country at the time, "no one," according to scholar Neil Harris, "had fully exploited the growing American taste for the spectacular and the exotic" until Barnum (238). The showman's adept marketing skills—along with the logistical and managerial efforts of his two partners Dan Castello and W. C. Coup—helped expand the appeal (and profitability) of the circus. In 1872, "P. T. Barnum's Great Traveling Exposition and World's Fair," which was being advertised as "The Greatest Show on Earth" for the first time, began using two rings to accommodate crowds. A few years later when Barnum merged his organization with James A. Bailey and James L. Hutchinson, this circus installed three rings.[16]

The multiple-ring system not only enhanced the spectacle, but it also kept people in their seats. In the single-ring layout, customers sitting far away from center stage often rushed closer to get a better view. This unruly behavior disrupted some of the class and ethnic hierarchies that the circus (and by extension society) wanted to reinforce. Wealthy patrons sitting in reserved box seats near center stage had no desire to mingle with working-class customers, who were supposed to remain in the bleacher sections at either end of the big top. And recent immigrants, Native Americans, and African Americans were relegated to the worst part of the arena—the "pit" between the Hippodrome and bleachers. The grandiose nature of the big top may have been emblematic of the country's growth as an industrialized nation, but these seating arrangements reflected America's divisive economic and racial politics.

By the time Cummings attended his first circus in 1900, the three-ring extravaganza had become the defining feature of the big top, and he would later praise its characteristics—the perpetual motion of the performance, the actual risk to performers, and its ability to engage the audience—as a distinctly modern art. In his essay, "The Adult, the Artist, and the Circus" (1925), he explains that "the bigness of the circus-show is intrinsic—like the bigness of an elephant or of a skyscraper—not superficial, as in the case of an enlarged snapshot. The nature of this bigness becomes apparent when we perceive that it is never, for so much as the fraction of an instant, motionless" (112). This "bigness" came not only from the literal size of the big top (the tent itself and its use of multiple stages with hundreds of performers and animals) but also from the ongoing activity of the show. For Cummings, this motion gave the circus the kind of grandeur and vividness that could be found in great art and modern American life. Like skyscrapers, subways, and picture palaces, the circus mirrored the frenetic pace and dazzling energy of urban living. As historian Janet M. Davis explains:

> The visually oriented three-ring circus flourished in tandem with multiple visual forms at the turn of the century: department stores filled with mirrors and reflective glassy surfaces, early motion picture actualities seen at saloons, railway stations, circuses, and world's fairs, and splashy new newspaper formats with big photo-filled sports pages; the three-ring circus was symbolic of an emergent "hieroglyphic civilization." (24)

The spectacle of the circus, in other words, fit into larger trends that celebrated visual culture (the hieroglyphic) in modern society, and as Davis's list implies, it was most intimately connected with images featuring movement—sports figures, motion pictures, and department stores.[17] Cummings makes motion a defining feature of *Him* to capture this modern-day vitality. The play has 105 parts, and the artistic range of the nine, rapid-fire scenes in act II, which includes a black musical revue in the tradition of minstrelsy, vaudeville, bawdy comedy sketches, absurdist drama, a parody of Eugene O'Neill's *Great God Brown,* and a burlesque in the style of Ziegfeld *Follies,* certainly emulates the variety of a circus show. Its diversity and scope bombard the audience with virtually every theatrical style, giving them the feeling that the play was never still for a moment.

Cummings also considered danger to be an essential component of the big top and of art more broadly. Any artist who exposes his own struggles and weaknesses (whether a circus performer or writer) makes himself vulnerable to criticism and condemnation. Not surprisingly, Cummings viewed the actual risks taken by acrobats and horseback riders as metaphors for the personal costs of creating art:

> Within "the big top," as nowhere else on earth, is to be found Actuality. Living players play with living...At positively every performance Death Himself lurks, glides, struts, breathes, is. Lest any agony be missing, a mob of clowns tumbles loudly in and out of that inconceivably sheer fabric by animal trainers, equestrians, acrobats—they are immune to forgetfulness in the same way that certain paintings, poems, and musical composition are immune. (113)

The artist (animal trainer, acrobat, poet) does not lose sight of what is at risk. He is not distracted by the frivolous and superficial (clowns); instead, he plays with living in every performance. Such a sentiment resonates with Hemingway's passion for bullfighting, and his notion of its artistry in *The Sun Also Rises* (1926). For the protagonist Jake Barnes, a great bullfighter (artist) enters the terrain of the bull, risking himself completely for his craft. Cummings seems to have entered this terrain for *Him.* As critic Norman Friedman has argued, Cummings explored his own personal struggles in the play—namely the loss of his first and second wives, his daughter, Nancy, and his father. The play's reception was another sore point: "The play itself was roundly trounced by the reviewers, both as a theatrical event and as a book. He seems to have cumulatively suffered a mortal wound from which he never wholly recovered. Henceforth, he would have to protect himself around the area of his hurt" (*(Re)Valuing* 159). For Friedman, this explains Cummings' inability to write another long work and his unwillingness to put more of himself into his fiction. Whether or not this is true, it does seem as if Cummings (as well as Hemingway) found a certain kinship with performers/artists who literally risked their lives for their art. At the outset of *Him,* the title character proclaims: "Damn everything but the circus!...The average 'painter' 'sculptor' 'poet' 'composer' 'playwright' is a person who cannot leap through a hoop from the back of a galloping horse, make people laugh with a clown's mouth, orchestrate twenty lions" (10). Here Cummings makes a case for art that speaks to the masses the way that acrobats and animal trainers could—through the authenticity and danger of their work. Horseback riders and acrobats can fall. Lions can turn on a trainer. Art not only needs to present something daring and new, inspiring audiences with its precision and beauty, but it also must communicate risk and its skillful avoidance.

Lastly, Cummings' admiration for the circus stemmed from the way it involved the audience in the performance. As mentioned earlier, Cummings believed that the arena enabled audiences to see around and participate in the three-dimensionality of the show. Davis's study of the circus points out that "no one possessed exclusive ownership of the gaze because it was a site of multiple surveillance, a three-ring 'theater in the round' which enabled people to watch each other from many vantages" (190). The crowds became part of the performance, and "the spectacle of these crowds became especially exciting when people fought, became drunk, gambled, or panicked in the face of a storm or rampaging animal" (28). Cummings viewed this symbiotic relationship between performance and audience, actor and viewer, and stage and arena as a model for contemporary theatre.[18] Just as the circus fed off the energy of the crowd as they laughed, applauded, stared at each other, felt anxious, moved around, and talked among themselves and to the performers, formal theatre needed to achieve something similar. He tries to recreate this arena-like space in *Him* by eroding the distance between audience and performer. Most noticeably, he has the stage rotate ninety degrees at significant points in the play to give the audience a three-dimensional perspective on both the action and the deteriorating relationship of Him and Me. Likewise, during the black musical revue in act II, Cummings has someone in the third row of the audience interrupt the performance.

This moment, like the rotating stage, literally draws attention to the artifice of the theatre itself.[19] Cummings makes this point explicit at the end of the play when Me explains to Him that the stage has an invisible wall and that real people are watching them: "They're pretending that this room and you and I are real" (139). Cummings uses these techniques both to give his play the kind of energy found in a circus performance and to make it an example of the possibilities for integrating popular forms and formal theatre.

Cummings presents the "perfect acrobat" as an image for all of these qualities—motion, risk, and audience involvement. At the opening of the play, Him explains to Me: "But imagine a human being who balances three chairs, one on top of another, on a wire, eighty feet in the air with no net underneath, and then climbs into the top chair, sits down, and begins to swing... Sometimes I look at it, with terror: it is such a perfect acrobat!" (10). This idealized figure risks his life to do/create something new, and the audience is drawn to him, presumably looking up in admiration and awe. The protagonist of *Him* values the perfect acrobat's craftsmanship, but it fills him with terror as well. Some of this fear comes from the gap between the artist's vision for a project (imagining its possibilities and promise) and the reality of his creation (recognizing its flaws and limitations). But it also comes from his conception of the artist as an isolated figure. Him's perfect acrobat (artist) doesn't have anyone to rely on; instead, he remains high above others, including his audience: "On air. Above the faces, lives, screams—suddenly. Easily: alone... The chairs will fall by themselves down from the wire and be caught by anybody, by nobody; by somebody whom I don't see and who doesn't see me: perhaps by everybody" (11). The artist cannot see the faces of his audience to measure their reaction. He is not part of their lives, and this encapsulates one of the central messages of the play: an artist needs to engage with the real world in order to create something meaningful. Formal art cannot remain separate from either life or popular culture.

Cummings further celebrates the orgiastic energy, movement, and physicality of such performers in his painting *Acrobats*,[20] but he does so in a way that emphasizes the importance of community. Dozens of naked bodies twist, turn, swing, and reach out for each other in a chaotic swirl of activity. Like Cummings' praise for the circus in which the audience "feels that there is a little too much going on at any given moment... [which] *is as it should be"* ("The Adult," 113),[21] this painting depicts bodies that blend into each other. Some disappear into the background or sail off the edge of the canvas, but one upside-down woman at the center reaches out as if to draw the viewer directly into the experience. This literal gesture (like the head on the right side looking out) acknowledges the viewer's presence, while the composition places him/her in the middle of the melée. The bodies are not being framed by space but seemingly captured at a random midpoint in the crowd, adding to the sense that the bodies are all around, above, below—much like the audience surrounding the stage at a circus. The element of community in this painting, however, is absent from Him's idealization of this performer, and as the play suggests, he will need to build such connections with others in order to create meaningful art.

As mentioned earlier, Cummings' praise for the circus in both his magazine writing and in *Him* is tempered by his criticism of the ways this entertainment emphasizes the sensational and superficial. Although his poetry tends to value the emotional over the intellectual (e.g., "since feeling is first/ who pays any attention/ to the syntax of things/ will never wholly kiss you" [*Complete Poems* 291]), it ultimately demands both levels of engagement from readers/listeners, and this is where Cummings' art departs from the popular entertainment of the big top.[22] Cummings wanted to achieve the visceral impact of popular culture in his work *and* the intellectual engagement demanded by formal arts. Even though he presents the circus as a metaphor for meaningful art in *Him*, he also qualifies this message by linking this entertainment with the Miss Weirds—three characters that appear sporadically throughout the play as commentators. Essentially, the play is interrupted by absurd conversations among these withered females, and unlike the witches of *Macbeth* or the Fates of Greek mythology, the Weirds don't provide insight into the drama as they knit, rock in chairs, and talk.[23] Instead, their conversations string together advertising slogans and gibberish that expose the superficiality of modern popular discourse and culture. Just as the women speak of a pet hippopotamus named "It's Toasted" (the slogan for Lucky Strike cigarettes) and parrot various slogans including one for United Retail Candy Stores ("Happiness in every box" [93]), they also describe someone who gave six pet hippopotamuses to "a circus" (3). Cummings connects the two to suggest a parallel between popular entertainment and other aspects of consumer culture designed to manipulate people. Advertising slogans influence desire, and like the sales of cigarettes and candy, the success of the traveling circus depended on marketing.[24] While attending the freak show at the end of *Him*, the Weirds accept the spiel of the barker as truth, and this belief in the advertisements for products and entertainment suggests that popular culture, when shaped by the demands of business, participates in a culture that promotes consumer desire. It encourages the superficial over the substantive, catchy phrases over meaningful discourse.

Such a contradictory message about popular culture might seem strange, but it is typical of Cummings' works more broadly. As Rushworth M. Kidder has argued, Cummings "thought in terms of 'opposites,' whether they 'occurred together' as in burlesque or not. No Hegelian, he did not always demand a resolution for his thesis and antithesis. He was often content simply to present binary structures, with some attention to various ideas he had learned from studying composition in the visual arts—the balancing of equivalents, the distribution of emphasis, the repetition of forms" ("Cummings and Cubism," 288). The same is true throughout *Him*. The Weirds' early reference to the circus is followed by the image of the "perfect acrobat," which complicates their claims. For Cummings, the acrobat's precision, skill, and risk-taking raise his craft to the level of art, but these qualities have the potential to get lost amidst the swirling spectacle of the big top and the consumer culture that promotes it. In other words, the danger for popular art is slipping too far into the realm of the unthinking, profit-hungry spectacle and failing to invite intellectual scrutiny *after* its initial emotional impact.

FREAK SHOWS AND THE BODY AS SPECTACLE

Cummings makes the differences between the circus and freak shows an integral part of the broader themes and structure of *Him*. In stark contrast with the opening image of the perfect acrobat, Cummings concludes the play with a freak show, and this shift from big top to sideshow also captures his critique of spectacle in American culture. Although human curiosities had been common attractions in taverns and public squares since the 1700s, these itinerant performers began appearing in dime museums in the nineteenth century. Here audiences could gaze at freaks alongside dioramas, menageries, stuffed animals, jugglers, historical wax tableaux, cabinets filled with curious objects, and other oddities. Live performers soon became central to the dime museum's appeal, and this form of entertainment reached its apex with P. T. Barnum's American Museum in 1841. Located in the heart of New York City near the Astor Hotel and Delmonico's Restaurant, Barnum's dazzling establishment became a fashionable public attraction. Due to the prominence he gave freak performers and the unprecedented scope of his promotional efforts, he helped make the freak show a national pastime.[25]

Like other freak-show entrepreneurs, Barnum used a variety of techniques, such as staging, costuming, and spiel, to transform the performer into a freak. Typically, these displays relied on juxtaposition and context to exaggerate differences: placing dwarfs next to giants, fabricating marriages between fat ladies and skeleton men, dressing nonwhites as exotic cannibals and wild men from Fiji, Africa, and South America, and asking audiences to guess about (and in some cases pay extra to "discover") the true sex of bearded ladies and hermaphrodites. Freaks also participated in stage performances, acting out poorly written parodies and giving renditions of popular plays. All of these characteristics, which Cummings drew on for his freak show in *Him,* ritualized the encounter with the freak and established what audiences expected to see.

In addition to dime museums, freaks played an integral role in the circus during its golden age (1870–1920), yet in this context they gradually became less enticing for the public. Instead of featuring one performer, these shows were known as "ten-in-ones" because patrons could see ten exhibits for the price of one—the format employed in *Him* (which places nine freaks on the stage at once). Freaks were also set apart from the featured acts of the big top (hence the term *sideshow*), and this distinction further changed the atmosphere surrounding these exhibits. Inside a museum, freaks had some respectability; they were integrated into a whole and displayed under the guise of learning and scientific study. But on the fairgrounds, the freak show gradually seemed dirtier and more difficult to justify. One even had to buy a separate ticket to see it. This contributed to its waning popularity, and by the late 1920s, the sideshow had become increasingly distasteful.[26]

As with Cummings' contradictory portrait of the circus, the penultimate scene of *Him* captures both the compelling and reprehensible elements of the freak show. First Cummings celebrates the vitality and fun of this entertainment by employing numerous sideshow ploys and performers. In Barnumesque fashion, a barker describes each exhibit—the giant, midget, snake charmer, geek, human skeleton, fattest woman in the world, hermaphroditic missing link, tattooed man, and a hootchy-cootchy dancer. He exaggerates the Nine Foot Giant's size by discussing his enormous clothes and gargantuan appetite and then juxtaposes him with the Eighteen Inch Lady, "[H]is lidl frien Madame Petite" (126). Her story is clearly modeled on true-life pamphlets (short, fictionalized biographies designed to promote and authenticate exhibits), and it details her international travels, arrest for being a spy, subsequent kidnapping, and narrow escape across Siberia while being chased by wolves—among other things. In addition to these characteristics, Cummings portrays his freaks selling items such as photographs and pamphlets and talking with the audience: The giant *"converses, offers photographs of himself"* (127); the Queen of Serpents responds to one audience member's distaste for snakes by saying, "Dat's because youse cawn't chawm dum dearie" (130); and before the King of Borneo eats a lightbulb, he *"winks solemnly to the spectators"* (131). This interactive component actively engages the audience and undermines the artificial distance between audience and performer.

Cummings also admired the visceral response audiences experienced at freak shows. In "The Adult, the Artist and the Circus," he praises "the writer, who, in the course of his lifetime, succeeds in making a dozen persons react to his personality as genuinely or vividly as millions react, each and every year, to the magnetic personality of Zip, the What-Is-It!" (112). Eliciting a genuine response was essential to the appeal of freak shows, and Cummings' protagonist has had a similar response to this entertainment. At the beginning of the play, Him agrees to take Me to the circus as long as she will see the freaks. When she questions why anyone would be interested in "a lot of motheaten freaks," he recalls an early experience at a sideshow:

> I seem to remember riding out of a circus once upon a time on somebody's shoulder; and hearing a throbbing noise, and then a coarse voice squirting a stream of bright words—and looking, and seeing

> a small tent with huge pictures of all sorts of queer things, and the barker spieling like a fiend, and people all about him gaping like fish. Whereupon, I began to tremble—(14)

This childhood memory links freak shows with community (the comfort Him feels while riding on someone's shoulders), visual spectacle (loud noises and pictures of the strange and unusual), verbal sensationalism (the "bright words" of the barker's spiel), and the wonder of the audience. Even as he reflects on this moment, he struggles to explain it, and the dash suggests that he still responds to this art more on a visceral than an intellectual level. Like his admiration for the physicality of acrobats, Him believes people should respond to art with the same kind of awe they have for freaks.

Cummings balances his admiration for this art, however, with concerns about the social elitism, sexual objectification, and racism often reinforced by freak shows. The Weirds' haughty responses to the performance offer one example. Miss Look Weird complains that the Human Needle was "starving himself to avoid honest labour!" (133), and Miss Listen Weird finds the Six Hundred Pounds of Passionate Pulchritude shameful. Their ridiculous commentary satirizes the value that many Americans placed on class and social propriety. Etiquette was not merely important for the upper classes. Manuals, such as Emily Post's *Etiquette in Society, in Business, in Politics and at Home* (1923), were still best-selling books among the middle classes hoping to rise in the social hierarchy, and just as Cummings presents Him as an everyman figure, he incorporates a freak show into the play because this entertainment had a history of appealing to all segments of American society. As scholar Rachel Adams notes, "In addition to working class audiences that formed their primary constituency, [freak shows] were attended by authors, artists, politicians, scientists, and philosophers" (4). For Cummings, the willingness among all audiences to be manipulated by humbug parallels a dangerous willingness in America to buy into socially accepted behaviors and norms. They both promote image over authenticity.

Cummings also uses the onstage audience of *Him* to condemn the self/other dynamic essential to the popularity of freak shows. Part of their appeal stemmed from the way freak shows reinforced the onlooker's sense of normalcy and belonging. As Rosemarie Garland

Thomson has explained, "[T]he freak soothes the onlookers' self-doubt by appearing as their antithesis. The American produces and acts, but the onstage freak is idle and passive. The American looks and names, but the freak is looked at and named. The American is mobile, entering and exiting the show at will and ranging around the social order, but the freak is fixed" (*Extraordinary* 65). Thus, the success of the freak show was contingent on its ability to maintain this relationship between viewer and freak. Cummings, however, collapses the distance between the two at the end of *Him*, and not surprisingly when Me and her child replace the final freak Princess Anankay, the entire onstage audience reacts in horror. They don't want the illusions of this entertainment shattered. At this moment, the Weirds exclaim that "[i]t's all done with mirrors!" (138) because the actual world threatens the comforts they derive from this performance—namely the way freakishness reinforces their sense of cultural and social superiority.

The exchange between Me and Anankay (whose name refers to the Greek goddess of necessity) points to the author's concern about the role of sexual objectification in freak shows and popular entertainment as well. Him's passion for freak shows, which include performers like the eroticized (and exoticized) Anankay, has shaped his view of women, and Cummings makes sexual objectification one of the sources for his limitations as a lover and an artist. As his frequent sexual puns suggest, Him primarily appreciates Me for her physical beauty. Every time she tries to communicate her anguish about their relationship or her pregnancy, Him reverts to sexual wordplay and/or a narcissistic discussion of his art. He even seems oblivious to her concerns moments before the end of their relationship. Me says mostly to herself: "Where I am I think it must be getting dark... The dark is so many corners—... so many dolls, who move—... by Themselves... Darker... We must go very carefully... gradually... until light" (83–84). Her feeling of being trapped by their relationship (the dark corners) and controlled by love (like one of the dolls) goes unnoticed by Him. Instead, her ideas are broken by his fixation on her body. He reduces her to a hand, wrist, arm, "the dangerous shoulders of Eve" (83), throat, head, breasts, and thighs, and he views these parts as "perpetually discovered yet undiscovered: sexual, sweet. Alive!" (84). He does not see her as a whole person but a sexual object,[27] and this explains part of his failure to build a lasting relationship with her. In a sense his sexual desire has turned her into a kind of freak, aligning her with Princess Anankay who comes from a land where women bathe in champagne three times a day and "doan wear nutn between dun knees un duh neck" (137).[28] Her act is about the erotic allure of seeing her near-naked body, and even the name of her dance (the Spasmwriggle) suggests that the pleasure of seeing her move will be akin to sex. When the barker urges the men in the crowd to get closer to the stage, he adds: "[D]uh Princess wears so lidl youse can stick her full uv looks like she wus uh pincushion" (137). This image of the pincushion, which suggests penetration and pain, also makes the violence of looking essential to her appeal. Ultimately for Cummings, the audience *needs* (as the name "Anankay" suggests) to see beyond the surface of etiquette, advertisements, and physical beauty in order to build meaningful relationships between men and women.

In a Cummings' painting completed in the same year, *New York, 1927,* sexual objectification seems to be the problem at the center of urban life as well. When discussing this work, Milton A. Cohen argues that Cummings "was searching for a new way of reconciling abstraction and representation" (55–56). Like the protagonist of *Him* who tries to integrate high art with popular culture, Cummings attempts to bring together two artistic styles in this painting. He admired the work of Marcel Duchamp, Giacomo Balla, and other futurists for their "worship of speed,"[29] and as Kidder has argued, Cummings' celebration of movement is evident throughout his art: "Many of his own drawings—of dancers caught in mid-step, of crowds glimpsed in a saloon, of strippers in wild undulations, of acrobats and clowns at the circus—capture actions which in the next second will change" ("Cummings and Cubism," 265). Everything about the city in Cummings' painting is in the process of happening. The background, which shows the influence of John Marin's art,[30] swirls with buildings, bridges, a ship, and smokestacks—capturing the frenetic energy of Manhattan. As with *Acrobats,* these images are mostly abstracted and incomplete, spilling off the canvas or blending into the waters and rising smoke. Waves carry the ship as it curves toward the center of the painting. The bridge, which is also a direct allusion to Joseph Stella's Brooklyn Bridge paintings/drawings, bulges as it arches into the city. Smokestacks depict factories at work, and the partially open windows of the apartment building imply people at home. Nothing seems at rest in New York City—except for the woman at the center of the canvas. Her stillness is quite startling amidst the surrounding tumult. Her bobbed haircut and fashionable hat characterize her as a flapper, but unlike most flappers (who abandoned corsets, attended late-night parties, drank, danced the Charleston, and rejected conventional roles for women such as mother and wife), this girl stands apart from the vitality and flux of urban life. Her pose, with one hand behind her head and the other on her hip, is reminiscent of a model or performer, but her expression seems to be more of exhaustion than pleasure. The dark circles around both eyes and the shading underneath the left eye suggest fatigue—perhaps from city living and from being viewed as an object. The latter is reinforced by her staged pose and Cummings' placement of the inverted triangle of her pubic hair at the center of the canvas. She is an object for the male gaze, defined by her nakedness and sexuality. Like Him's horrified reaction to Me and her child, this painting presents her as a static, sexual object—not a "natural" or classically beautiful type.

Him's difficulties with reconciling life and art, the popular and formal also stem from his failure to see beyond racial caricature. Cummings first indicates this problem through O. Him's play, which includes a musical revue in the tradition of minstrelsy. Like freak shows, minstrelsy, which gained popularity in the 1830s and 1840s, was an art form that helped whites justify the social status of blacks in America. As Robert Toll explains in *Blacking Up: The Minstrel Show in Nineteenth-Century America*, "[M]instrelsy provided common Americans with folk-based earthy songs, vital dances, and robust humor as well as with beautiful ballads and fine singing that they could enjoy at reasonable prices. It also provided a nonthreatening way to white Americans to cope with questions about the nature and proper place of black people in America" (57). Cummings' version appears to contain similar qualities and messages. The use of black English vernacular, makeup (all of the characters are descried as "coalblack"), folk song, music, and emphasis on black sexuality play into widely held stereotypes about African Americans. These characteristics could be found on the contemporary burlesque stage as well, even in upscale productions like Ziegfeld's *Follies* (which will be discussed in more detail later). In an example from 1922, Gilda

Gray sang "It's Getting Dark on Old Broadway," and for this number "Ziegfeld had bought radium paint in Paris and... required the white performers to slather it onto their costumes. Against a rack of electric lights and a canvas drop depicting Longacre Square, as the lights faded, the performers appeared to be 'getting dark' while their white costumes and hats gleamed and their bodies jiggled to piano rags" (Shteir 75). Cummings undermines some of these racist ploys by placing them among O. Him's parodies of theatrical styles and by directing most of the humor at a white character named John Rutter—a humorous allusion to John Sumner who became president of the New York Society for the Suppression of Vice (NYSSV) in 1915, succeeded in banning the publication of Joyce's *Ulysses* in the United States six years later, and tried to close down Minsky's burlesque theatre in 1927. In Cummings' retelling of the Frankie and Johnnie story, Frankie not only shoots Johnnie three times after he "done her wrong" by sleeping with another woman, but she also castrates him. Before one of the other actors can say the word "penis," a white man in the audience interrupts the performance. Like the larger tension in the play between authenticity and illusion, this scene presents the censor—who speaks for the "Society for the Contraception of Vice" (50) and sits among the audience—as preserving the illusion of wholesome entertainment, beauty, and arguably racism for the viewer. When Frankie asserts that she is not a young lady, for example, the censor immediately replies that she should "attempt by every method practicable and impracticable way to conceal the fact instead of making it glaringly apparent." Women should appear young and "lady-like," and by extension African Americans should appear as caricatures. Just as Him and the audience react with terror to Me and her child, this audience would presumably respond negatively to an authentic portrait of African Americans. Popular entertainment like minstrelsy and freak shows sanctioned a racist ideology, and as the presence of the censor suggests, society wanted to avoid moments of authenticity that would shatter the illusions and stereotypes that preserved such comforting, self-serving biases.

Cummings' minstrel revue also challenges this racism by incorporating black music into the play. Minstrelsy was not merely about reinforcing racism. As Eric Lott has argued persuasively, this entertainment expressed a "cross racial-desire that coupled a nearly insupportable fascination and self-protective derision with respect to black people and their cultural practices and that made blackface minstrelsy less a sign of absolute white power and control than of panic, anxiety, terror, and pleasure" (6). Cummings captures this tension between pleasure and anxiety by juxtaposing a lively musical number with the censor's fears of social impropriety and emasculation. Nothing about the stage directions suggests that the satire here is aimed at the jazz band or singing. Instead, like Cummings' implementation of other aspects of popular culture, he wants the vitality of this music to enrich the play. This may have also been Cummings' intention in his painting *Small's* as well. Cummings' personal affinity for this club on 135th Street and Seventh Avenue would suggest a desire to communicate some appreciation for jazz here, but any such message is undermined by the racist characterization of the couple—whose bodies are distorted by their large lips, eyes, and teeth. As Cohen points out, Cummings was interested in caricature in his paintings. "The challenge of compressing character and motion into a few telling—and exaggerated—details appealed to the artist" (41). Yet without a broader context like the parodies offered by O. Him, this painting comes across as racist.

Along with the caricatures of African Americans in *Him,* Cummings specifically includes two ethnic exhibits (the Missing Link and the King of Borneo) in the freak show of act III to expose the dangerous way that popular culture objectified nonwhites and sanctioned commonly held prejudices among white Americans. White angst about race/ethnicity intensified in the Teens and Twenties with the exodus of African Americans from the South (over 1.3 million left the South between 1900 and the 1930s), the popularity of jazz and other black arts during the Harlem Renaissance, and the growing number of immigrants. Between 1880 and 1914, for example, over 23 million immigrants came to the United States, and by September of 1920 approximately five thousand new arrivals entered Ellis Island every day.[31] Freak shows worked to mitigate some of these anxieties by presenting degrading images of nonwhites on stage. In this tradition, Cummings' Ge Ge serves as a fairly typical missing link—a bridge between animal and human whose African origins ("[being] discovered...in duh jungles uv Darkest Africuh" [134]) link blackness with primitivism and savagery. This kind of exhibit, like minstrel shows, encouraged audiences to question the humanity of blacks. Cummings mocks the racist message of Ge Ge, however, through the "scientific" validity offered by the barker. Ge Ge was supposedly studied "by evry intimut means known tuh duh corporeal un mentul sciences incloodin syntetic bloodtests telepathic waves cerebrul photogruphy postprandiul iodic injections testicullur hypnotism rhapsodic vaginul eelectrolysis decalcomaniuh un X ray" (135). The absurd juxtaposition of scientific tools, such as cerebral photography and x-rays, with telepathic waves and testicular hypnotism satirize the presumed civility of scientists and university professors. The King of Borneo (or the Human Ostrich) also appeals to the prejudices of the typical freak-show viewer. According to the barker, the King of Borneo ruled the most primitive of all semicivilized communities (129) and could eat indigestible substances such as lightbulbs. Despite his royalty, this ability to eat anything is clearly associated with the presumed cultural inferiority of Borneo. Such connections were typical among freak exhibits, which were designed to reinforce the cultural superiority of white onlookers.[32]

Interestingly, this ambivalent portrait of freak shows is mostly absent from Cummings' essay "The Adult, the Artist and the Circus," which seems to praise freak performers unreservedly:

> [H]appy is that writer, who, in the course of his lifetime, succeeds in making a dozen persons react to his personality as genuinely or vividly as millions react, each and every year, to the magnetic personality of Zip, the What-Is-It! Nor can I refrain, at this point, saluting also the Giant, the Pygmy, the Pin-Head, the unutterably refined Human Skeleton and the other distinguished members of Zip's very select secret society. (112)

As mentioned before, Cummings values the visceral response of audiences to freak performers, but his reference to Zip typifies both the appeal of and problems with freak shows. Zip performed under a variety of stage names, but he began his career as P. T. Barnum's notorious "What Is It?" First presented in 1860, William Henry Johnson, a mentally retarded African American from New Jersey, was cast as a mysterious man-animal hybrid billed with the headline "What Is It?"[33] As Janet Davis points out, "Johnson always remained mute on stage, from his early days... until his final years at Coney Island, where he silently worked until his death in 1926 at eighty-four" (182). Cummings certainly admired the individuality of freaks and their provocative performances/bodies, but highlighting a silent/silenced performer like Zip undercuts this admiration. Zip's body always remained a site for interpretation, giving the audience the power to label and interpret his social meaning. His silence kept the racist construct of the show/performance intact, and this makes it difficult to assess Cummings' comments here.[34] Is Zip's personality "magnetic" because the viewer could project a personality of his or her own making onto Zip's body (undeterred by his speech), or despite being mute did Zip, in fact, project a charismatic self? Or is Cummings merely being sarcastic? Despite this ambiguity, Cummings' explicit agenda in these magazine writings was both to celebrate popular culture as art and to defend against those who dismissed it as lowbrow and vulgar. His friend Gilbert Seldes, the foremost authority on popular entertainment at the time, dedicated a book to this subject in 1924. In the preface to the 1957 edition of *The 7 Lively Arts*, he explained that "[m]y theme was to be that entertainment of a high order existed in places not usually associated with Art, that the place where an object was to be seen or heard had no bearing on its merits" (3). Seldes' survey of popular entertainment, which included burlesque shows, jazz and ragtime music, comic strips, and films, celebrated these arts and felt that they were an important part of modern life.[35] Cummings' passionate defense of popular entertainment takes on this rallying cry, but as the uncritical praise of Zip suggests, his support is overstated. *Him,* as we have seen, offers a more balanced portrait, and the use of nonwhite bodies in the play's sideshow ultimately functions to condemn the protagonist's passion for the entertainment of spectacle. Freak shows become another aspect of modern amusement culture that prevent mutual understanding. For the protagonist, it keeps him from loving Me and achieving his full potential as an artist—what Cummings called achieving "selftranscendence."[36]

"Burlesque, I Love It!": Staging Female Nudity, Sexuality, and Gender

It is not entirely surprising that Cummings was drawn to burlesque, which combined various aspects of the humorous play and bodily objectification found in circus/freak shows and minstrelsy. In fact, the circus provided one of the earliest public forums for respectable nudity. Female acrobats, bareback riders, and statue girls (who posed motionless as living pictures) appeared scantily clad or partially nude, but circus managers were always careful to present these acts as wholesome family entertainment. Nevertheless, as Rachel Shteir has argued, "[T]he modern self-referential quality of undressing acts begins here on the flying trapeze [at the turn of the century], and a number of female acrobats undressing in the air during this era display a new physical awareness" (52). This awareness helped set the stage for burlesque's emphasis on the female body. In its infancy in 1870, burlesque borrowed the three-part structure of the minstrel show. Part one, which Cummings used as a model for the minstrel scene in *Him*, featured the company sitting in a semicircle on stage with performers alternating between telling jokes, engaging in improvisational repartee, singing sentimental love songs, and dancing. It concluded with a group song and dance number. The second part, called the olio, offered the audience a variety show with singing, dancing, acrobatic stunts, and other novelties. Its defining feature was the stump speech—a combination of physical and verbal comedy that relied heavily on malapropisms. A one-act skit rounded off the show in part three. As Toll explains, "[B]efore the mid-1850s these finales almost invariably were set on Southern plantations" (56), but a few years later, they tended to lampoon current events and feature slapstick comedy. The singing, dancing, and comedic components of minstrelsy remained an important feature of burlesque, but in the early part of the twentieth century, burlesque abandoned the three-part structure. It still included variety acts, ethnic comedy, and other skits, but women tended to be objects of both the ribald humor and the voyeuristic interest of the mostly male audience. After Florenz Ziegfeld first launched the *Follies* on the rooftop of the New York Theatre in 1907, lavish scenery and, of course, beautiful showgirls became the defining features of this entertainment.[37] By presenting these women as respectable through clothing and a Parisian backdrop/setting, the *Follies* sold itself as high-class entertainment, sidestepping public condemnation over the display of women's bodies. As Robert Allen explains in his study *Horrible Prettiness: Burlesque and American Culture*, "Ziegfeld's shows succeeded with bourgeois audiences... because he managed to package feminine stage sexuality in such a way that his audiences connected the *Follies* not with the working-class sexuality of burlesque but with the cosmopolitan worldliness of Paris" (245).

One of the most significant changes to the burlesque show, the introduction of the runway, supposedly came in 1917 at Minsky's National Winter Garden, Cummings' favorite burlesque house in New York City. By adding a runway to the theatre, the Minsky brothers created a more intimate relationship between performer and audience. Billy Minsky, arguably the most entrepreneurial and Barnumesque of the brothers, encouraged his performers to step off the runway and mingle with the audience. He even paid women extra for the "take-off" or breast flash. Not surprisingly, the nudity at the National Winter Garden led to several highly publicized police raids, which temporarily closed the theatre. It was during this period when Cummings saw his first striptease. In a 1936 essay about the history of burlesque, Cummings views the introduction of the striptease as a watershed moment for burlesque, marking a shift in focus from the comedian's humor to feminine pulchritude. He notes that "whereas, formerly, sketches and comedians had constituted a *pièce de résistance* for which soi-disant sex appeal served as trimming, sketches and comedians now served as trimming for Sex with a capital S" (294). Historians would argue that female sexuality was part of burlesque from its earliest days in America, which publicized female performers (most notably Lydia Thompson and Pauline Markham) as possessing extraordinary beauty and sexual magnetism.[38] Nevertheless, introducing nudity was considered a last-ditch effort to maintain dwindling audiences. Cummings does not disparage burlesque for this shift, however. He celebrates the vibrancy that female sexuality brought to the stage. In his essay "Burlesque, I Love It!" he singles out performer June St. Clare, for example: "She propagates...a literally miraculous synthesis of flying and swimming and floating and rising and darting and gliding and pouncing and falling and creeping and every other conceivable way of moving" (295). Once again for Cummings, part of the artistry of burlesque—like the circus—has to do with the perpetual movement of these shows.

He depicts this dimension of burlesque most explicitly in his 1935 poem "sh estiffl." From the first adverb, Cummings suggests a certain ambivalence about the pouting stripper who "stiffly struts all ifs and buts." Her awkward movements signal a reluctance on her part to perform, and the typography captures this stiffness, while making the poem itself a striptease. It reveals the action gradually to the reader who must undress its meaning by regrouping the word clusters:

> sh estiffl
> ystrut sal
> lif san
> dbut sth
> epouting(g Wh.ono:w
> s li psh ergo
> wnd ow n,

After she "slips her gown down," the word "revealing" stretches down the page, and Cummings breaks it apart to isolate the name "Eve"—the archetypal woman who represents temptation and whose original sin made men and women ashamed of their nakedness. With this as well as the word "sin/uously" in the fourth stanza, Cummings expresses moral reservations about this burlesque act and its ultimate objectification of women. The more she disrobes, the more she disappears in front of the hungry eyes of the audience. Only her body matters to these men as their "eyelands" on her breasts and swirling hips. Amid the sound of the audience whooping and calling out ("ono" and "ow"), she thrusts in and out for their pleasure. Her objectification by the viewer not only reduces her to body parts, but it also allows him to see her in terms of ownership. From the word "ow n" in stanza two and to the line "(yoursmine mineyours yoursmine" at the end of the poem, the male fantasy here involves seeing her as an object. Even the pronouns at the outset are pulled apart "sh e" and "h er," implying her lack of identity [as does the fact that she remains nameless]. Ultimately, she gets reduced to "it" in the final line: "i()t)." Her act culminates in her complete disrobing, and Cummings uses the parenthesis to visualize her vagina as well as to signal an emptiness at the heart of this moment. There is something unfulfilling for both the performer and the audience here. As with the protagonist of *Him,* the speaker in "sh estiffl" is caught between enjoying the vitality and fantasy of burlesque while recognizing the real, belittling objectification of this woman.[39]

More specifically in the play, Cummings parodies two burlesque comedy routines in act II to link this entertainment with his broader concerns about popular culture and America's investment in spectacle. Scene VI, for example, invokes the humor found in a vaudeville and burlesque skits featuring people from different cultures struggling to communicate with each other. The humor largely comes from wordplay—specifically British idioms that Americans don't understand and the reverse. Like *Suppressed Desires* (1914/1915), an earlier Provincetown play by Susan Glaspell and George Cram Cook, this scene also satirizes the fad with Freud and psychoanalysis in America. At one point, when an Englishman is questioned about the contents of his trunk, he explains that it contains his unconscious: "My unconscious, old egg. Don't pretend you haven't heard of them in America—Why my dear boy, I was given to understand that a large percentage of them originated in the States: if I'm not mistaken, the one I've got is made hereabouts, in Detroit of something like that" (55). With the reference to Detroit, the heart of the automobile industry and the place where Henry Ford launched the assembly line, Cummings mocks the commercialization of psychoanalysis in the United States by linking it to mass-produced, consumer culture. Its popularization has transformed it into a commodity—something to own, so to speak, in order to claim a connection with European sophistication. Furthermore, when a criminal and police officer look inside the trunk, they immediately die from the horror of its contents. This moment, which highlights the notion that we all hide things about ourselves that would seem horrifying to others, links the scene to the larger tension between image and truth in the play. At one point, the criminal even tells the Englishman to "Can dat soikus stuff" (55), accusing him of deliberately misunderstanding him, but in the end, the circus stuff and game playing is preferable to the truth. People don't really want to know these hidden truths about others or, as psychoanalysis would promise, about themselves.

The stage directions for the burlesque skit of scene VIII explicitly refer to the Old Howard, Cummings' favorite burlesque house in Boston, and this section of O. Him's play offers a political satire that ultimately condemns image culture in America. Cummings offers a burlesque of burlesque here by substituting a group of homosexual men for female performers, strippers, and teasers. The text refers to these men as "fairies," which as historian George Chauncey has explained had less to do with sexuality in the 1920s than it did with one's gender persona. "For many men, then, adopting effeminate mannerisms represented a deliberate cultural strategy, as well as a way of making sense of their sense of sexual difference. It was a way to declare a gay identity publicly and to negotiate their relationship with other men" (56). Such effeminate displays were common on the burlesque stage as well as on the streets of Greenwich Village, Harlem, and Coney Island. In fact, Shteir notes that "burlesque became a hangout for homosexuals—and a place where these gay men could perform drag striptease" (94). Men often passed as strippers in burlesque shows, and some of these performers, like cross-dressers Bert Savoy and Jay Brennan and female impersonator Barbette (Van Der Clyde), had highly successful careers.[40] Despite the mockery, contempt, and abuse experienced by many homosexuals in public, the visible presence of fairies in bohemian culture revealed a tolerance of homosexuality among the working class in the early twentieth century. "Much evidence suggests that the fairy, so long as he abided by the conventions of this cultural script, was tolerated in much of working-class society—regarded as an anomaly, certainly, but as more amusing than abhorrent, and only rarely as a threat to the gender order" (Chauncey 57). Cummings incorporation of "fairies" in this scene not only plays with gender, sexuality (a common feature of burlesque), and the visible place of gay culture in Bohemia at the time, but it also parodies the form by presenting fairies instead of female impersonators. This group of "girls" gossip, flirt, kiss each other, and cry without much provocation. One even hopes *"rapturously"* (65) that Caesar might whip them. Cummings seems to poke fun at both stereotypes about the gay community and the clichés of women on the burlesque stage.

This playfulness with gender types fits into the larger theme of artificiality in the drama. When the burlesque turns its attention to contemporary society, for example, the characters on stage mention A. S. M. Hutchinson's *If Winter Comes*. Published in 1921, this bestselling novel describes the unhappy marriage and divorce of Mark Sabre and the suicide of Effie Bright, a single mother. One of the fairies in *Him* has recently borrowed the book from Caesar, and the group is excited to read it because the title "sounds lovely" (64). Along with the Ethiopian slave who calls the gay men "peddyrasts" and the fairies who judge a book based on its title, the society depicted here judges the world based on surface image. Gay men must be pederasts, and a good title must indicate a good book. Cummings links this message to the political critique of the scene as well. The fairies fawn over and cower before Caesar, who is actually Mussolini dressed as Napoleon Bonaparte. The conflation of these figures suggests that the ruthlessness, insatiable greed, and megalomania of corrupt rulers are consistent throughout Western history. Just as Napoleon famously employed propaganda painters Jacques-Louis David and Antoine-Jean Gros to manipulate the public, for instance, Cummings suggests that abusive power is often masked by appealing artifice. His concern extends beyond fascism, though, and he quickly directs the satire once again to America's preoccupation with the superficial image. The public too readily accepts propaganda, and like the weak, unmasculine fairies, they enable corrupt leaders to maintain power. At the end of the scene, Me expresses her dislike for the scene, stating that she hates history. Him responds: "So do I.—Europe, Africa, Asia: continents of Give. America: the land of the Keep—Keep in step Keep moving Keep young Keep your head Keep in touch with events Keep smiling Keep your shirt on Keep of the grass Keep your arms and limbs off the car. National disease: constipation" (69–70). For Him, greediness, movement, conformity, and image define the American character. The importance of smiling and following the rules is an essential part of life in the United States, and Cummings links this to popular culture. Him continues: "National recreation: the movies...National anthem: You Forget to Remember. National advertisement: The Spirit of '76—a man with a flag a man with a fife and a drummerboy—caption: General Debility Youthful Errors and Loss of Manhood" (70). Film is part of a culture that encourages the public to forget history. Even the struggles and triumphs of the American Revolution have been reduced to an advertisement. The flag, fife, and drummer boy are clichéd images of patriotism—far removed from the realities of eighteenth-century American life.

Cummings does not include the sexualized dancing of burlesque until the freak show at the end of the play; by placing it outside of the parodies of act II, he connects the objectification of women with the degrading spectacle of freakishness to warn against the dangers of a popular culture that capitalizes on the exploitation of the body in the name of entertainment. Instead of a group of chorus girls, Cummings promises the audience a performance by Princess Anankay, a hootchy-cootchy dancer who wears virtually nothing. The barker then claims that she is "duh woil's foist un foremohs exponent uv yaki-hooluh-hiki-dooluh udderwise known us duh Royal Umbilicul Bengul Cakewalk" (137). The reference to Bengal reinforces her status as an exotic other, an essential characteristic for cootch or belly dancers. This form of dance was first introduced in America on the Midway of the Columbian World Exposition in 1893, and it featured women with an exposed midsection gyrating to Middle Eastern music. As John Kasson notes in *Amusing the Millions,* "Visitors were titillated by the prospect of the World Congress of Beauty with '40 Ladies from 40 Nations'... They pushed into the Streets of Cairo, the Algerian Village, and the Persian Palace of Eros to watch entranced as 'Little Egypt,' and her colleagues and competitors, performed the 'danse du ventre,' popularly known as the hootchy-cootchy" (24–26). The popularity of these dances, which offered a socially acceptable context for staring at the partially clothed woman's body,[41] made performers like Little Egypt and Fatima staples at burlesque shows almost immediately. "Within weeks of the fair's closing on October 29, 1893, cootch dancing arrived in New York City as part of a sampling of fair exhibits erected at Grand Central Palace at Lexington and Forty-third Street" (Allen 229). These dancers became regular members of burlesque troupes by the early 1900s, and their performances were precursors to the shimmy in the 1910s and the striptease of the 1920s and 1930s. The cootch dancer's exotic otherness made this form of sexuality safe, and Cummings suggests as much in his painting *Danseuse "Égyptienne."* Her dark features and pose (contorted body) distance her from white standards of beauty. Her elongated, twisted neck and angular breasts seem reminiscent of cubism and also suggest his attempt to capture the movement of her dance. Like the display of ethnological exhibits at freak shows, the eroticization and exoticization of these dancers distanced this display from the white notions of sexuality and propriety. As Allen argues, "[T]he belly dancer was another kind of woman, whose expressive sexuality tantalized but whose power was contained and distanced by her exotic otherness. She was a woman, to be sure, but as far removed from the modern, American bourgeois woman" (229). Thus when Me takes the place of Princess Anankay onstage in *Him,* she presumably replaces the "grotesque" sexuality of the other with the purity of the Anglo-American woman. Since they both appear in the context of a freak show, however, part of the horror for the protagonist comes from the idea that white female sexuality (Me) is no different than the sexuality of Princess Anankay after all. Cummings exposes the artificial distancing between self/other and normal/freak and the prejudices that that these entertainments offered.

Conclusion: High, Low, and *Him*

Cummings introduced the theatrical experiment of *Him* with a warning that appeared in the original program for the 1928 Provincetown production:

> (*WARNING:* him *isn't a comedy or a tragedy or a farce or a melodrama or a revue or an operetta or a moving picture or any other convenient excuse 'for going to the theater'—in fact, it's a PLAY, so let it PLAY; and because you are here, let it PLAY with you. Let it dart off and beckon to you from the distance, let it tiptoe back down on you from above, let it creep cautiously behind you and tap you on the back of the neck, let it go all around and over and under you and inside you and through you. Relax, and give this PLAY a chance to strut its stuff—relax, don't worry because it's not like—something else—relax, stop wondering what it's all 'about'—like many strange and familiar things. Don't try to despise it, let it try to despise you. Don't try to enjoy it, let it try to enjoy you. DON'T TRY TO UNDERSTAND IT, LET IT UNDERSTAND YOU.)*[42]

On one level, this is an invitation to experience the play as one would a circus—on instinctual and visceral levels. Categories such as tragedy, farce, and melodrama establish an audience's expectations and influence their reactions before a production begins. The emphasis on "play" serves as both an image for the work itself, which plays with numerous theatrical styles and tones, and as a challenge to viewers/readers to be open-minded, to resist condemning something unfamiliar before giving it a chance. His description of the play as coming down on the audience from above, behind, "all around and over and under you and inside you and through you" is also reminiscent of the circular arena of the circus or the runway at a burlesque house. He hopes the audience will experience the show on multiple levels. In his reviews for the *Dial* and other magazines, Cummings had been quite vocal about the failings of contemporary theatre to engage viewers: "The play itself is required to give [the entire theatrical space] life... Nothing is accessory: everything is a complement, a sequence, a development, a conclusion" ("The Theater II," 147). He offers *Him*—with its vast range of styles and the way it rotates the stage and reaches into the space of the audience—as an alternative to the static quality of much contemporary theatre. This play, in other words, was designed to have an emotional impact on the viewers ("Let it try to despise you... Let it try to enjoy you"). Cummings recognizes that the greatest barrier to this might come from the audience itself, and this warning makes clear that one must suspend a rush to judge the more surprising, innovative, and disorienting aspects of this work in order to connect with its emotional content. At first glance, this text seems antithetical to his critique of the passive acceptance of surface/superficial images, but Cummings realized that audiences for the Provincetown Players would approach this play differently than they would a freak show, for example. They would be evaluating it in the context of a theatre group famous for innovative productions and high art. Many would find his incorporation of popular culture objectionable, and even those who enjoyed mainstream entertainment outside of the formal theatre probably compartmentalized high and low art. Cummings warning, like the play itself, is an attempt to breakdown such distinctions.

On another level, this warning communicates Cummings' own anxieties about the fusion of popular and formal arts. He certainly understood the possible pitfalls of this experiment, and it couldn't have been too surprising that many theatre critics—who also tended to ignore, scorn, and/or dismiss popular culture as frivolous—found *Him* objectionable. In response to the controversy surrounding the play, the Provincetown Playhouse published a pamphlet entitled *Him and the Critics,* which reprinted numerous articles about the work. The introduction, written by Gilbert Seldes, accuses the critics of being more concerned with the warning and the lack of capitalization of Cummings' name than the actual content of the work. He also argues that most audiences at the time viewed high and low arts as antithetical to one another, which explains some of the negative reactions to the play. This perception of popular culture and formal arts prevented most people from recognizing the true innovation of the play—its exploration of serious and tragic issues through popular modes: "Perhaps the most astounding thing in the play is the fact that Cummings has expressed these tragic themes [of love and angst about artistic failure] in the techniques of the burlesque show and the circus" (3). Despite this spirited defense of the work, *Him*—as we have seen—walks a fine line between its appreciation for the vitality and appeal of art forms like the circus and its reservations about its use of spectacle and objectification. One might admire an acrobat's skill, but the eroticization of female trapeze artists undermines some of the integrity of the performance. It creates a context that diminishes her craft in order to titillate audiences. Likewise, the breakdown of theatrical space in freak shows took a backseat to its racial and cultural messages, and the crude objectification in burlesque often reduced it to pornography. Cummings expresses these concerns most powerfully through the failure of Him and Me's relationship. Him's unquestioned investment in these popular arts contributed to his limited and arguably sexist view of Me. The real emotional barriers between them came largely from his inability to recognize her emotional and intellectual needs. Although she claims many times to be unintelligent, there is no evidence for this in the play; in fact, many of her observations about act II are quite astute. In the final moments of the play, Him is terrified by Me's presence on stage, exposing his failed recognition that the objectification of women found in the circus, freak shows, and burlesque have shaped his attitudes about women, and that he has viewed her as a spectacle too.[43] Me appears on stage, but she is wearing the wrong outfit. She appears fully clothed and as a mother, not a stripper.

As mentioned earlier, the worst aspects of popular culture tend to reduce people—such as women, African Americans, and homosexuals—to caricatures. They reinforce explicit or tacit prejudices on the part of the audience, instead of offering images that might encourage people to question such biases. At its best, popular culture captures the energetic vitality of modern urban life. Like Millay, Cummings tapped into popular forms because he recognized the artistic value of play, and he had a desire to reach a wide audience. The subject matter of his writings (such as love, passion, nature, and childhood innocence), his use of conventional forms like the sonnet, and the role of popular arts in *Him* suggest as much. But the lack of resolution in the play (Him's failure to reconcile high and low) and Cummings inability to produce another long dramatic work suggest he couldn't find a lasting expression that brought together the formal and popular. Perhaps the relative obscurity of this play—the fact that it has largely been excluded from discussions of the development of American theatre—points to the difficulty of this undertaking. We still tend to see mainstream popular culture, such as reality television, as far removed from a Pulitzer Prize–winning novel. It is still rare to find an art form that can speak to such different audiences, and Cummings' attempt to create a play that does so still challenges us to recognize the cultural power and beauty of popular arts.

CHAPTER 3

PLANES, TRAINS, AND AUTOMOBILES: TECHNOLOGY AND THE SUBURBAN NIGHTMARE IN THE PLAYS OF JOHN DOS PASSOS

> The home-making propaganda is the best training in national pride that the child or the adult can have. Homeless people make poor citizens. Nomads are seldom patriots. Give us a nation of homes, with each family loving and beautifying and developing its own, and there will be small need for teaching patriotism.
> *American Home,* July 1929.[1]

DOS PASSOS SPENT MUCH OF HIS CHILDHOOD IN HOTEL ROOMS. His mother, the mistress of a prominent attorney, traveled extensively throughout Europe and America with her son, and he grew accustomed to long journeys by steamship and rail. The sights and sounds of a crowded city block, hotel lobby, bustling wharf, and busy thoroughfare signaled home for Dos Passos. This type of landscape not only characterizes much of his fiction, but it also helps explain some of his interest in the theatre, which provides a literal space for recreating these dynamics. As a teenager at the Choate boarding school in Connecticut, he participated actively in drama, often playing the lead in school productions.² These experiences inspired a lifelong passion for the theatre, and a few years later he decided to write plays "to attract, move and mould an audience" for social change.³

Despite the comforting familiarity of city life, Dos Passos soon realized that he couldn't tolerate living in a place like New York for long. As a young man on holiday from school, he often found solace at his father's vast country estate in Westmoreland, Virginia. Nicknamed the White House, this place gave Dos Passos a sense for the pleasures of upper-class suburban living. He spent many afternoons horseback riding, swimming, boating, gardening, and entertaining his father's numerous guests. Yet as biographer Townsend Ludington observes, some of these experiences, like sailing on the family yacht, also made Dos Passos aware of "the distance between him and those less genteel than he or his family" (38). Such feelings became more acute when he returned to the United States after serving in the Norton-Harjes Ambulance Corps. Small town America suddenly seemed unsettling in its uniformity, naïveté, and opulence. The incongruity between his cousins' home in Bay Head, New Jersey, for example, "with its 'little square houses in rows, the drug stores, the board walk, the gawky angular smiling existence of an American summerresort,'⁴ and his life during the last year was appalling," Ludington notes (165). Although most critics focus on Dos Passos' portrait of urban America, the author was also fascinated by suburban culture.⁵ It is no accident, then, that most of his characters are caught between a desire to go to and run away from the big city, and Dos Passos captures the destructive allure of both in his work.

His three plays—*The Garbage Man* (or *The Moon Is a Gong*) (1923), *Airways, Inc.* (1928), and *Fortune Heights* (1933)—focus on the myths surrounding suburbanization in America. The first play, originally titled *The Moon Is a Gong*,⁶ tells the story of two lovers, Tom Burns and Jane Carroll, who desperately try to maintain their passion and idealism in a society preoccupied with industrialization, materialism, and social propriety. At the outset the couple passes through a working-class suburb after an all-night party, and their revelry is disrupted by the sound of pounding factory engines (reminiscent of the harsh, mechanical sounds of the ship in O'Neill's *The Hairy Ape*): "Tom, the engine in the powerplant; that's all people. The engines are made out of people pounded into steel. The power's stretched on the muscles of people, the light's sucked out of people's eyes" (5). Jane recognizes the destructiveness of industrial America on the individual, and she fears succumbing to the deadening rituals and routines of modern life. After the death of her sickly mother, she decides to flee her upper-class suburban home in order to be with Tom. His aimlessness eventually becomes too much for her, however, and she resents their "slave existence" (28), worrying about "three meals a day and money in the bank and train schedules" (27). When she witnesses the violent aftermath of a train wreck, she decides to leave Tom: "I will live now. Tomorrow there's only death suffocating me like a blanket" (34). She moves to New York, but her career as a Broadway actress does not bring her happiness. It just proves to be another form of slavery. Dos Passos juxtaposes her new life, which thrives on public image, with Tom's status as a bum. While Jane must host tea parties with pseudo-intellectuals, sycophants, and her publicist, Tom has traveled the world. Yet his freewheeling existence has left him bereft as well. He has lost his romantic idealizations ("I haven't any wishes now" [47]) and feels that he has bungled everything since losing Jane. Both of them come to realize that they need each other to live fully and to escape the drudgery of modern life. As Tom explains, "We either live or we are swept away...garbage, waste. These machines make a lot of waste, Jane" (68). In the closing moments, Tom escapes Death by jumping off the stage, leaping across rooftops, and eventually climbing up the tallest building until he literally reaches the moon. He then saves Jane by taking her there, too. As this ending suggests, the moon-gong not only functions as an image for romantic love and for following one's dreams to lead a fulfilling life, but it also provides an escape from the relentless pressures of social conformity and dehumanizing work.

For its publication a year later in 1926, Dos Passos renamed the play *The Garbage Man,* which refers to the character of Death who appears in various guises (including a garbage man) throughout the work. This shift was both a nod to the original idea that inspired the play[7] and, more importantly, an attempt to highlight the social critique of the work. Death tempts people with money that enables them to indulge in the excesses of the Jazz Age: "You can buy stock on margin...You'll get rich and ride home in your Lincoln Eight up Fifth Avenue every evening and stop to have a cocktail at the Plaza" (43). As with Tom and Jane's story, Death reminds the audience that this pursuit of wealth and high-class amusement is self-destructive. It reduces one's life to garbage—a theme that reflected Dos Passos' growing interest in drama that would inspire social reform. Even though the impact of *The Garbage Man's* social critique is often overshadowed by the romantic story of Tom and Jane (who escape industrial America by going to the moon), this theme is an important reflection of Dos Passos' increasing investment in social and political activism during this period—activism that inspired his travels to Russia in 1928, editorials for *The New Masses,* tireless efforts for the Sacco-Vanzetti Defense Committee, and work with the New Playwrights Theatre—a radical socialist theatre group in Greenwich Village.

Published in 1928 and staged by the New Playwrights Theatre in 1929,[8] his second play, *Airways, Inc.,* depicts the gradual deterioration of the Turners, a family living in a white, working-class suburb not far from an industrial center. Originally titled *Suburb,*[9] this play attacks numerous assumptions about home ownership and the technology facilitating suburbanization. The Turners' financial troubles primarily revolve around making the monthly mortgage payment, and this hardship has contributed to their disconnectedness from one another. Dad Turner, who laments his failed career as an inventor,[10] continually feels neglected by his children. His youngest son, Eddy, begrudgingly works as a carpenter building suburban houses while he fantasizes about the excitement of city life. Claude Turner has become embittered and aloof from working in white-collar America for fifteen years, and their sister, Martha, resents the exhausting routine of cooking, cleaning, and shopping for the family. At the same time, she sacrifices her autonomy to keep them together: "Our home would break up if it wasn't for me" (105). The most promising of the Turner clan, Elmer, is a charming pilot in the mold of Charles Lindbergh. He has recently set world records in altitude and speed, and he has agreed to become a partner in a new company called Airways, Incorporated. When he discovers that this business is only interested in making money, not developing innovations in aviation, he becomes disillusioned, gets drunk, and crashes his plane. Dos Passos has each of the central stories culminate in a moment of intense violence to underscore his indictment of the socioeconomic forces that destroy people in their pursuit of the suburban dream. At the end of act I, for example, Dad Turner commits suicide in the unfinished house next door.

Act II depicts the rise and fall of Elmer's aspirations as a pilot and inventor. It culminates in his plane crash and a riot between strikers and police, who frame activist Walter Goldberg for shooting a police officer. Dos Passos uses Goldberg's persecution (for organizing a strike and leading peaceful labor protests) as a way to condemn the racism that enabled the execution of Sacco and Vanzetti in 1927. Act III concludes with Goldberg's execution and a portrait of the remaining Turners—dazed, debilitated, and seemingly trapped in their home.

Dos Passos was disappointed by the reception of this play and the collapse of the New Playwrights Theatre.[11] He had dedicated a great deal of energy to both ventures, but this did not prevent him from trying to use drama to extend his critique of suburbanization and capitalism in his final play, *Fortune Heights*. Premiering in Moscow in 1933 and having subsequent performances in Leningrad and Chicago before its publication in 1934, this three-act play has forty-one rapid-fire scenes reminiscent of cinematic montage and vaudeville. Set at Owen Hunter's filling station along a national highway, it opens with a conversation between a hitchhiker and Morry Norton, the station attendant and mechanic. While the hitchhiker complains about the inhospitable residents of this new suburb, he stands beneath an enormous advertisement:

> Why not look over our lots now?
>
> FORTUNE HEIGHTS
>
> We help U along the road
>
> to ownership and independence

The pairing of this sign with the opening exchange underscores the central tension in the play between the social realities of the Depression and the self-destructive myth of suburbia. All of the characters in this work struggle to hold onto the dream of "ownership and independence," even as they succumb to forces outside of their control such as foreclosures, unemployment, poverty, infidelity, and violence.

Fortune Heights focuses on the experiences of three central characters—Owen Hunter, Morry Norton, and Ellery Jones—in its condemnation of suburbia. Owen believes that owning a home and a small business (gas station) will help him achieve prosperity—even though he must rely on bootlegging to make his mortgage payments. After reconciling with his estranged wife, they have a child together, but their hopes for domestic happiness are shattered by the College Boy Bandits. These young men rob the Hunters, making it impossible for them to pay off the mortgage. In the closing moments of the play, the bank evicts the Hunter family, and they begin walking down the highway with the hope that something will turn up when they meet other people in a similar predicament.[12] The second central character, Morry, dreams of going to college, having his own business, and making a lot of money one day, but he is leery about buying real estate. Because of his experiences with debt (his family still owes money on their farm), Morry doesn't want to stay in one place for too long. Eventually, he leaves Fortune Heights and abandons his girlfriend Rena, whom he reluctantly agreed to marry. When he returns several years later and discovers that Owen is being evicted, Morry rallies the local farmers to protest—an event that leads to his death. Finally, Ellery, the real-estate developer, sells properties in this new suburb and genuinely believes that it will grow into an attractive community with "homes, stores, lunchrooms, picture theatres, garages, newsstands, gas stations" (192). At the same time, he relentlessly pursues his own self-interests, seducing a girl who had a short-lived career in musical theatre, getting involved in a brief affair with Owen's wife, and marrying Mrs. Stead, the widow of a wealthy banker who killed himself after the stock market crash. At the end of the play, Ellery decides to run for political office, claiming that he "will introduce a bill for a moratorium on mortgage foreclosures" (273). Through all of these stories, Dos Passos attacks both the prosperity myth of home ownership, which leaves most of the characters destitute or dead, and materialism in American culture. It is not merely the economic conditions of the Depression and the moral bankruptcy of the characters that prevent them from achieving economic and emotional fulfillment; it is following the dream of home ownership.

As these summaries suggest, Dos Passos used the theatre (as well as some of his fiction from the same period) to debunk the mythology surrounding suburbanization in America. Just as buying a new car symbolized a person's social status in the early twentieth century, so did owning a home. By the 1920s, segregated suburban communities existed for all classes and ethnic groups in the United States, and Dos Passos viewed these developments as a microcosm of the socioeconomic hierarchies that were dividing people. His portrait of the suburbs also includes a critique of the technologies enabling its growth, particularly trains, automobiles, and airplanes (which many believed would expand the possibilities of suburban development even farther). Cultural historians Becky M. Nicolaides and Andrew Wiese have noted that "the rise of suburbia was inextricably linked to ideas about class, race, and gender, changes in American political culture and the role of the state, the evolution of success ideologies, opportunities for social mobility, and the construction of American culture itself" (1). For Dos Passos, the intersection of these characteristics made the suburbs an ideal dramatic setting for exposing suburbia as a form of enslavement that leads to unhappiness and disillusionment. Suburban life, in other words, emerges as a kind of dystopia (masquerading as a technological paradise), and its underlying misogynistic, racist, and class-inflected malaise ultimately leads to outbursts of sudden violence.

THE RISE OF SUBURBAN AMERICA AND THE POLITICS OF EXCLUSIVITY

As Dos Passos witnessed at his father's estate in rural Virginia, class defined the suburbs. In the second half of the nineteenth century, the railroads allowed passengers to travel across the country quickly and efficiently. A farmer or businessman could live great distances from a city and still engage in urban commerce, shipping goods and services with relative ease. Even those who needed to work in the city could live outside of it as transportation evolved. In many respects, this reconceptualization of space corresponded with an unprecedented population surge in the United States (doubling between 1870 and 1890 and nearly doubling again between 1890 and 1910)[13]—a surge that necessitated suburbanization. The railroads began by adding new stops along the "main line" to encourage housing developments for the upper-middle class—a group that could increasingly afford stylish accommodations by the 1880s. They also longed to share in the type of country living that the wealthiest Americans had been enjoying for decades. Vanderbilt's "Biltmore" mansion and the Du Pont's estate in "Chateau country," for example, were well-publicized images of upper-class extravagance.[14] Needless to say, these railroad suburbs were not as elegant as the Biltmore, but they did offer prestigious, highly restrictive communities for those who could afford to live there. The proliferation of these developments soon corresponded with the expansion of streetcar suburbs (first accessible by horse-drawn carriages and subsequently by electric streetcars). Between 1888 and 1918, the electric streetcar (or trolley) became the most popular mode of public transportation for its speed and cost. (It moved four times faster than horse-drawn transport and charged a flat rate of five cents.) This technology also "opened up a vast suburban ring" (Jackson 114), facilitating new housing developments for all social classes.

Since streetcar suburbs were accessible to most people (from working-class immigrants to middle-class whites), the latter group became increasingly invested in racially homogeneous living. The housing shortage during World War I contributed to this desire. As early as 1914, a scarcity of building materials, a sharp rise in construction costs, and a national call for conservation greatly limited real-estate development. This occurred at a time when large numbers of people, particularly African Americans, were flocking to northern cities to find work and to escape racial oppression.[15] As Margaret Marsh explains in *Suburban Lives,* "[R]acial tensions increased as some [urban] communities were forced to accept black neighbors who had moved from the South in search of industrial jobs" (130). Thus the postwar boom in suburbanization can be understood, in part, as a reaction among whites against the growing ethnic diversity of the city. Soon suburban developments were appealing to whites in terms of racial exclusivity. Restrictive covenants—legal restrictions against "undesirable activities" (such as construction that might damage the aesthetics of a planned community) and "undesirable residents" (namely racial minorities and poor people)—helped protect these suburbs from the "dangers" of the modern world. As historian Robert M. Fogelson has argued, restrictive covenants exposed deep-seated fears in middle-class, white America—"fear of others, of racial minorities and poor people,... of people like themselves..., of change and their fear of the market" (24). Like the "Red Summer" race riots, the mainstream popularity of eugenics, the ongoing practice of lynching, and the Immigration Act of 1924, restrictive covenants offered another example of the broader social tensions surrounding ethnicity during this period.

Like trains and electric streetcars, the automobile not only facilitated this exodus from the city, but it also created greater (literal) distances between the middle and working classes. As Kenneth Jackson explains in *Crabgrass Frontier,* even as early as 1922 "about 135,000 suburban homes in sixty cities were already completely dependent upon cars for transportation" (176). While only 2.5 million people owned cars in the United States in 1915, nearly 9 million cars were on the road by 1920, and this number jumped to approximately 26 million by 1929 (Kyvig 28, 30). During the same decade, middle-class home ownership surged. In fact, "3,231,770 more families were home owners in 1930 than had been in 1920" (Marsh 133).[16] Middle-class whites were moving farther away from the city to escape both urban life and another undesirable location—industrial suburbs. For the working class, access to employment, public transportation, cost, and the proximity to family were significant factors in determining where to live, and the industrial suburb offered a practical option. One did not need a car to get there. These families were also willing to sacrifice conveniences like paved roads, sewers, and street lighting in order to own property. Many built their own homes,[17] cultivated gardens, and raised livestock as an extra source of income—activities that were forbidden in middle-class suburbs. Working-class developments also "welcomed factories, not just because they paid for municipal services but because they offered jobs to residents who could ill afford to commute elsewhere" (Harris and Lewis 281). Ultimately, these segregated, low-income communities were not concerned with aesthetics because they didn't view these homes as permanent. As Fogelson argues, "[T]hey did not intend to spend their lives in a Torrance or Home Gardens; nor did they expect their children to live there after they died. These suburbs were not so much the last stop...but a way station—a place that announced not that its residents had arrived but that the were on the way" (80). For many of these home owners, the next step to prosperity involved owning a car and buying into middle-class suburbia (figure 3).

Figure 3   Queens, New York in the 1920s. "Dezendorf's Delightful Dwellings"[18]
Source: Library of Congress.

Like Dos Passos' portrait of America in the *U.S.A* trilogy (which focuses almost exclusively on whites),[19] his plays depict the white experience in 1920s and early 1930s suburban America—from an upper-class family in *The Garbage Man* to the working-class communities in both *Airways, Inc.* and *Fortune Heights*. When viewed as interconnected plays (one of the characters in *Airways, Inc.* even refers to a housing development called "Fortune Heights"), these dramatic works portray the gradual disintegration of the suburban prosperity myth in America.

Dos Passos, however, viewed home ownership and the mythology surrounding it as a powerful tool in capitalist America for reinforcing divisive hierarchies and encouraging class exploitation. Part of this perspective came from his experiences with the Sacco-Vanzetti case, which profoundly shaped Dos Passos' political and social outlook. The crime occurred on April 15, 1920, in South Braintree, Massachusetts, while two employees of the Slater and Morrill Shoe Company were transporting a payroll of approximately $15 million. The men were shot and killed by armed assailants who grabbed the money and drove away in a green Buick. Three weeks later, the police arrested Nicola Sacco and Bartolomeo Vanzetti for the murders. Sacco, a shoe craftsman with a wife and two children (his daughter was born while he was in prison), and Vanzetti, a self-employed fish peddler, were Italian immigrants and anarchists. Based on circumstantial, often contradictory, evidence and influenced by the blatantly racist remarks of the judge in the case, both men were convicted of first-degree murder on July 14, 1923. Their appeals for a new trial were denied, and Sacco and Vanzetti were sentenced to death in 1927. Almost two weeks before the execution, protesters gathered in front of the State House in Boston, and both Dos Passos (while reporting on the demonstrations for *The Daily Worker*) and Edna Millay were among those arrested on August 10.[20] The execution took place on August 23.[21]

In his eloquent essay on their crime and conviction,[22] Dos Passos attributes this miscarriage of justice, in large part, to the kind of racism fostered in suburbia:

> Dedham is the perfect New England town, white shingleroofed houses, polished brass knockers, elmshaded streets. Dedham has money, supports a polo team. Many of the wealthiest and oldest families in Massachusetts have houses there...Dedham has always stood for Anglo-Saxon supremacy, and the white man's burden. Of all the white men the whitest are those descendents of Puritan shipowners and brokers and ministers who own the white houses with graceful colonial doorways and the trim lawns and the lilac hedges and the elms and the beeches and the barberry bushes and the broad A and the cultivated gesturelessness of the New English. ("The Pit and the Pendulum," 88)

Dedham typified the elite suburb in the early twentieth century. The whiteness of its identical houses and the meticulously organized streets (with trim lawns, elm trees, and lilac hedges) symbolized the community's supposed ethnic purity and desire for sameness. This need for conformity, however, was being threatened by the changing demographics of the region. Beneath the population of wealthy Protestants and Irish Catholics, a group of "wops, bohunks, polacks, hunkies, dagoes, some naturalized and speaking English with an accent, others unnaturalized and still speaking in their native peasant dialects"... [were doing] the work" (88). The gap between leisure and labor as well rich and poor occurred along ethnic/racial lines there. At the same time, the work ethic of this immigrant community challenged white suburbia as well: "Meanwhile the latest-come immigrants are gradually gaining foothold... The Italians start truck gardens in back lots, and by skillful gardening and drudgery bring forth fiftyfold where the American-born couldn't get back the seed they sowed... The American-born are seeing their own state eaten up from under their feet. Naturally they hate the newcomers" (88). The example of Italian gardens explicitly links this description back to Sacco, whom Dos Passos praises for his love of gardening earlier in the essay. To this New England community, Sacco represented the broader immigrant threat—success and fertility in the face of white American stagnation. Sacco and Vanzetti thus became the focal point for the resentment of "right-thinking Puritan-born Americans of Massachusetts... [and] the people of Norfolk County, and all of Massachusetts, [who] have decided that they want these men to die" (88).

Dos Passos wrote this essay and a pamphlet for the Sacco-Vanzetti Defense Committee, *Facing the Chair: Story of the Americanization of Two Foreignborn Workmen* (1927), when he still believed that the legal system would rise above the prejudices of white America. Their execution shocked and deeply disheartened him, and he would express this disillusionment in both the culmination of *The Big Money* (1936), the final novel of the *U.S.A* trilogy, and *Airways, Inc.* In its portrait of the first twenty-nine years of the twentieth century, the trilogy focuses on twelve characters whose stories are interspersed with sixty-eight Newsreel sections (newspaper clippings, headlines, song lyrics, and excerpts from political speeches that Dos Passos "intended to give the clamor, the sound of daily life"[23]), twenty-seven biographies of historical figures, and fifty-one Camera Eye sections, which are experimental meditations on his life and experiences. These four distinct narratives intersect at the moment of the Sacco and Vanzetti executions, suggesting the importance of this event in the series. Specifically, Mary French, who leaves behind her upper-class background and drops out of college in order to be a labor activist, participates in the Sacco-Vanzetti protests. Like Dos Passos, she interviewed the men in jail, volunteered to work on the Defense Committee, and worried about the long-term implications of their deaths. The chapter ends with her arrest during a protest march while she and her comrades are singing the *Internationale*. The following Newsreel (LXVI) intersperses headlines like "SACCO AND VANZETTI MUST DIE" (370) with the lyrics of the song. It also concludes with an excerpt from one of Vanzetti's letters. The subsequent Camera Eye (50), which narrates some of Dos Passos' impressions of this case, concludes with a passage from Vanzetti as well. As critic Barbara Foley notes, these interwoven references highlight Sacco and Vanzetti's

> privileged political place in *U.S.A.* Not only does the execution reveal that American society has moved toward irreparable polarization. It also furnished an account of the text's moment of inspiration: Dos Passos began writing *The 42nd Parallel* almost immediately after he emerged from jail. (435)

When Dos Passos started *The 42nd Parallel* (the first book of the trilogy) in 1927,[24] he was hard at work on his second play *Airways, Inc.*, and not surprisingly he incorporates these events into his drama as well. The execution of Walter Goldberg becomes a clear image for the racism and indifference that enabled the Sacco and Vanzetti killings.[25] One of the characters in the play alludes to this when she expresses her anguish over the impending execution: "They always get the good guys and electrocute them or something... When they hear about a real man they want to drag him down, an' they strap him in a chair an' kill him at midnight; that's what they do" (147). As this play and his essay "The Pit and the Pendulum" demonstrate, Dos Passos ultimately attributes the persecution of social activists to the prejudices of suburbia.

SUBURBAN NIGHTMARES IN
THE DRAMA OF DOS PASSOS

Kenneth T. Jackson has argued that "suburbanization symbolizes the fullest, most unadulterated embodiment of contemporary culture; it is a manifestation of such fundamental characteristics of American society as conspicuous consumption, a reliance upon the private automobile, upward mobility,... and a tendency toward racial and economic exclusiveness" (4). As this list suggests, suburbia reveals a great deal about Americans' understanding of space and their relationship to it. Suburban homes are not merely literal spaces, however. They are, as Robert Beuka has argued, "psychic and emotional landscapes" (4) that have come to symbolize personal happiness and success. Throughout the 1920s, Catherine Jurca notes, "[T]he suburban home emerged as a crucial symbol of consumer prosperity and fulfillment in popular periodical articles, modern advertising, and a national 'Own Your Own Home' campaign, sponsored by the government and business interests" (6). This home-making propaganda, as the epigraph from *American Home* magazine illustrates, helped equate home ownership with national pride and patriotism. It constructed suburbia into an image for America itself. Writers like Dos Passos, Upton Sinclair, Willa Cather, F. Scott Fitzgerald, and other contemporaries, however,[26] recognized the pervasive fears, ethnic intolerance, and class hierarchies underlying this image.

Dos Passos' plays specifically present the homogeneity, prescribed gender roles, and economic hardships of suburbia as destructive forces in American society. *The Garbage Man* begins by juxtaposing two suburban communities—lower income and upper class respectively—that reduce its residents to automatons. In the opening moments, two laborers cross the stage wearing overalls and carrying tools. They have just "[tumbled] out of bed" (3), and as the backdrop of factory chimneys indicates, they live in an industrial suburb—close to the jobs that occupy most of their time. (The "blue light of a winter dawn" colors the stage, and the men carry dinner pails, suggesting the length of their workday.) While they talk about the coldness of the morning relative to the ruthless heat of the factory furnace, one man notices Jane, who is dressed in elegant evening wear. She and her lover, Tom, are returning from a party, still "full of ragtime and champagne punch and love and dancesteps and kisses" (4). Loud factory engines intrude violently on their revelry, disrupting the jazz tune accompanying the scene and overshadowing their memory of the evening. Jane is particularly unnerved by these pounding sounds, which symbolize her fear of succumbing to the demands of either working- or middle-class America—a country that wants people "to be shoveling coal, pounding typewriters, filling greasecups" (4). This could be her fate if she leaves her wealthy family to be with Tom. As the complaints of these laborers reveal, the routines of blue-collar life have reduced them to cogs in the machinery of the power plant. Jane even observes that the engines "are made out of people pounded into steel. The power's stretched on the muscles of the people" (5). Industry acts as a vampire that sucks the life out of those working for it.

Dos Passos' depiction of upper-class suburbia in the following scene isn't the pastoral haven that such developments promised residents in the 1920s; instead, it is a space defined by meaningless rituals, prescribed gender roles, and racism. Not only must Tom and Jane pass through an industrial suburb on their way home (a reminder of upper-class dependence on modernization and the labor that sustains it), but they also find the social expectations of Jane's affluent, suburban community stifling and potentially dehumanizing. Tom explicitly refers to the house as a "cage" (7), and he recognizes the structure as closed off from the natural world: "[S]huttered against the sun and the wind" (23). According to the stage directions, *"[T]he old house...has penned the righteousness of three generations into its gloomy rooms. The walls are arsenic green blotched with yellowing crimson bouquets"* (6). As the arsenic green suggests, there is something poisonous about this environment. Jane's relatives, who only gather for funerals and weddings, descend on the home immediately after her mother's death to perform this family obligation. They also want to inquire about the will and see the body. All of these actions reflect the morality of the group, valuing money and external appearance over empathy. The only act of mourning occurs when they dance *"ring-around-a-rosy crying, 'Boo hoo, boo hoo, boo hoo'... [and] form a frieze expressive of mourning"* (21). Like the minister who has nothing to say at the memorial, this performance offers another example of the artificial rituals that define upper-class suburban life. Dos Passos reinforces this message by having the characters waltz during their interactions, floating across the stage from one meaningless conversation to another. Unlike the jazz associated with Tom and Jane,[27] this generation of old-money aristocrats dances to a nineteenth-century musical form. They prefer the past to the present, prescribed behaviors to emotion.

Dos Passos presents suburbia as a form of captivity for women as well, who must sacrifice their own happiness for the demands of family. Jane, who has been living at home to care for her ailing mother, longs to be free, but after her mother's death, her relatives plan to keep her in the house (the front door never remains open for long, for example) and orchestrate her romantic life in the hope of resuscitating her social standing. As Aunt Georgiana explains to Jane, "Old Tom Burns was a plumber...I never understand how your poor dear mother allowed you to play together when you were children. Very unwise. Very unwise." (13). Suburbia was designed, in part, to preserve class hierarchies, and Jane's relationship to Tom threatens this. At the same time, Jane fears being subsumed by this world of exclusivity, admitting at one point that "I'm made the same as they are" (22). She enjoys the comforts of wealth, and suburban life exerts a gravitational pull on her. Just as the suburbs privilege sameness and conformity, this family accordingly wants to mold Jane into their own image. Dos Passos captures this intention by depicting Jane's relatives as indistinguishable from one another: *"Aunt Marianna is the exact replica of* [the ample] *Aunt Georgiana, only dark instead of blond, Uncle William is cleanshaven, heavyjowled, spreading so to a paunch that the buttons of the doublebreasted vest seem ready to pop from under the looped watchchain. The exact replica of the other uncles to come"* (17). While these heavy bodies function as a conventional image for the excesses of upper-class life, they also suggest complacency. Like the three generations penned into the rooms of the house, suburbia invites stasis, not change—particularly for women who must remain home to care for family. Thus when Tom eventually suggests that he and Jane settle down and have children, she rejects this option: "I don't want children. I want to be myself" (28). She recognizes the suburbs as antithetical to female independence.[28]

Finally, Dos Passos highlights racial prejudice as an inherent part of elite suburban culture. At the funeral, Aunt Georgiana claims: "Oh Jane she's so beautiful, so white, like a lily" (14). She characterizes Jane in terms of whiteness and delicacy here. It is something to value and protect, and this is what most suburbs promised through restrictive covenants—ethnic exclusivity and safety. As Fogelson explains, "[U]nder a typical covenant, an owner was forbidden to sell or lease the property to a member of any of a number of allegedly undesirable racial, ethnic, or religious groups. He or she was also forbidden to allow a member of these groups, other than chauffeurs, gardeners, or domestic servants, to use or occupy the property" (95). As mentioned earlier, these covenants were designed to assuage white fears about the encroachment of poor immigrants and African Americans, and Jane's family clearly shares these anxieties. Most notably, the African American character John Lincoln is only allowed in the house because of his position as butler. His "bulging eyes" (12), use of dialect, and preaching make him a caricature, reflecting the family's racist view of blacks. Not surprisingly, they find his fervent desire to pray, which is antithetical to their emotional aloofness, as "scandalous" (25), and they flee the house in fearful indignation. As his last name ironically suggests, Lincoln is anything but free. His assertiveness in this scene serves as a reminder of the fragility of social hierarchies, but this shift in power doesn't last long. John helps Jane and Tom escape, giving them enough time to run away, but he ultimately has nowhere to go.

In his second play, *Airways, Inc.,* Dos Passos shifts his attention to white, working-class suburbia, and he uses this setting to condemn, once again, the homogeneity, economic hardships, and prescribed gender roles of suburbia. The play first announces its critique of conformity by contrasting the setting with the chaos of the Turner house. The set features *"two...small onefamily houses with porches such as you can find in rows in suburbs of any American city"* (81). The generality of this description implies that America as a whole values sameness, and the Turners represent millions of Americans who bought or were buying into the same kind of suburban dream. While these row houses might have offered many people a comforting image of orderliness and stability, the Turner's home suggests that these places did not necessarily provide a nurturing environment for family. Instead, the tight quarters seem to fuel contentiousness and neglect. Eddy, for instance, is too preoccupied with getting out of the house for a night in the city to help his sister. Dad Turner can't see beyond his feelings of neglect to communicate with his children, and Claude's position at the Chamber of Commerce exacerbates his anger over the recent labor strikes, which have lowered real-estate values. Literary critic Linda Wagner has pointed out that Dos Passos' use of "intermeshed" dialogue and non sequiturs in the play also reflect the characters' failure to listen to one another. "They talk about only what they themselves are interested in" (79). This selfishness also has dire consequences. When Dad Turner alludes to killing himself ("You'd be sorry if you drove me to a desperate thing" [102]), for example, such warnings go largely unheard.

Dos Passos' condemnation of suburban conformity occurs through images of physical violence as well. Throughout act I, Dad Turner blames his neglect on suburbanization: "Everywhere they're building ramshackle houses for young folks..., and no place for an old man in them, no place for a tired man without a job" (98). He recognizes that these homes do not represent family but divide them, making the elderly a liability for not contributing financially to the mortgage. His subsequent suicide in the unfinished suburban house next door is partially an attempt to expose this truth. Dos Passos reinforces this point by linking Dad Turner's suicide with a moment of violence involving infidelity and murder. In the scene immediately following his death,[29] Claude Turner muses over a story in the Sunday paper about a woman who conspired with her lover to beat her husband to death with a lead pipe: "An' then he grabbed her and they was kissin' each other before he'd washed the blood off his hands" (115). Claude finds the picture of their house particularly disconcerting: "Funny, it looks kinder like our house. They were decent people, the feller had a good job. I wonder what gets hold of people" (115). As with Dad Turner's death, Dos Passos associates this act of violence with suburban life. The paper prints a photograph of the house, not the murderers, as if the former is more important for understanding the crime. Unlike advertising materials in the 1920s that presented suburban developments as symbols for family, stability, and professional success,[30] the nearly identical houses here imply that suburbanites are just as capable of depraved acts as their city counterparts. Claude refuses to accept this, however. Even though he lost his job because of the suicide, he accepts the social consequences of this. The community "won't stand for things like that and I don't blame 'em" (116). The value that he and suburbia place on the appearance of normalcy also explains his desire to have the police hide the truth about his father's death: "Say, can't you say it was an accident?" (114). Ultimately, Dos Passos' portrait of these crimes suggests that suburbia makes conformity the grounds for personal and social success. Identical houses and manicured lawns merely mask the ugliness of divisive social hierarchies and the exploitation endemic to capitalism.

Dos Passos criticizes the racial homogeneity of suburbia as well. Early in the play, Claude insults Martha for dating a "damn kike"—an insult that has less to do with Goldberg's ethnicity than it does with the economic impact of his social activism: "Well, who wouldn't be sore if they found their sister running around with a damn kike and a longhaired anarchistic agitator at that?... You could have had the pick of decent fellers" (97). For Claude and the real-estate developers trying to sell lots in Glenside, Goldberg's socialist philosophies and role in the labor unrest run counter to the capitalistic drives of suburbanization (which I will discuss later). This fuels their racist descriptions of him as a cheap, dishonest Jew. Even Martha, who identifies with her family and this community, struggles with Goldberg's ethnicity.

> *Martha:* But they're my brothers, my people, my kind of people...They're much more my kind of people than you, Walt.
> *Goldberg:* You mean because I'm a jew.
> *Martha:* ...I dunno, maybe there is something in it, but I don't think it's that.
> *Goldberg:* There's something in it. You'd have to be a jew like me to understand... Every one of us has something fenced up way down in us. We've been in prison for two thousand years... That's why I feel the slavery of the workers, I feel it as a worker and I feel it as a jew. Oh, you can't imagine the overheated stuffiness of life at home on the East Side when I was a kid. We were all jailed in poverty and Judaism and in old customs and hatreds and wornout laws.
> *Martha:* We're all of us that. (105)

Martha clearly shares his view of home life as restricting. For her, suburbia (as opposed to poor immigrant city life) locks one in an economic, social, and religious prison,[31] and it reinforces prejudices toward Jews and "ignorant foreigners" (97). Despite her recognition of these things, Martha is only willing to assist social causes from the sidelines, refusing to attend rallies or support Goldberg in public. Part of her inaction comes from the epithets applied to Goldberg (agitator, anarchist, Red, crook), which link his Jewishness with a broader immigrant threat. Racial intolerance prevents her and other suburban, white home owners from moral action. In the concluding moments of the play, Dos Passos even suggests that racist indoctrination helps establish this intolerance. After the police frame Goldberg for the shooting death of a police officer, he moves from a celebrated figure among working-class kids (who chant "Two four six eight/

Who do we appreciate?/ Goldberg! Goldberg! Hurrah!") to a reviled one ("Oh, we'll burn Walter Goldberg/ In the electric chair/ Burn him till he's dead./ ... Oh, the kike Walter Goldberg lies amoulderin' in the grave" [154]). This shift is similar to Eddy's use of the phrase "damn kike" early in the play. As Claude's youngest sibling, Eddy (who is not old enough to care about the economic ramifications of Goldberg's actions) is clearly mimicking the racist language of his brother. Suburbia thus becomes a place that models and reinforces hatred in the name of conformity, and it helps enable the violent persecution of those who reject its values.

In addition to the play's depiction of conformity, Dos Passos uses the setting of *Airways, Inc.* to portray the prosperity myth of suburbia as trapping people in an endless cycle of debt and personal hardship. The staging signals both the social status of its residents and the financial difficulties of home ownership: *"Between the houses is a suggestion of empty lots and of the tall chimneys and windows of a powerplant and the square shapes of mill buildings beyond"* (81). The specter of chimneys and power plants suggests that these lives are largely defined by industrial labor. The unfinished second house onstage and the empty lots also point to the riskiness of this investment. For property value to increase, people must buy houses, but that doesn't happen in this play. Instead, the second house remains incomplete, and the Turners never pay off their mortgage. Dad Turner recognizes the false promises of suburbanization and believes that the ramshackle houses, "quickbuilt demountable homes," and "maisonettes knocked together" (98) being built around the country give lie to the success/personal fulfillment narrative of the suburbs. As these descriptions suggest, this narrative is built on a cheap, collapsible foundation. It encourages young people to "hustle for money to buy bonds to pay the interest on mortgages," but it ultimately enslaves them to monthly payments and oppressive familial responsibilities. Martha explicitly refers to home ownership as "slavery" (112), for example, and she asks Elmer for help with the mortgage every month. Eddy works construction on the type of house that has trapped him and his family, and Claude keeps a miserable, middle-class job for fear of being evicted. Dos Passos' concerns about the dangers of home ownership also appear in *The 42nd Parallel* through Mac (Fainy) McCreary, who abandons his socialist beliefs for the consumerist, suburban outlook of his wife Maisie. Mac buys a bungalow in San Diego and must take out a second mortgage to pay for her medical expenses. By the time they have a second child, "all that he could do with his pay each week was cover the interest on his debts" (90).[32] Once again, Dos Passos portrays the "road to success" of real estate, as Maisie's profit-hungry brother and the realtors of *Airways, Inc.* call it, as leading to greater debt and unhappiness.

The prosperity myth of suburbia also appealed to speculators, and Dos Passos presents the marketplace as encouraging people to prioritize personal profit over social fairness. The character Jonathan P. Davis, who brokers the deal to form Airways, Incorporated, is also a realtor, and within moments of meeting Dad Turner, he tries to sell him property in Florida. His sales pitch reflects the consumerist values rampant in 1920s America: "Once our great system of postpossession payments is in operation, not the installment plan, no sir, but a system of small postpossession payments that clinch the investment. No possible rational human wish unfulfilled. A man with a salary of fifty dollars a week can start payments on a Rolls-Royce, the Waldorf-Astoria, or a troupe of trained seals if he so desires" (92). As the phrase "postpossession" implies, the myth of suburbia involves acquiring things you don't own and, as Martha quickly points out, can't afford. It is about escapism (fulfilling every wish), and enjoying aspects of elite culture such as fancy cars, a beach home, and high-class hotels. The Turner's current financial troubles as well as the 1926 crash of Florida's real-estate boom remind audiences of the many people who lost money on down payments for worthless land or the depreciation of overpriced property at the time.[33] Dos Passos uses Elmer (as well as Charley Anderson in the *U.S.A.* trilogy) to condemn this kind of speculation, which privileges quick profit over hard work and ethnical business practices. Specifically, Elmer's downfall coincides with his interest in real-estate speculation. He shows a callous disregard for the labor strike by performing aerial stunts during a rally, and his plane crashes shortly after he wants to escape his disillusionment with Airways, Inc. by flying to Florida. Like Elmer, Charley Anderson from the *U.S.A.* trilogy is a mechanic/pilot/speculator, and his downfall corresponds with speculation in the stock market and Florida real estate as well. Both men abandon their principals as they become increasingly involved in the capitalistic marketplace, and Dos

Passos uses these narratives to condemn many of the business practices that contributed to the growth of suburbanization.

Finally, *Airways, Inc.* presents misogyny as another destructive hierarchy in suburban culture. The free-spirited flapper and New Woman of the 1920s don't live in the suburbs. Their infrequent visits highlight the striking gap between women's lives in suburban and urban America. Elmer's girlfriend Mae, for instance, lives in the city. She enjoys drinking, the Broadway cabaret scene, and her individual autonomy. As she complains to Elmer, "Last time I [helped your sister get supper] I washed all the dishes and my hands were ruined for a week. What do you want to drag everybody around to see your relations for anyway?" (92). She finds cooking, housework, and the suburbs oppressive—the very things that define Martha. As the only woman in the Turner family (Ma Turner died years earlier),[34] Martha functions as a mother caretaker for her brothers and father. She resents the incessant demands of cooking and cleaning, which severely limit her personal freedom, and at times, she even suggests abandoning the house for an apartment in the city—an idea her brothers (particularly Claude) reject as irresponsible:

> *Claude:* How about the house? We can't stop payments now. We almost own the place...Why, it was you that was craziest about moving into this house.
> *Martha:* I know, but it's just slavery.
> *Claude:* It ud mean the beanery for me for the rest of my life...
> *Martha:* But Claude, I tell you I can't stand it any more. I'll go crazy...
> *Claude:* But what about Dad? (111–112)

With his characteristic lack of empathy, Claude does not address Martha's emotional and psychological needs here. He is merely looking for an argument that will keep her at home. When he realizes that she no longer cares about their financial investment in the property, he remarks that such a move will enslave him to a white-collar job (the beanery) indefinitely. He then reminds her about Dad Turner, hoping that guilt will convince her to stay. He not only views his employment as a greater sacrifice than her housework, but he also never considers his own responsibility in caring for their father. Like cleaning and cooking meals (which are never served quickly enough for her insatiable brothers), caring for an elderly parent is a woman's duty. Martha is trapped by the misogynistic expectations of her family—expectations that Dos Passos explicitly links with the suburban home. In a moment of frustration with Claude's authoritarian control over the house, Martha threatens to leave once again. "You know perfectly well I'd have gone out and gotten a job ages ago only you boys thought it would break up your home. All right, Claude, from here on I'm through" (117). The phrases "you boys" and "your home" signal a shift in Martha's attitude from the first act. By this point in the play, she no longer considers herself part of the family but separate from it, and she recognizes the house as a tool for male control over her.

Even though Dos Passos presents social activism as a possible means for altering the gender hierarchies of suburbia, Goldberg's fate suggests that America is not ready for such a change. Part of Martha's attraction to Goldberg comes from his promise to take her away from the house: "You're coming with me and you're never going back" (121). As an outsider to white, capitalist suburbia, he has a different perspective on gender relationships. He doesn't believe that Martha should cook and clean for her brothers, and he wonders: "Why couldn't they eat round at the cafeteria, like I have to?" (107). As this moment reveals, he views the relationship between men and women in relatively egalitarian terms: "The girls on the picket lines icy mornings before dawn, the guys who get beaten up, the workers little by little coming to realize their strength, the strategy of it all" (107). Goldberg's vision of social activism includes the efforts of men and women, and Dos Passos presents this type of collective action as a means for achieving fair treatment both in the workplace and at home. Goldberg's tragic death, however, shatters Martha's hope for a future with him and for escaping the suburbs. Now, her paralyzed brother replaces her elderly father's need for care, and she merely wants "to burn this house down and everything in it" (153). The house has become a prison in these final moments, and Dos Passos captures this confinement by setting act III in the Turner's claustrophobic living room. Like a close-up in film, this view of the action establishes a parallel between Martha's entrapment and Goldberg's imprisonment. Unlike her brother Claude who now owns his own home, she can't leave. She merely waits for the phone call confirming Goldberg's execution, and in the closing moments of the play, she realizes that suburban life is responsible for her loss of freedom: "Street where I've lived all these years shut up in a matchwood house full of bitterness...America, where I've scurried from store to subway to church to home, America that I've never known" (157). Goldberg's death inspires these thoughts of abandonment, isolation, and longing—all of which are connected with suburban life.

The title of Dos Passos' final play, *Fortune Heights,* appears in *Airways, Inc.,* and given his work on the epic *U.S.A.* trilogy at the time, it is not surprising that he conceived of these plays as part of a larger whole. Early in *Airways, Inc.,* Dad Turner's diatribe against suburbanization in the United States includes a place called Fortune Heights: "Everywhere they're building ramshackle houses for young folks...Ozone Park, Crystal Meadow, Joyland, Fortune Heights, Coral Gables" (98). These names, most of which refer to actual suburbs,[35] imply pastoral beauty, happiness, financial success, and architectural grandeur. Together they embody the typical qualities and characteristics used to market such properties. For Dos Passos, however, a name like Fortune Heights reflects the ironic distance between the promise of these developments and the impoverished lives of many Americans in the 1930s. The collapse of the real-estate market was a painful, highly visible sign of the country's economic woes. As Kenneth T. Jackson explains, "Between 1928 and 1933, the construction of residential property fell by 95 percent, and expenditures on home repairs fell by 90 percent. Only aggressive sales campaigns, Federal Housing Administration mortgage programs, and extensive advertising kept the vision of a home of one's own before the American people" (187). Dos Passos was troubled by these advertising campaigns given the rate of foreclosures during the Great Depression. In 1926, which Jackson presents as a typical year in the decade, 26,000 homes were foreclosed. Four years later, the number jumps to 150,000. Banks subsequently repossessed 200,000 homes in 1931 and another 250,000 in 1932. "In the spring of 1933, when fully half of all home mortgages in the United States were technically in default, and when foreclosures reached the astronomical rate of more than a thousand per day, the home-financing system was drifting toward complete collapse" (193). Dos Passos viewed this crisis as being perpetuated by the suburban myth, and he offers Owen Hunter's progression from home ownership to homelessness as a cautionary tale. Suburbia doesn't lead to "big money" but instead offers a life of financial hardship and destitution. Once again Dos Passos condemns the racism, greed, and misogyny underlying the suburban myth, ultimately placing the blame on individuals who participate in real-estate speculation at the expense of their own integrity.

Every instance of racism in the play reflects a desperate need among whites for suburbia's promise of preserving racial hierarchies. The College Boy Bandits, Buck and Babe, for example, believe in the suburban ideal. As Buck explains to Rena, "How people get rich is cities growin', developments, new subdivisions, real estate booms, stuff like that" (184). His dream is not about living in suburbia per se but profiting from the real-estate market, which would enable him to assert superiority over others: "Take you [to the coast] some day, and we'll have a nigger chauffeur drivin' us, maybe we'll have Buck for a chauffeur and make him do it in blackface" (233). For Babe, his fantasies about wealth require either the subservience or denigration of blacks, and this reference to blackface is intended to humiliate Buck, who wants to flirt with Rena as well. Similar prejudices recur throughout the play. When the College Boy Bandits steal Owen's mortgage money, they are associated with Native Americans.[36] Florence listens to a broadcast of Amos 'n' Andy after the robbery that leads to the Hunter's eviction (243). Rena, who dreams of settling down as a wife and mother, belittles Ike Auerbach as a "Jewish boy" after she discovers that he is poor: "All he's got's a motorcycle, that's the kind of cheapskate he is" (186, 201). Morry fears going into real-estate debt after experiencing his family's struggles to pay for their farm, and he finds the prospect of working for Owen indefinitely as beneath his race: "This ain't no life for a white man" (212). Even a vagrant tells Morry that he'll "do any kinda work that's clean an' fit for a white man" (165). This qualification, despite the fact that this man is a panhandling transient, corresponds with his surprise at the indifference of those driving along the highway near this new suburban development. He expected Fortune Heights to be compassionate and friendly, but Morry reminds him that "[t]his burg is no place for a man without money... or for a man with money for that matter" (164). All of these experiences reflect a desire among blue-collar whites to mitigate their class status through racism—racism that stems to some extent from their relationship with and investment in the suburban myth.

Furthermore, in the world of Dos Passos' fiction, social activism tends to reinforce these prejudices. The sheriff, who serves business interests by enforcing evictions, assumes that the people protesting and resisting eviction must be nonwhite. "What's eatin' 'em? Furriners ain't they?" But a hitchhiker corrects them: "Hell no, they's most of 'em white men like you an' me" (263). Anyone who rejects the capitalist philosophy of suburban growth gets associated with dark skin or Communism ("red agitators" [263]), and Dos Passos presents both of these prejudices as undermining individual integrity and communal solidarity.

Throughout *Fortune Heights,* Dos Passos focuses on lower-income suburbs to condemn the get-rich-quick mentality fueling suburbanization in America. As mentioned earlier, Fogelson describes the working-class view of suburbia as "a way station" (80)—a temporary place along the road to middle-class success. Owen perceives his home and gas station in similar terms. His lot, which is part of the titular new development, is located on a highway between cities, and Dos Passos uses this setting as a metaphor for Owen's social and economic aspirations. Like Owen, most people who stop at the station see themselves as moving on to something better. They have left home in the hopes of finding a new job, a place to stay, an education. At the same time, they continue to think of real estate as a vehicle for making money. Buck and Babe, the College Boy Bandits, admire the residential developments outside of Detroit and Chicago ("How people get rich is... developments, new subdivisions, real estate" [184]), and Ellery Jones, the local real-estate agent, tries to convince everyone that an investment in Fortune Heights will turn a profit: "Take our little development here. We plan to make money out of it, we intend to make money out of it" (192). Furthermore, he argues that "these lots out here are safer than a savingsbank. Banks fail, but improved property increases in value year by year" (172). Suburbia is presented as a place that offers protection from the vicissitudes of the financial market, and even though Owen has lost money in the Florida real-estate boom (178), he continues to buy into the prosperity myth of home ownership. He believes that Fortune Heights offers "a chance to come out on top with big money" (179). It is a stepping stone to the middle-class suburban town of Center a few miles away. "Center's a fine public spirited little burg, natural gas in every house and the purest drinkin' water in the state. I never was in a place so easy to get along with. It's an old section but a new town" (179). This promise of safety, however, is predicated on personal debt—what Ellery calls "availing [oneself] of extraordinary credit facilities" (171). For Dos Passos, these credit facilities encouraged speculation and self-destructive fantasies about earning "big money" without considering the consequences. In Owen's case, he must rely on bootlegging and renting cabins to unwed couples to pay the mortgage. Buck and Babe resort to robbery to get ahead financially, and Ellery marries a banker's widow to escape the financial fallout of the Depression and to pursue a career in politics. In their desire for money, these characters engage in unethical practices, and these developments don't inspire community but a greedy desire to get rich at the expense of others. This critique occurs most explicitly through Owen, who condemns his own actions after the eviction: "All I wanted was to squeeze as much money out of it as I could and then go live somewhere else. That ain't no way to run a business, that ain't no way to live in a house. That ain't no way to run your life" (292).

Dos Passos' indictment of the suburban prosperity myth includes popular culture as well, which reinforces delusions about wealth and privilege. Babe's dreams of success, for instance, have been shaped by the entertainment culture of the 1920s. As he tells Rena, "[W]e'll be sitting way back on the expensive upholstery [of my car] and we'll stop and eat chicken and champagne suppers in all the swell hotels, and I'll tell you how lousy things used to be and you'll give me a kiss, not one of them movin' picture whore's kisses, but a little cute kiss right on the corner of my mouth, an' that'll mean one million dollars" (233). All of the fantasies here—of elegant cars, champagne suppers, ritzy hotels, and romance—revolve around money and material possessions. Even his depiction of Rena (a woman whom he hardly knows) and her million-dollar kiss make her another object for displaying his wealth. Likewise, the radio programs heard throughout the play encourage similar illusions: *"You've been listening to Lee Heintz's orchestra playing for the daily Tea Dansant and Afternoon Musicale in the Pompeian Room of the Hotel Cincinnatus. We wish you were here with us folks to enjoy the beautiful surroundings, the perfect dance floor, the brilliant and exclusive social life"* (227). The exclusive society, perfect dance floor, and afternoon tea starkly contrast the boredom, impromptu music making, and spoiled hamburger that define life around Owen's place. Just as suburbia promises riches through speculation and, in the case of more prestigious developments, access to upper-class living, popular culture helps privilege these values as well. It presents ostentatious displays of wealth and exclusivity as the defining markers of success and happiness. Dos Passos' portrait of popular culture and suburbia, however, ultimately questions the values promoted by both.

In addition to the racial inequity and consumerist values of suburbia, Dos Passos also presents gender hierarchies and violence as characteristic aspects of this culture. Florence, who provides a $2,000 down payment for Owen's property, feels enslaved by the domestic responsibilities of the house: "[T]his slave's life always washing out baby clothes and making jams and jellies and baking cakes to sell to those miserable tourists and cleaning up their filth after them, shutting my eyes to their damn dirty ways" (218). These tasks primarily relegate her to the domestic sphere—whether the house with Owen or the cabins that they rent to unmarried couples for the night—and to the role of cleaning up after the lives of others. She has witnessed other women in a similar position: "[I]n cities you've seen those old women that scrub the floors in office buildings. Sometimes you see 'em if you go to work a little early" (296). The debilitating sacrifices that women make for money, men, and family occur in urban America as well. Part of Florence's frustration stems from the recognition that she didn't escape this fate. She simply became one of these old women for the sake of the suburban dream. She has given Owen all of her money, forgiven his infidelity, excused his criminality as a bootlegger, and overlooked the immorality of their renters in order to have a child and home. She expresses her resentment through a brief affair with Ellery (whom she uses for drinks, perfume, and going to parties) and her treatment of the gas station attendant Morry, whom she emasculates by asking him to perform domestic chores such as "[cleaning] out the kitchen sink" (206) and fixing the stove (219). She seizes on the power disparity between Morry and herself (as the wife of his employer) to feel a sense of power, but even these moments don't change her subordinate position as wife, mother, and caretaker.

For Dos Passos, men primarily enforce the captivity of suburban women through verbal and physical violence. Morry condemns

Ellery's girlfriend Fay for having sexual affairs: "I wouldn't go with a woman like that, no not for a million bucks. 'Fraid I might ketch something, as the feller said" (207). He considers the free-spirited 1920s woman a threat to men and traditional values. Moments later he tries to kiss Rena, and after she rejects him, he likens her to a prostitute: "I suppose if I had a big wad of lettuce in my pocket and a sport car you'd give me a tumble as soon as you'd put powder on your face" (207). For Morry, women harm men either by spreading disease or having unreasonable expectations about money. As he asks petulantly, "[W]hat do you want me to do, go an' rob a bank?" (207). Morry later abandons Rena to avoid the responsibilities of marriage, and Dos Passos uses this moment to capture the bind facing women. Outside the context of marriage and motherhood, women either become sexual objects or threats to men. Buck expresses similar sentiments when he refers to film actresses as "whores" (233). These women present a sexual freedom (along with fame and wealth) that Buck simultaneously resents and longs to possess. When Rena rejects his sexual advances (once again) and recognizes that he and Babe are the College Boy Bandits, Buck shoots her while Buck yells, "Stick it to her" (235). The language of rape makes this act both a sexual violation and a punishment for rejecting him and his dreams of making "big money" by any means—particularly through real-estate speculation. Buck and Babe's description of the subdivisions twenty-five miles outside of Detroit and the Evanston, Illinois suburb that used to be "nothing but meadows" (184), for example, don't impress Rena.

> *Rena:* That's what I like, just meadows an' cows and birds and things.
> *Buck:* There'll always be plenty of meadows. How people get rich is cities growin', developments, new subdivisions, real estate booms, stuff like that...
> *Babe:* If we were selling real estate we'd be driving our own car. (184)

Rena's view of land and marriage run counter to the capitalist interests that motivated suburbanization. She wants permanence, but her death, Dos Passos suggests, comes as a consequence of the greed and misogyny that shapes suburban culture.

Fortune Heights ends with an image of another couple buying into a self-destructive suburban fantasy. The realtor presents the property as a path to prosperity and a higher social status: "Here's an opportunity for a man who's willing to work to attain independence, a respectable position in society, and even wealth in a short time" (297–298). Making a quick profit is an integral part of the sales pitch, as is mitigating any guilt about buying a foreclosed property: "One man's misfortune is the next man's opportunity. You may be the man success has marked to win" (298). The pursuit of prosperity and happiness through suburbia has not only convinced people to risk more than they can spend ("What do you think Mother, can we swing it?" [298]) but also to overlook the misfortunes of others. This closing scene captures the vicious cycle that has taken hold in America, and as the appearances of this couple suggests (they *"look as much as possible like Owen and Florence without being mistaken for them"* [297]), they will turn out just like Owen and Florence—alone and destitute. Although Dos Passos' dramatic suburban trilogy concludes with an image of the dangerous allure of suburbia, the promise of homogeneity, stability, and success continues to resonate with most of his characters—whether it's Jane's fear of turning into her upper-class relatives, Martha's desire to own a home with her father and brothers, or Owen's hope of making big money on a lot in Fortune Heights—and it ultimately traps or destroys them. It isolates people from each other as well. Social protests threaten property value and the capitalistic marketplace, and for Dos Passos, as long as collective action remains antithetical to personal profit, America will continue to perpetuate the escapist, hierarchical, and self-destructive myths of suburbanization.

THE ROAD TO SUCCESS?: CARS AND CLASS STATUS IN SUBURBAN LIFE

Dos Passos loved to drive. In the ambulance corps during World War I, he relied on his skills behind the wheel and as a mechanic to survive, tuning up and repairing engines almost daily. Automobiles also made it much easier for him (and most Americans) to travel. In the early 1930s, for example, he and his wife Katy drove across the country. They enjoyed the open road, and this trip gave him greater insight into the lives of

Americans from different social classes. These experiences shaped both *1919* and *Fortune Heights,* which he was writing at the time. For Dos Passos, whose fiction often explores issues of social and economic inequity, he found the automobile an effective image both for modernity and for the ongoing struggle over social status in the United States.

In the first few years of the twentieth century, automobiles were largely popularized by affluent Americans who could afford to import them from Europe. People like William K. Vanderbilt, Jr. and Albert C. Bostwick enjoyed these roadsters for speed and adventure. They engaged in highly publicized races throughout the country and started a "touring craze," cruising through the countryside as a way to escape city life and to drive fast. As historian Tom McCarthy notes, these highly visible signs of upper-class status also inspired a great deal of acrimony among the have-nots. The public viewed this technology in positive terms, but "many resented how [it] was introduced by the wealthy. More to the point, they disliked what being automobile-less said about their status" (7). Increasing reports of car accidents involving wealthy drivers and lower- and middle-class pedestrians only made matters worse. Soon mainstream resentment turned to mob violence, and stonings became a common reaction to reckless driving among the rich. Typically groups of young men and boys "threw not only stones but mud, sticks, beer bottles, lead pipes, and decaying vegetables. These incidents occurred around the nation throughout the automobile's first decade" (McCarthy 11).

While the upper class constituted the primary market for automobiles prior to 1908, Henry Ford's introduction of the Model T that year signaled a growing desire among automakers to appeal to a wider market. The Tin Lizzie, as it was nicknamed, offered people an affordable, rugged, quick car that assuaged middle-class bitterness about elite roadsters. "Ownership of a good, plain, practical car like the Model T," McCarthy argues, "became synonymous with middle-class decency for those who prided themselves on being regular folks who disdained material pretense but who refused to be left in the dust" (41). In many respects, car ownership became a sign of class status and self-respect, and Ford recognized these social and psychological needs among consumers. Although he did not contribute anything innovative to early automobile technology or pioneer the idea of building a car for the common man, he did facilitate developments in mass production that would bring car ownership within reach of most Americans—living up to his 1909 claim to "build a motor car for the great multitude." Ford brought together a team of engineers at his factory in suburban Highland Park, Michigan, and in 1913 they introduced a crude version of the assembly line. They experimented continuously, and as David Hounshell explains, "[B]y the end of April 1914, three lines were fully in operation, and the workmen along them put together 1,212 chassis assemblies in eight hours, which worked out to ninety-three man minutes" (255). Prior to this, it took Ford's men approximately fourteen hours to assemble a car, but by 1925 they were producing one every ten seconds. This new proficiency enabled Ford to reduce the cost of the Model T from $950 in 1910 to $290 in 1924. Such innovations—along with instituting the five-dollar workday in 1914, offering rebates, and sponsoring races[37]—kept Ford in the public eye, and his roadster quickly became the most popular car in the world. By 1923, there was enough traffic in New York to make parking difficult and to necessitate electric stoplights. Four years later, there were approximately 26 million cars in the United States, and every second car on earth was a Ford.[38]

The staggering proliferation of automobiles facilitated greater suburban expansion and a rise in consumer debt as well—concerns that preoccupied Dos Passos. As the above statistics suggest, cars changed the daily lives of most Americans in the 1920s. They inspired massive government efforts to build roads[39] and expanded the possibilities for suburbanization. Jackson points out in *Crabgrass Frontier* that "between 1920 and 1930, when automobile registration rose by more than 150 percent, the suburbs of the nation's 96 largest cities grew twice as fast as the core communities... Grosse Point, near Detroit, grew by 725 percent in ten years, and Elmwood Park, near Chicago, by 717 percent. Long Island's Nassau County almost tripled in population, while Connecticut's nineteen fastest growing towns of the decade were all suburbs" (175–176). These startling numbers highlight the inextricable relationship between suburbanization and the development of the automobile. At the same time, widespread car ownership was only possible through credit, and automotive financing became a big business in the 1920s. McCarthy points out that in 1926 nearly 60 percent of American cars were financed. Furthermore, "From 1920 to 1929 the amount of consumer debt in the United States more than doubled from $3.3 billion to $7.6 billion... Between 1922 and 1929, automobile debt quintupled" (42). The role that automobile financing played in consumer debt suggests that it helped shape the psychology of the marketplace. Of course, Americans had gone into debt for consumer goods long before the automobile, but as Lendol Calder has argued, the 1920s established the debt-based mass consumerism that still exists today. The relative ease and availability of credit made people more comfortable with accruing greater amounts of debt, and this climate helped fuel the real-estate market that Dos Passos portrays in *Airways, Inc.* and *Fortune Heights.*

Throughout his plays, cars function as an image for the destructive impact of technology on individuals and society as a whole. Although Jane and Tom walk home from the party at the opening of *The Garbage Man,* for example, all of the guests drive to the funeral. Most elite, and a growing number of middle class, suburbs, required one to own a car, yet Jane's relatives are critical of this technology. Aunt Georgiana worries about getting her clothes dirty on the way to pick up the minister: "John, get me that carriage robe. There's always so much dust on the seat of the car" (14). When she returns later than expected, everyone assumes the car had a blowout. For them, automobiles are filthy and dangerous instruments—attitudes that reinforce their status as old-money elites who cling to nineteenth-century values. The presumption about Aunt Georgiana's blowout also reflects some of the literal dangers surrounding automobiles at the time. As Gerald Leinwand notes, 21,716 peopled died in automobile-related accidents in 1927; "[M]echanical failures, poor roads, and a paucity of road signs contributed to the high death rate" (10). The automobile may have represented modern progress, but it also involved personal risk. Dos Passos makes this connection more explicit in the following scene when Jane and Tom witness the aftermath of a train wreck. Jane is horrified by the carnage, and she views the accident as a dangerous sign of people's increasing reliance on the technology of transportation: "Isn't it frightening the thought of all these trains? Machines spinning, weaving steel webs, cold steel splinters sharp as razors, and nothing but our poor bare hands to lay hold of that, our naked bodies to fight all that, to conquer all that" (28). The vast number of trains and dangerous spinning machines (much like the relentless sound of factory engines at the opening of the play) capture the dominant role of technology in contemporary human life. People have become trapped in its web (either using this technology or working to build and maintain it), and their fragile bodies (naked skin and bare hands) are no match for the razor-sharp splinters of modernity. Dos Passos would later make this point through his indictment of Henry Ford in *The Big Money*. The assembly line literally reduces men to machine-line components who perform relentless tasks at high speeds until "every ounce of life was sucked off into production and at night the workmen went home grey shaking husks" (44).

In Dos Passos' fiction, these developments in technology often correspond with a loss of one's humanity. As Jane watches the casualties from the wreck being carried away on stretchers, an overweight businessman complains about the delays: "Every hour I'm late in Milwaukee will mean a thousand dollars to me more or less. I'll be ruined if we don't get in before noon...Lives are cheap. It's money that's dear" (29). His callousness stems from greed and a capitalistic ideology that privileges profit over empathy. Jane recognizes that technology, which reduces laborers to automatons, has created a culture that devalues human life. Dos Passos revisits this theme in *Fortune Heights* when a businessman crashes his car during an exhausting business trip to Nebraska: "I made six hundred and ninety miles today and I guess I was tired...You say Center's the next town, now how can I get there? When do trains leave westbound. I've got to get to Omaha. I've got very important business" (195). Just as he prioritizes business over his own life (and the lives of others on the road), Owen eagerly hopes to profit from the accident as well: "One man's misfortune sure is the next feller's bankroll" (190). He sees a way to transform tragedy (or near tragedy) into a money-making opportunity. In this way, the literal dangers of technology (car accidents and train wrecks) encourage a careless disregard of others. While drivers like the exhausted businessman and Charley Anderson in the *U.S.A.* trilogy often endanger others literally,[40] those without cars experience a startling indifference from those with them. The hitchhikers in *Fortune Heights,* for example, can't seem to get a ride. As Morry explains to one man, people won't even stop for a man with "a wooden leg an' crutches...Sure [cars] go past, way past, as the feller said. Takes a collision to stop 'em" (164, 165). Cars insulate drivers from those on the road and establish a hierarchy between the haves and have-nots. Dos Passos uses a similar image to conclude the *U.S.A.* trilogy. In the final chapter, a young man tries to hitchhike across the country. Exhausted, hungry, and disillusioned, he watches as one car after another "slithers past...and slaps grit in his face...Eyes black with want seek out the eyes of drivers, a hitch, a hundred miles down the road" (446–447). But he never sees their eyes. He is merely left with the bitter memories of unfulfilled desires as he chokes down the dusty air. There is no community here—only self-interest insulated by material possessions.

Throughout *Fortune Heights,* vehicles embody the social status of their owners, representing the materialist values of American culture. The banker's wife, Mrs. Stead, wears elegant clothing adorned with diamonds, diets during the Depression, owns "a fat little dog" (274), and drives a "fancy Stutz town car" (173). Fitting with her upper-class status, she uses the car as a pastime, not a necessity: "It's a great relaxation to drive your own car once in a while" (221). Ellery Jones' "snappy roadster" becomes an outward sign of his success as a real-estate agent. Fast and shiny, this car reflects his attributes as a salesman, and it offers his clients an image of the material success that can come with owning property. Likewise, Charley Anderson's progression up the social ladder can be seen through his various cars in *The Big Money*—a used car in his formative years, a Packard sports phaeton during his time on Wall Street, a Buick sedan for his job in Detroit, and a Lincoln town car while wooing the wealthy Gladys Wheatley.[41] Like the difference between the used car and the Lincoln, a similar dichotomy appears in *Fortune Heights.* The dilapidated Model T of the Meankin family, who stop at Owen's station to beg for gas and lodgings, and Ike's motorcycle represent the other side of the socio-economic spectrum. The contrast between these vehicles and Ellery's roadster, for example, inspires resentment among the poor. Most notably, Buck and Babe, who fantasize about owning their own car (184), take Ellery's for a joyride—an act that first puts them in trouble with the law. Buck and Babe will become the College Boy Bandits in pursuit of big money and a chauffeured car. And Ike will eventually trade in his motorcycle for a "snappy new coupé" (275) by capitalizing on the misfortunes of his acquaintances and collecting rewards for selling them out to the police. For Dos Passos, the class hierarchies signified by automobiles divide the community and encourage the selfish pursuit of material gain.

On one level, the connection between automobiles and suburbia in these plays mirrors the historical relationship between the two. As mentioned earlier, automobile and road development, along with a host of social factors, fueled suburbanization. On another level, suburban homes and cars became powerful cultural symbols for materialism in America—a materialism that Dos Passos viewed as distracting the public from addressing social and economic injustice. Most of the characters in *Fortune Heights* view automobiles and suburbia in terms of profit and social status. In a conversation with Owen, for example, Ellery observes: "Why if the growth of traffic down this road keeps up at its present rate you'll be clear in six months, ready to invest in some lots on your own account" (171). Cars bring business and potential investors in real estate. Even though Owen considers his home a place to repair his marriage and start a family, it primarily serves as a means for making enough money to buy a nicer home in Center. Babe expresses a similar attitude later in the play: "If we were sellin' real estate we'd be drivin' our own car" (184). This emphasis on buying a new car, owning a home, or spending money at a speakeasy distracts these characters from doing something about social problems. Morry only recognizes this when he assembles the working-class community to protest Owen's eviction. His impromptu speech questions the existing social structure: "It's all right to talk about law n' order but the question is whose law n' order is it...Every time the lawyers have to...drag a family out of their old homestead or to dump a workin' man, or a tenant farmer, or a sharecropper's wife an' children out in the snow, it makes the rest of us that much stronger...stronger to resist oppression" (283–284). Morry's and the protestors' failure to prevent the eviction and inspire lasting change points to a larger cultural problem with materialism. Despite the fact that the pursuit of property and material goods like cars leave many people bereft, American culture continues to cling to the prosperity myths associated with them.

UP IN THE AIR: AVIATION AND THE POSSIBILITIES FOR SUBURBAN EXPANSION

Although *Airways, Inc.* acknowledges the important role of automobiles in suburbanization ("automobiles gave you the suburban development" [91]), it primarily focuses on the technology of aviation and its relationship to suburban culture. Early in its history, the airplane didn't have much practical use. Orville and Wilbur Wright's twelve-second flight in Kitty Hawk, North Carolina, on December 17, 1903, did not receive widespread attention until the brothers demonstrated their plane for the War Department in 1908. Despite the military's interest, it didn't develop aerial units for reconnaissance and battle until 1914. Prior to this, airplane builders, most notably the Wrights and Glenn Curtiss, needed to rely on aerial shows and popular culture to earn money. Balloonists and trapeze artists had been capitalizing on the public's fascination with gravity-defying stunts for decades. P. T. Barnum hired these performers to dazzle crowds at his Hippodrome in New York, and in the twentieth century, the entertainer Houdini frequently escaped from a straitjacket while hanging upside down from the top of office buildings. In this tradition, the Wrights and Curtiss began organizing flying exhibitions in 1910 that toured the country. The pilots, commonly referred to as "birdmen," also performed at circuses, carnivals, and country fairs, risking their lives to entertain large crowds.[42]

The use of airplanes in World War I, the first war fought on land, sea, and in the air, continued to fuel public interest in flight. Daredevil fighter pilots, like Germany's infamous "Red Barron" (Manfred von Richthofen), captured the popular imagination with his eighty "kills" (aerial victories) before his death in 1918—inspiring films, dime novels, and even songs about airplanes. After Armistice, a number of veteran airmen found work as stunt pilots in the United States, and as historian Dominick A. Pisano has remarked, this pastime epitomized the "frivolous spirit of the Roaring Twenties" (51). This decade quickly became the era of barnstorming (dangerous, improvised aerial tricks for sport) and flying circuses. The latter often featured wing walkers, who performed acrobatic feats on the wings of a plane. Corporate America soon found ways to profit from such breathtaking entertainment by sponsoring these exhibitions and advertising products. African American pilot Hubert Fauntleroy Julian, for example, parachuted into Harlem with a sign for Hoenig Optical in 1923, and five years later, Jack Savage, the famed British war pilot, "launched the art of skywriting and aerial advertisement" when he spelled out "SMOKE LUCKY STRIKES" above New York City (Douglas 27).

While entertainment and advertising were the most spectacular forms of aviation in the 1920s, government airmail, which began in 1918 "as a means to train pilots and stimulate aircraft production" (Bilstein 20), greatly benefited national commerce and banking. Furthermore, the first nonstop cross-country flight took place in 1923 (at twenty-seven hours), and two army planes circumnavigated the globe one year later. The era of aviation had begun.

None of these moments captivated the public more than Charles A. Lindbergh's solo flight across the Atlantic in 1927, which embodied both technological progress and the spirit of American individualism (figure 4). Lindbergh, a soft-spoken, clean-cut, twenty-five-year old from the Midwest, took off from New York's Roosevelt Field just before 8 A.M. on May 20 and landed at Paris's Le Bourget airport thirty-three and a half hours later. Flying without a radio, copilot, or life raft to keep the plane as light as possible, he traveled approximately three thousand miles. By the time he and his plane, *The Spirit of Saint Louis,* returned to the United States aboard the USS Memphis, he was a celebrity. Almost a month later, an estimated 4.5 million people lined the streets of New York for the largest ticker-tape parade in the city's history to get a glimpse of him. Lindbergh had conquered the natural world where others had failed (numerous people died trying to fly across the Atlantic before Lindbergh), and he did so through technology. According to Roger Bilstein, "Lindbergh's flight symbolized individual achievement within the framework of the age of technology... The challenges of [the contemporary] world were met by society adapting itself to the technological discipline of the machine. Lindbergh's conquest of the Atlantic became a metaphor for the mastery of the complexities of the twentieth century" (22). Just as Lindbergh's self-reliance and skill helped make him a celebrated figure in terms of individual achievement, these qualities were also associated with aviation more broadly. Building airplanes required highly skilled workers and a degree of craftsmanship that other forms of production (particularly the assembly line) seemed to be doing away with. Such laborers took great pride in this, and "the careful work they lavished on each 'plane' imparted to it an individuality compounded of skilled craftsmanship, knowledge, and love" (Bilstein 21). Aviation offered

Figure 4 Charles Lindbergh (1902–74) working on engine of "The Spirit of St. Louis" (1927)
Source: Library of Congress.

hope that these highly developed, individual skills would play an important role in the modern age. (Dos Passos makes this point in *The Big Money* when Bill tells Charley: "Slavedrivin' may by all right in the automobile business, but buildin' an airplane motor's skilled labor" [246].)

After Lindbergh's flight, the future of this technology seemed as limitless as the sky itself. People like Glenn Curtiss, for example, envisioned flying buses and boats, and he believed that individuals would eventually own small, compact airplanes as they did cars. He also thought that "transportation of this nature would...contribute to the development of suburbs and so relieve crowding in several cities" (Leinwand 313). In fact, most people agreed with Curtiss, believing that the sky could provide new modes of transport and alleviate urban congestion. Some even felt it would change humanity itself. As Ann Douglas notes, there was speculation "that the aviation age might breed an 'aerial person,' a kind of superhuman American creature who would live in the newly habitable altitudes. Couples got married in airplanes, and a few expectant mothers, hoping to elevate if not improve the species, jumped into planes" (460). While much of the public viewed these potential innovations in positive terms, Dos Passos portrays the spirit of individualism and the technology associated with aviation in *Airways, Inc.* as ultimately corrupted by corporate interests and harmful to the lower and middle classes.

Specifically, he casts Elmer Turner in the mold of Charles Lindbergh to condemn the ways in which celebrity culture diminishes individual achievement and reduces public figures to corporate commodities. Elmer's fame comes from holding altitude and speed records as a pilot. Newspapers run photographs of him, and women, like Mae (his girlfriend) and Edna, are attracted to his success: "Sure, I think he's swell...his picture in all the papers, makin' a record an' everything. Gee, couldn't you get him to take me up widdim some time? Gee, he is good lookin' in his pictures in the papers" (102). Unlike Lindbergh at the time,[43] Elmer doesn't shy away from such publicity and attention, and Dos Passos presents this as one of his central flaws. He fails to recognize that Edna's attraction to him, like her passion for film and Valentino, is rooted in his movie-star status—a fitting connection given that aviation films first started appearing in 1913.[44] The same is true for Mae, who later marries another man after an accident ends Elmer's stardom and prevents him from flying again. He only discovers the corrosive influence of celebrity after agreeing to become a partner in Airways, Inc. His participation in the company is largely motivated by his respect for aviation and a desire to design a faster plane. Like Mae's and Edna's interest in Elmer, however, the corporation just cares about his public image as a "daring young aviator" (130). In fact, the other partners completely disregard Elmer's input as a pilot. When he asks how other pilots will benefit from the company, for instance, Davis ignores the question altogether: "Don't mind him... It's spring in the air" (125). Airways, Inc. has no investment in the working- and middle-class people who repair and fly planes:

> *Elmer:* Don't you want to see my blueprints? Honest, it's a wonderful boat. She ought to have a cruising speed of a hundred and forty-five an hour.
> *Davis [absentmindedly]:* Yes, just a minute. We might have a little... er... *[makes a gesture of lifting a glass]* to the success of the new enterprise.
> ...
> *Elmer:* Oh, it's a hell of a business... Those bastards don't give a damn about me or aviation or anything. All they can see is a chance to scoop up easy cash. (126, 128)

He discovers that this business is about profit, not aviation. Much like his father, who spent most of his career trying to promote his invention of an alcohol-based engine, Elmer's skills as a pilot and inventor are only valued to the extent that they can benefit the immediate economic goals of corporate America ("scooping up easy cash"). His celebrity will raise the stock value of the company and increase public interest in flying, generating revenue. This portrait of the burgeoning aviation industry as callous and greedy, however, undercuts the mythology surrounding air travel at the time. It exposes the corrosive influence of capitalism on even the most inspirational new technologies.

Dos Passos expands this critique by linking aviation with suburbanization as well. Specifically, Airways, Inc. considers suburban developments a lucrative source of income for the company. As Davis explains, "Airplane transportation is going to revolutionize land values. Steam made outoftown real estate a possibility, automobiles gave you the suburban development, what is aviation going to do?" (91). He follows this comment by attempting to sell Dad Turner property in Florida on an installment plan. As with trains and automobiles, aviation provides a means for increasing the scope of real-estate speculation. Davis implies this connection when he asks Elmer if one can fly from New York to Chicago in eight hours.[45] The young pilot dismisses this as "mere commuting" (125), but one of the other partners quickly explains the profitability of this: "Certainly the airplane has great possibilities for commuting. Southampton and the exclusive south shore resorts within reach of the man of moderate means" (125). Whether providing business flights between cities or opportunities to rent or buy property at beach resorts, aviation is becoming another tool for businessmen and the upper class to make money. Even Claude applies his corporate profits to real estate at the end of the play. After taking control of his brother's interests in Airways, Incorporated, he buys himself a new house, leaving Martha to care for Elmer. Claude also acknowledges that Goldberg's death, which ended the strike, enabled his own prosperity: "Nothing can hurt us now, especially with the clearing up of labor unrest" (150). The profitability of suburbanization and aviation are intertwined with suppression here, and Dos Passos uses this moment with Claude to suggest that airplanes have become another tool for exploiting the lower and middle classes.

For Dos Passos, corporate influence over the aviation industry has devastating consequences for social cohesion and individual integrity. As the company's full name suggests (All-American Airways, Incorporated), its ruthless drive for profit is presented as fundamentally American, and not surprisingly it associates patriotism with capitalism. According to the company lawyer, "[T]his corporation will, I firmly believe, fulfill a great scientific and patriotic duty and I hope will not be devoid of profit for the stockholders" (125). Dos Passos juxtaposes this claim with the unethical and unpatriotic use of airplanes in the play. Most notably, the town hires a pilot to intimidate the strikers and drop Chamber of Commerce leaflets on their rally. As Goldberg proclaims, "Look, there's an airplane overhead now, dropping leaflets to bully you...Are you going to be clubbed into submission?" (135). Davis even assumes that the leaflets and Elmer's stunt flying are part of the economic agenda of the town: "He's breaking up the meeting all right...They're all looking at him instead of listening to the riot act. Talk about restoring confidence [in real estate]. There, sir, is confidence in the making. That's what I call publicity...He must have had a tip from the cops to charge down on the crowd. That'll disperse them all right" (136, 137). Davis celebrates the airplane's ability to maintain the profitability of suburbanization, to intimidate working-class dissidents, and to generate publicity for the company. It comes as no surprise that Airways, Incorporated is eager to sell planes for government use during war and civil unrest. As Claude explains to his siblings, "[I]n case of war or labor troubles we could turn seventy-five bombing planes over to the government at twenty-fours hours' notice" (150).[46] For Airways, Inc. and corporate American more broadly, technology can be used just as easily against the working class as it can a wartime enemy. Both are threats, and both provide opportunities to make money. Technology, therefore, becomes part of the social structure that empowers business, governments, and the wealthy, creating a greater gap among the classes. Dos Passos returns to this theme at the end of the *U.S.A.* trilogy where aviation becomes an image for the lacuna between the privileged and the poor, between those with access to technology and those without. After Vag tries to make eye contact with passing drivers, he hears a plane droning overhead. The airline passengers are "big men with bank-accounts, highlypaid jobs, who are saluted by doormen" (447), and the literal distance between them and Vag reinforces his social insignificance in capitalist America. Transportation ("trains, plains: history the billiondollar speedup" [448]) is integral to the drive to earn money as quickly as possible. Even though Vag has been excluded from such luxuries, he still longs to possess them: "[W]ent to school, books said opportunity, ads promised speed, own your home, shine bigger than your neighbor" (448). American society promises these things to everyone, but as Vag's comments reveal, material signs of prosperity reinforce the kind of hierarchies (shining above your neighbors) that leave the working class destitute. In these closing moments, Dos Passos again associates planes, trains, and automobiles (speed) with home ownership to suggest that the pursuit of these things further divide the country. The fear in his plays and the trilogy is that the distance between wealthy businessmen who travel in planes and shiny cars and the vagabond walking the highway is already too great to bridge. As the closing words of *Fortune Heights* suggest, "[W]e have no use for poor men in this country" (298).

Lastly, the destructive potential of technology becomes a symbol for the loss of personal integrity in Dos Passos' fiction. When the pilot originally hired to drop leaflets over the protests gets ill, Elmer offers to take over. Martha warns that "it's helping jump on a man when he's down," but Elmer dismisses the ethical implications of this act: "It's all hokum. I don't see that it hurts the strikers any. Tommy's sick in bed an' they're paying him a hundred bucks an hour for doing the trick an' he needs the money... Well, I need a little spin. I'll loop a couple of loops for 'em. There's a big crowd out there. I'll put on a show for 'em" (133). Elmer's motivations have more to do with bravado than a genuine desire to help Tommy. His disillusionment with Airways, Inc. doesn't help forge a kinship between him and the strikers; it just makes him want to distance himself from working-class concerns by reconnecting with his celebrity as a hotshot pilot. During one of his stunts (which he performs after drinking heavily all day), Elmer's plane goes into a tailspin, and the accident leaves him paralyzed, trapped in the Turner house. His paralysis becomes an image both for the suffocating environment of suburbia, as discussed earlier, and for the powerlessness of the working class that Elmer refused to see. Charley Anderson follows a similar trajectory in the *U.S.A.* trilogy. Even though he is a former mechanic, Charley disregards the labor concerns at his own company, telling his friend Bill that "we've got a responsibility towards our investors... we've got to have some patriotism" (*The Big Money* 249). Once again, the call for patriotism is merely a self-serving justification for unequal labor practices. Moments later, Bill dies in a plane crash with Charley, and his death symbolizes the disenfranchisement and abuse of blue-collar America. Bill and the other mechanics suffer in poor working conditions while Charley's wealth increases at their expense.[47] It is fitting that Charley dies after driving drunk onto the tracks of an oncoming train. Like Dos Passos' biography of Isadora Duncan, which ends with her drunken car accident and Daughter's death in a plane crash when an intoxicated pilot takes her for a joyride over Paris, technology in all of these examples represents a loss of humanity—literally in these instances and metaphorically in terms of the dehumanizing labor needed to sustain it.

Conclusion: Suburbia and Socialist Theatre

In 1926, Dos Passos was invited to form a new theatre group with John Lawson, Em Jo Basshe, Francis Edward Faragoh, and Michael Gold—all of whom shared a socialist philosophy and admiration for the innovations of contemporary Russian theatre. They launched the New Playwrights Theatre, which operated between 1927 and 1929, to showcase drama that would confront the rampant social and economic inequalities inherent in America's capitalistic system.[48] As Dos Passos explains in his introduction to *Three Plays,* they wanted to create a new myth "to replace the imperialist prosperity myth" (xxi) and to challenge the vapid Broadway production "that everybody is ashamed of, but that manages to keep a houseful of people sitting straight up in their seats from eight-thirty to eleven-thirty six nights a week."[49] This noncommercial theatre, however, struggled with financial and ideological problems from its inception, and it closed with the production of *Airways, Inc.*[50] The small turnout made Dos Passos realize one of the central problems with their goal to educate audiences and inspire social change—working-class audiences did not want to spend their evenings watching experimental theatre about their daily lives. At the same time, the themes for many of these plays did not resonate with mainstream audiences. As Virginia Carr notes, "The play was a barrage against the mechanized American world of capitalism, but the attack had fallen largely on deaf ears and empty seats in the theater of the New Playwrights" (263).

Its popular and critical failure at the time has continued to this day. Dos Passos' plays are virtually neglected by critics, and when they are acknowledged, most do so disparagingly. Ruby Cohn, for example, finds them confusing, didactic, and dull.[51] Some of the recurring criticism about the characterization and dramatic tension in these works are legitimate, but it is my contention that the portrait of suburbanization and the technology of transportation in *The Garbage Man, Airways, Inc.,* and *Fortune Heights* make them rich resources for understanding 1920s American culture. As many of the Turners realize, suburbia traps people economically and ideologically. It is a space that reinforces racial and gender hierarchies, insulating people from one another and promoting self-interest. This not only prevents social action, but it also fosters the kind of prejudices used to justify persecution and injustice. Likewise, the technology enabling suburbanization and real-estate speculation are corrupted in capitalist America. Charles Lindbergh's inspiring flight in 1927, for example, gets reduced to another tool for corporate profit in *Airways, Inc.* Here airplanes do not represent man's ability to conquer the challenges of the modern world through technology. They create new possibilities for suburban developments and provide a powerful weapon against social activists or those who questions the values and practices of capitalism.

Dos Passos dramatic trilogy about suburbia—*The Garbage Man, Airways, Inc.,* and *Fortune Heights*—offers a counterpoint to the *U.S.A.* trilogy's emphasis on urban America. Certainly, many characters in the latter experience suburban life—Mac struggles to pay for his California bungalow and Charley Anderson worries about his wife's expensive shopping habits while living in the elite suburb of Grosse Pointe, for example—but much of the action takes place in cities. The last two plays, on the other hand, focus exclusively on suburban life, and arguably the first play is framed by images of suburbia (from Jane's upper-class home to Tom and Jane's trip to the moon, which is about as far away as one can get from urban life). Taken together, these plays depict the deterioration of the suburban myth. Suburbia does not lead to prosperity and community here. It contributes to the ongoing disenfranchisement of the middle and working classes, and the bleak ending of *Fortune Heights* offers little hope that things will change, that something will break the cycle of materialism and debt characterizing American life. If anything could begin the process, for Dos Passos, it would be art—particularly the theatre with its ability to reach audiences directly—but the public didn't respond to his plays. Perhaps his themes cut too close to the bone of public sentiment, of the way people wanted, and by the 1930s, needed to see America as a place where anyone could achieve happiness and prosperity. Perhaps the prosperity myth of home ownership was too important to most Americans to embrace works like

Airways, Inc. and *Fortune Heights*. Perhaps it still is. American culture today invests a great deal in the symbolic significance of home ownership—as an image for family, safety, stability, and socioeconomic success. In this regard, little has changed since the 1920s, and few want to hear otherwise.

Conclusion

In 2008, the Longest Lunch Theater Company, an independent dramatic arts group in New York, staged a dynamic production of E. E. Cummings' *Him*. The small venue, limited budget, collaborative nature of the production, and use of talented (but relatively unknown) actors certainly captured the spirit of the 1928 premiere. While researching the production history of the play, director Meghan Finn found a tendency among theatre groups to rewrite sections of *Him* to make it more accessible for contemporary audiences—a decision that, for Finn, failed to recognize Cummings' profound admiration for popular culture. Her decision to remain faithful to the text came with certain risks, of course. Most notably the performance inspired a public response that was just as polarizing as it had been for the Provincetown Players eighty years earlier: "Some ecstatically loved it, others detested it, some were baffled, and many were inspired" (Finn 4).

Finn did modify several aspects of the play based on her concerns about public reception, however:

> If I felt uneasy at all in moving toward rehearsals, it was due to a couple of specific moments in the play that had what I would term *historical residue*. At its heart, I felt the play was an examination of an eternal conflict between the necessities of the artistic spirit and the realities of human life. While the forms Cummings used were indispensable, and the dialogue between Him and Me essential to the play's story, there were specific embedded issues within the text that I was acutely aware would hinder the audiences' ability to fully engage with the story. These issues were the racist connotations of minstrelsy (Act II, Sc. 4) and the porter (Act II, Sc. I), the embedded sexism within Him and Me's dialogue and the interpretation of the Mussolini scene as homophobic. (19)

Her decision to remove race from the play offers one example of the complexity surrounding the integration of popular and formal theatre. What is popular at one moment in history often reflects prejudices and beliefs that are condemnable at a different time. Since Finn never intended the production "to become a museum piece or incite socio-political discussion about race,... [she] felt that by relying on the minstrel structure and performing the number as close to its written form as possible (while removing race from the equation) was the best way to prevent alienating the audience from the play's central theme" (19). Her concerns about blackface make sense. Cummings certainly wanted his use of popular forms to speak to audiences, not alienate them, and Finn's decision to alter such a moment helped her production achieve this goal.

At the same time, this type of change elides the contradictory portrait of popular culture in the play. Removing race from the minstrel scene (by using white performers),[1] homophobia from one of the burlesque numbers, and sexism (particularly Him's objectification of Me) also mitigates Cummings' message about objectification in the play. He believed, as I have argued earlier, that some of the dangers of popular culture stemmed from its tendency to reduce people to ethnic caricatures and sexual objects. It reinforced tacit or explicit prejudices that prevented mutual understanding, and Him's investment in the popular helps explain his failure as a husband, father, and artist. He can't write about the world meaningfully because he prefers the illusion and escapist pleasures of popular culture. Though Cummings himself enjoyed minstrelsy, burlesque shows, and freak shows, he recognized the ethnic and misogynistic biases that shaped these arts—biases that, as *Him* suggests, created problems for the artist and society as a whole.

Such an observation is not an attempt on my part to criticize Finn's compelling production. As a scholar, I have the luxury of examining a text without confronting the challenges of staging such a work, of trying to preserve the integrity of Cumming's text while making it resonate with contemporary theatregoers. Instead, my intention is to highlight how these decisions reveal some of the challenges of performing experimental hybrid drama. Finn's production maintains the playful vitality of these popular arts but does so in a way that removed Cummings' ambivalence about them from the work.

Perhaps, as Finn explains in her MFA thesis about the production, the racism and homophobia in *Him* would ultimately distract the audience from appreciating the play's overarching theme about art. In an age when the mere threat of racism or sexual harassment is enough to convince people of a person's guilt, these moments could have dominated discussions of the play among audiences and the media. Nevertheless, such erasure does detract from one of Cummings' critiques of American culture. For him, consumerism, as embodied by the advertising slogans heard throughout the play, and mainstream amusements had come to define American life and discourse by 1928. They were also fashioning a public that preferred superficial entertainment over critical engagement.

As enthusiasts of popular culture, Edna Millay, E. E. Cummings, and John Dos Passos appreciated and understood its appeal in the early twentieth century. Restaurants and picture palaces allowed middle-class patrons to feel like aristocrats for an evening. Men enjoyed the illusion of intimacy that burlesque dancers and chorus girls created during performances. Freak shows and minstrelsy offered whites comforting messages about ethnicity. Many Americans went into debt to own a car or a home. Working-class women modeled their own finery on the clothing in fashion magazines, and etiquette manuals suggested that upper-class life was simply a matter of mimesis. These fantasies played into the desire among many Americans to escape the every day and to be perceived as rising in the social hierarchy.[2]

Even though Millay, Cummings, and Dos Passos empathized with some of these desires (all of them struggled with money at some point in their lives—whether coming from a poor background like Millay or relying on family for financial support like Cummings and Dos Passos), they were troubled by the ways that popular culture encouraged consumption and consumerism. It often celebrated the pleasures of material gain by glamorizing upper-class trappings, and it perpetuated social inequities in its construction of female and nonwhite bodies. The integration of the popular into experimental theatre, therefore, came at a risk. Using popular elements that appealed to the public could prevent people from responding to the more serious themes of these works. Millay's use of commedia dell'arte in *Aria da Capo* could allow some audiences to dismiss her messages about sociopolitical apathy and the greed that motivates imperialist violence. Likewise,

Cummings' rollicking use of popular theatrical entertainment, which captures the energy and humor of these arts, could overshadow the concerns he raises about objectification (particularly of female, black, and homosexual bodies). Finally, Dos Passos's attack on the prosperity myth of suburbia could be too biting for audiences in a country that needed—that still needs—to equate home ownership with social and personal success.

Together these writers wanted to craft a hybrid theatre that challenged audiences to question popular depictions of class, race, and sexuality, that warned against the escapist fantasies of mainstream arts (fantasies promoting complacency, sociopolitical apathy, and materialism), that bridged the divide between high and low culture, and that could be both entertaining and thought provoking. They wanted to create drama that would make a lasting contribution to dramatic arts. They may not have achieved the widespread audiences they hoped for, but they did create works that continue to resonate and raise questions about the nature of popular culture in America.

NOTES

INTRODUCTION

1. For a list of cabarets between 1911 and 1920, see table 1 in Lewis Erenberg's *Steppin' Out*, 120–121.
2. See Henry F. May's *The End of American Innocence: The First Years of Our Own Time, 1912–1917*, 338.
3. Michael A. Lerner explains the origins of this term. "Likely derived from the 'speak-softly shops' of nineteenth-century England, where smuggled, untaxed liquor could be bought cheaply, the term 'speakeasy' served in New York as a catch-all phrase for illegal bars ranging from cellar dives peddling twenty-five-cent beers or fifty-cent glasses of 'smoke,' to fancy townhouses in midtown outfitted with multiple bars, dining areas, game rooms, and live entertainment...Whether these gathering places were tucked away in construction sites, hidden in apartment back rooms, disguised behind receptionists' desks in office buildings, or brazenly situated across from police precinct houses, New Yorkers delighted in discovering the locations of speakeasies as if it were all part of a game" (Lerner 138).
4. According to Lerner, the New York City Police Department "estimated the number of illegal drinking establishments [at the height of the Prohibition-era] to be as high as 35,000 with 2,200 in the Wall Street area alone" (138).
5. His *Follies* of 1907 ran for 70 performances. In the following year, his production had 120 performances. The 1910 and 1911 *Follies* ran for 88 and 80 performances respectively. For more, see Patinkin, 92–94.
6. While appropriating the *Folies Bergère* and other aspects of Parisian entertainment culture, such as the Moulin Rouge, Ziegfeld aligned his productions with European theatrical forms, but he frequently cast his girls in far more exotic roles. As Ann Marie McEntee has argued, Ziegfeld was tapping into the country's fascination with

Orientalism. On his stage, "[E]xotic stage pictures, dripping with sensuality—another aspect of the culture's preoccupation with Orientalism—eclipsed the Americana satires and patriotic numbers" (179). From Ann Marie McEntee's "Feathers, Finials, and Frou-Frou: Florenz Ziegfeld's Exoticized Follies Girls" in *Art, Glitter, Glitz: Mainstream Playwrights and Popular Theatre in 1920s America*, eds. Arthur Gewirtz and James J. Kolb, Westport, CT: Praeger, 2004: 177–188.

7. The Palace Theater on Broadway and Forty-Seventh Street, completed in 1913, quickly became the epicenter for talents like Fanny Brice, Harry Houdini, Irving Berlin, and blackface performer Eddie Cantor.
8. Nickelodeons in New York City alone grossed $6 million in 1908, for instance (Sklar 16).
9. For more on the diversity of early film audiences, see Richard Butsch's *The Making of American Audiences: From Stage to Television, 1750–1990*, 140–157.
10. The movie industry that had been highly profitable in the early twentieth century gradually eclipsed all other forms of entertainment during the 1920s. In 1923, there were 15,000 theatres in the United States that had an average weekly attendance of 50 million people, and by 1928 "65 million tickets were being sold nationally each week" (Kyvig 93, 94).
11. The dynamics of the movie theatre space changed abruptly in the late 1920s. Picture palaces, like vaudeville houses, provided places for people to socialize with each other as they watched a mixture of staged routines and film. This atmosphere created a sense of community among the audience as they audibly expressed views about the film, making each screening a unique social event. *The Jazz Singer* (1927) with Al Jolson, however, altered this dynamic. The tremendous success of the film and the talkies that immediately followed allowed theatres owners to cut vaudeville and musical acts from the program. Furthermore, as Robert Sklar explains, "With talkies,...people who talked aloud were peremptorily hushed by others in the audience who didn't want to miss any spoken dialogue. The talking audience for silent pictures became a silent audience for talking pictures" (153).
12. Poggi 47. He also notes that the height of commercial theatre in New York coincided with the start of its decline. After the 1925–26 season, "Plays were closing more quickly and theaters were kept open less frequently" (50).

13. For more on the play, see Ted Merwin's *In Their Own Image: New York Jews in Jazz Age Popular Culture*.
14. In "Jazz and American Culture," Lawrence W. Levine surveys the cultural debate surrounding jazz in the 1920s: "Various critics insisted, bore the same relationship to classical music as a limerick did to poetry, or a farmhouse to a cathedral, or a burlesque show to legitimate drama. Jazz was attacked not only for returning civilized people to the jungles of barbarism but also for expressing the mechanistic sterility of modern urban life... It was praised and criticized for breaking out of the tight circle of obedience to Eurocentric cultural forms and giving expression to indigenous American attitudes articulated through indigenous American creative structures. It was, in short, praised *and* criticized for being almost completely out of phase with the period's concept of Culture" (437–438).
15. In the realm of the theatre, African Americans had been establishing independent performance troupes, companies, and productions since the late nineteenth century. After the Civil War, most of these troupes performed in blackface since the prejudices of white audiences "circumscribed the performance boundaries of African American stars," requiring them to "speak and sing in dialect, wear funny costumes, sing 'coon' songs, and end their acts with a cakewalk or some other kind of 'darky' dance... Only in black theaters were the black performers permitted to imitate whites" (Nasaw 57). The first black show to make it to Broadway was *Clorindy*, or the *Origin of the Cakewalk* (1898). Composed by African American Will Marion Cook (with lyrics by Laurence Dunbar), it can be credited with introducing "ragtime and eccentric dancing" to Broadway (Graziano 94)—though this type of syncopated music had been part of vaudeville and minstrelsy for quite some time. This inspired other African American musicals, including *Sons of Ham* (1901), *In Dahomey* (1902), *The Shoo-Fly Regiment* (1907), and *The Red Moon* (1909). In 1921, the revue *Shuffle Along* (with its all African American cast including a young Josephine Baker) captivated white and black audiences with its rich mixture of blues, jazz, ballads, African American songs, and quick dance numbers. It was also the first musical to allow African Americans to sit on the main floor of the theatre. Though *Shuffle Along* "ushered in a new period of black musicals on Broadway," as John Graziano has argued, "it was a continuation of the stereotypical representations of African Americans that had been seen twenty years earlier" (98). The white patronage of musicians like Berlin, Kern, and Gershwin was still required to give this music mainstream appeal.

16. Nasaw 31 and 47–61. "Even on Broadway, African Americans who wished to see the black comedy team of Bert Williams and George Walker performing *In Dahomey* had to undergo the humiliating experience of entering the theater by a back entrance and taking seats in the upper gallery" (49).
17. This flurry of popular entertainment also reveals a significant change in American social life at the time. As mentioned earlier, escapism of one kind or another appealed to most Americans in the early twentieth century, and the rise of leisure culture can thus be viewed as a response to an increasingly regimented workplace. As Lynn Dumenil explains, Americans turned toward leisure and consumption as a response to "the degradation of work and the erosion of individual autonomy in mass corporate culture" (57). Modern machine production for blue-collar laborers and bureaucracy for white-collar employees created a working environment that demanded routine tasks over individual autonomy. Henry Ford's assembly lines, which were first introduced in 1913, epitomized these changes for the proletariat. This technology transformed the individual's role in the workplace, subdividing labor into specialized tasks and reducing his role to a single, repetitive action such as tightening nuts and bolts. It also transformed productivity. As this innovation became more widespread, backbreaking speed and mind-numbing repetition began to characterize the factory laborer's daily life. At the same time such innovations enabled him and his family to experience a greater degree of freedom to enjoy popular culture. Although "the nine-hour day and fifty-four hour week continued to be the legal standard in New York well into the 1920s" (Peiss 43), labor unions were successfully reducing this time. By 1923, many working-class women worked forty-eight hours or less per week. Salaried workers also began to receive two-week paid annual vacations by the middle of the decade, and this trend reflecting the growing interest among white-collar workers for commercial entertainment as well.
18. As Fearnow notes, Lawrence Langner, an attorney who helped fund and write the manifesto for the Washington Players, was the driving force behind the Theatre Guild, which he wanted to be fully professional and self-sustaining. See "Theatre Groups and Their Playwrights," 356.
19. More specifically in 1923, O'Neill, along with Kenneth Macgowan and Robert Edmond Jones, quickly launched Experimental Theatre, Inc. (1923–25). Despite the new name, they still advertised programs as part of the Provincetown Playhouse. The group placed a premium

on professionalization and expanded the scope of productions, operating two theatres (the Provincetown Playhouse and the Greenwich Village Theater). The expense of these productions (particularly those that failed financially) caused a division among the organization yet again. O'Neill's faction continued to work with a permanent company of professional actors, directors, and set designers. After one more season, they merged with Actors' Theater. A second faction, headed by James Light and Eleanor Fitzgerald, returned to the group's origins to offer simple, amateur productions. "From 1925 to 1929, they tried to bring Provincetown back to its old ideals and policies. They emphasized new American plays, though they sometimes did non-originals in experimental styles" (Poggi 118). The most notable productions by the Provincetown Players in its final years included Paul Green's *In Abraham's Bosom,* which received the Pulitzer Prize in 1926, and E. E. Cummings' *Him.*

20. To offer one example, Kathy Peiss argues in *Cheap Amusements: Working Women and Leisure in Turn-of-the-Century New York* that "generally, a 'trickle down' model is assumed in these interpretations: bohemian intellectuals, college students, or an elite urban vanguard develop new social forms, which are then diffused downward, via institutions of mass culture, to the broader middle class and, ultimately, to the working class" (8). However, she points out that cultural change is multidimensional and that "the lines of cultural transmission travel in both directions" (8). For other discussions of the blurring of these categories, see Levine's *Highbrow/Lowbrow: The Emergence of Cultural Hierarchy in America* and Neil Harris' *Cultural Excursions: Marketing Appetites and Cultural Tastes in Modern America.* Kammen also offers an overview of this debate in the first chapter of *American Culture, American Tastes.*

21. As David Nasaw explains, these popularly priced stock theatre companies staged shows "not unlike those being performed at ticket prices ten times higher in the downtown opera halls and playhouses. If there was a hierarchical division between the high-priced and the popular-priced audiences, it was not based on the content of the show. The only discernable difference was in timing. It took a season or two for current productions to reach the cheaper theaters" (41).

22. See *After the Great Divide: Modernism, Mass Culture, Postmodernism* (Bloomington: Indiana University Press, 1986).

23. Critics have typically cited German expressionism as a major influence on American dramatists in the early twentieth century, but as Walker points out in *Expressionism and Modernism in the American*

Theatre: Bodies, Voices, Words, "[T]he German plays were not produced on the American stage until many American plays had been written and, in some instances, already produced" (4). Walker contends that there were other sources in the American landscape that shaped these dramas, such as "speech educator S. S. Curry's theory of expression. Curry, drawing upon the work of French vocal instructor Francois Delsarte, challenged conventional elocutionary instruction by insisting that communication was not a function of the voice alone but a whole bodily process that depended upon the perfect coordination of all three 'languages' of the body—verbal, vocal, and pantomimic" (5).

24. In his discussion of the growth of popular culture in America between 1885 and 1935, Kammen notes the important role of transportation technology as well: "Innovations in transportation and technology made it possible for entrepreneurial amusements to reach audiences on an expanded scale" (70).

1   "I Cannot *Live* without a Macaroon!"

1. Sections of this chapter appeared in *Modern Drama* 54.1 and are reprinted with permission from the University of Toronto Press Incorporated (www.utpjournals.com).
2. As Henry May notes in *The End of American Innocence: The First Years of Our Own Time, 1912–1917,* "[B]lack and orange became, for the *Saturday Evening Post* a few years later, a clear sign of sin" (283).
3. In "Freud, Flappers, and Bohemians: The Influence of Modern Psychological Thought and Social Ideology on Dress, 1910–1923," scholar Deborah Sayville highlights fashion as a significant part of Millay's public persona as well: "Millay's dress choices reflected her bohemian sentiments. Batik dresses, hand-printed tunics, Spanish shawls, bobbed hair, artistic jewelry and silk dresses that crisscrossed her bosom without a brassiere expressed Millay's sensuality and independent personal identity experienced at the height of her popularity around 1920."
4. One critic, Gerhard Bach, considers Millay's *Aria da Capo* as prefiguring the theater of the absurd. "*Aria da Capo,* besides its modestly expressionist setting, is quite likely an early forerunner of the Absurd tradition. Its importance as such, however, has yet to be acknowledged" (36).
5. In "World War I: The Turning Point," for example, Ralph Raico explains that the British were intentionally trying to starve the

enemy public by confiscating food shipments to Germany. By 1916, the German people were trying to survive on nothing more than "'a meager diet of dark bread, slices of sausage without fat, an individual ration of three pounds of potatoes per week, and turnips,' and then the potato crop failed" (228). At this point, Germany had no choice but to attack the illegal British blockade, drawing America into the war.

6. As Marsha Gordon points out in "Onward Kitchen Soldiers: Mobilizing the Domestic During World War I," *Good Housekeeping*, for example, "[F]elt compelled to publish a statement in its November 1918 issues to correct rumors that it was in fact a government publication" (68).

7. Dieting (or guilt about not dieting) had become an active part of American life in the early twentieth century. Prior to 1890, the Food Administration's nationwide call for moderation would have been dismissed as virtually unpatriotic. Americans always had a reputation for consuming great quantities of food. The United States was the land of plenty, after all, and many people used meals (as well as bodily girth) to communicate material and social success. However, a crusade against fatness took hold between 1890 and 1910. This diet craze was largely inspired by British diet fads, the popularity of slender theatre stars, pornography featuring thin women, the rise of athleticism among women, and fashion. New gimmicks and commercial products also encouraged consumers to reshape their bodies. Advertisements equating fatness with unhealthiness and unsightliness became commonplace. And new epithets describing obesity, such as "slob," "porky," and "jumbo," captured changing cultural perceptions about weight. Not surprisingly, by the time Millay moved to New York the slimness ideal was firmly in place. For more on this, see Peter N. Stearns' *Fat History: Bodies and Beauty in the Modern West*.

8. As Christine Stansell argues in *American Moderns: Bohemian New York and the Creation of a New Century*, bohemians "abandoned marriage as the locus of legitimacy and upheld instead a principle of honesty among equals: the acknowledgment of sexual interests among a community of freely participating partners. Truth telling and equality, not a church ceremony, became the basis for morality, signs that distinguished honorable from immoral sexuality, whoever the parties and whatever the context" (273).

9. Millay wrote three plays for her Technique of Drama class at Vassar in 1917: *The Wall of Dominoes*, which was published in the *Vassar*

Miscellany Monthly in May, *Two Slatterns and a King: A Moral Interlude* and *The Princess Marries the Page*. For more on these plays, see John Joseph Patton's dissertation, *Edna St. Vincent Millay as a Verse Dramatist*, 41–78.

10. In a 1941 interview, Millay claims that she first had the idea for *Aria da Capo* in 1916, but she didn't start writing the play until 1918. See Patton 68.
11. *Aria da Capo,* which Millay starred in and directed for its premiere with the Provincetown Players, was performed in Boston, Baltimore, Saint Louis, and Paris within a few months after its premiere in New York. It was first published in *Reedy's Mirror* in March the following year. Subsequently, it was published several times in 1921, including the reprint in *The Provincetown Players* (edited by George Cook and Frank Shay). Harper published an edition in 1924, and the play appeared in *Fifty Contemporary One-Act Plays* in 1925. John Joseph Patton notes that it was published eight or nine times by 1926 (99–102).
12. Charles Ellis designed the stage for the December 1919 production of *Aria da Capo*. As Brenda Murphy explains in *The Provincetown Players and the Culture of Modernity*, "[R]ather than a backdrop and wings on the tiny stage, Ellis used black screens of various sizes on which he painted a design in white" (149). Millay's suggestions for the production discuss the colors and costuming as well: "The table, six feet long and two feet wide, has thin legs and is painted black" (43). She also recommends a tablecloth with "black and white spots and striped ends" (44) and white, wooden bowls (46), for example.
13. 133 Macdougal Street served as the theatre for the Provincetown Players at the time, and Millay's first apartment was only a few blocks away at 30 West 9th Street.
14. See Milford 248–249.
15. The Other Players was a short-lived theatre group started by Alfred Kreymborg and William Zorach that produced *Two Slatterns and a King* along with five plays for a week-long run at the end of March in 1918.
16. Nora eats macaroons throughout the first two acts of *A Doll's House*. This inconsequential food, which her husband outlaws from their house because he fears they will rot her teeth, reflects the idealized, artificial world she occupies for much of the play. Ibsen's work was well-known in the United States by the Teens and Twenties, and as the reference to macaroons suggests, Millay most likely found inspiration in the modernist, political (particularly in terms of gender politics), and metatheatrical dimensions of this work. As critic Toril Moi

has argued in *Henrik Ibsen and the Birth of Modernism: Art, Theater, Philosophy*, "*A Doll's House* is the first full-blown example of Ibsen's modernism...[The play] is teeming with metatheatrical elements, and a preoccupation with the conditions of love in modernity" (225).
17. As Sarah Bay-Cheng and Barbara Cole note in *Poets at Play: An Anthology of Modernist Drama*, "From both her theatrical work [she played Columbine in the Theatre Guild production of *Bonds of Interest* in 1919] and her collegiate studies, Millay was familiar with the traditional figures of commedia and their Italian street theater improvisations that toured Europe throughout the sixteenth and seventeenth centuries" (47).
18. For more on these characters and their place in the history of commedia dell'arte, see Allardyce Nicoll's *The World of Harlequin: A Critical Study of the Commedia dell' Arte*. Although Pierrot was first introduced in 1576, his character evolved, and by the 1670s he tended to be lazy and outspoken. "He mistakes absurdly, yet often his errors may be viewed as exhibitions of his common sense" (90). Columbina was usually presented as a flirtatious, young servant in dainty dress, but her character was not as richly developed as Pierrot, for example. Nicoll points out that the female servants were not fully established figures. "It is amply apparent that the names themselves do not serve to designate personalities of the sort exemplified by Harlequin, Scapino, Brighella, Punch and Pierrot, but are merely dependent on the choice of actresses interpreting one single part" (95).
19. In her senior year at Vassar, for example, she even went down to New York to hear Caruso sing *Aida,* and she was subsequently campused, "which meant she was forbidden any additional nights away from the college" (Milford 137).
20. See Milford 469.
21. Millay's conflicted response to her propaganda efforts has been well documented. As Cheryl Walker notes, Millay's "radio broadcasts and public appearances contributed to her complete breakdown in 1944, which occurred just after the Writers War Board had insisted that she write a poem for their continuous D-Day broadcast" (90). Biographer Nancy Milford also points out that Millay "knew the risk to her reputation of writing propaganda" (470), and this criticism impacted her work. As Millay explained in 1947, "The effect of writing so much propaganda during the war—from the point of view of poetry, sloppy, garrulous, and unintegrated—is to make me more careful and critical of my own work even than I formerly was, so that now I write more slowly than ever" (489).

2 "DAMN EVERYTHING BUT THE CIRCUS!"

1. This diary entry is quoted in Richard S. Kennedy's *Dreams in the Mirror: A Biography of E. E. Cummings*, 28.
2. Kennedy references some of these early works on 32 and 45.
3. These three volumes—*Tulips and Chimneys* (1923), *XLI Poems* (1925), and *&* (1925)—came from his manuscript *Tulips & Chimneys* (1922), which was never published in its original form and arrangement in Cummings' lifetime.
4. Unlike the critical success of *The Enormous Room*, Cummings' first book of poetry, *Tulips and Chimneys*, received mixed reviews. As Kennedy points out, "[M]ost reviewers were hostile to the 'eccentric system of punctuation' (Louis Untermeyer's phrase) and allowed praise only for the more traditional poems like 'Puella Mea' or 'Epithalamion'" (253).
5. As Louis S. Warren describes in *Buffalo Bill's America: William Cody and the Wild West Show*, "[T]he initial racing and historical acts were followed by shooting demonstrations by Buffalo Bill, Doc Carver, and Adam Bogardus, a former market hunter from Illinois who had set many records for competitive pigeon shooting and who was also the developer of the clay pigeon" (223). Buffalo Bill's shooting competitions typically used clay pigeons.
6. For the rest of his life, Cummings struggled to write another play, but he produced only fragments, notes, a ballet scenario based on *Uncle Tom's Cabin,* and a short morality play about Santa Claus in 1946. Richard Kennedy situates this latter work in the tradition of the puppet play, "[F]or its archetypal characters and its basic action with sudden reversals are straight from the tradition of the Guignol performances in the Champs Elysées, the Toon puppets in Brussels, or the marionette theater of Remo Bufano in Greenwich Village" (407).
7. As Kennedy notes, "[T]he Village audiences—intellectuals, Bohemians, academics—liked the play, and some people returned more than once. It ran to full houses (200 people) for 27 performances, though it made no money for the Playhouse because production costs were so high. It provided a fine climax for the 1927–1928 season" (296).
8. Many critics, such as Richard Kennedy, Norman Friedman, Milton Cohen, and Linda Wagner-Martin, have discussed the important biographical dimensions of this play. Cummings modeled the main plot of *Him* on his relationship with Elaine Orr Thayer. He fell in love with her in 1918 while she was still married to his friend and former Harvard classmate, Scofield Thayer. Scofield seemed to have tacitly

approved of the situation. The couple had already taken up separate residences in Greenwich Village, and he espoused the bohemian philosophy of free love. Nevertheless, when Cummings and Elaine's daughter, Nancy, was born in 1919, Elaine felt it important to tell people that she was Scofield's daughter. Cummings became increasingly estranged from Elaine in the first few years of Nancy's life. Elaine and Scofield eventually divorced in 1921, and she married Cummings in 1924. However, their relationship was already beginning to flounder. A few months later, she met Frank MacDermot (whose name appears in the barker's monologue in act III) and asked for a divorce from Cummings. As Kennedy explains, "[T]he recent months had no doubt revealed fully his blindly self-centered existence. He professed to love her, yet he neglected her... He declared that he loved Nancy, but he treated her less like his child than like a toy to be take out for amusement... Elaine finally realized her 'mistake' during the time when Estlin was proving so ineffectual after the death of [her sister] Constance. Here was a time when she really needed help and Cummings was unable to take charge of anything" (255, 257). The gun in the play also seems to refer to the fact that Cummings acquired a .38 caliber pistol in 1924 and considered suicide. "On one occasion, he came to 3 Washington square and in Elaine's presence drew out the pistol and pointed it at his temple" (259). Cummings' new relationship with Anne Barton in 1926 helped him deal with the heartbreak of his broken marriage, but it did add to his guilt about being so removed from Nancy's life. Cummings did not reveal that he was her father until 1948.

9. Mary C. English has argued that this satire places Cummings' play in the tradition of Greek drama, particularly the comedies of Aristophanes: "Although Cummings drew inspiration from a number of sources, his attitude toward comedy is strikingly Aristophanic: he sought to advise his audience on important issues plaguing American society, and artists in particular, while crafting a play that would entertain... He forced his audience to confront aspects of American culture that were, at the very least, 'unsettling'" (81).

10. As he prepared to write *Him* (which he began writing in 1926), Cummings attended theatrical performances throughout the Village, and his friendship with John Dos Passos and John Howard Lawson, both of whom had recently produced expressionistic dramas that incorporated elements of popular culture, inspired Cummings to write *Him* in that tradition. Their approach to the theatre may have

also helped him wrestle with some of the difficulties of integrating popular art into dramaturgy.

11. This statement comes from "The Adult, the Artist, and the Circus." Cummings' articles on the circus, burlesque, and the theatre are reprinted in *E. E. Cummings: A Miscellany Revised*. My citations refer to the page numbers in this volume.

12. It is also important to note that Picasso's shift from postimpressionism into cubism is deeply connected to circus and burlesque imagery. He was imitating the work of Toulouse-Lautrec in the late nineteenth and first few years of the twentieth centuries—which itself featured café singers and burlesque-type figures, for example. Most art historians consider the Blue and Rose periods to be the first original work of Picasso—Blue features musicians; Rose features circus performers.

13. See Trachtenburg's *The Incorporation of America: Culture and Society in the Gilded Age*, 57–59.

14. In *The Circus Age*, Janet M. Davis argues that "no other amusement saturated consumers like the circus at the turn of the century. Neither vaudeville, movies, amusement parks, nor dance halls equaled the circus's immediate physical presence—that is to say, towns did not shut down in their midst. These popular forms were integrated into local economics and local systems of surveillance, while the railroad circus was an ephemeral community ritual invading from without...The traveling circus, in contrast, came to one's doorstep. Disconnected from daily life, the nomadic circus had a distance from community ties that enhanced its ability to serve as a national and even international popular form" (13).

15. Two years earlier, his second American Museum burned to the ground—the original museum on the corner of Broadway and Ann Street was destroyed by fire in 1865. These events inspired him to retire from the museum business for a while and join forces with Castello and Coup. Barnum had worked in the circus early in his career. As Neil Harris discusses in *Humbug: The Art of P. T. Barnum*, "In the 1830s he had traveled with one of the pioneers of the American circus, Aaron Turner, and later formed his own troupe, although Barnum's Grand Scientific and Musical Theater toured only a short time and consisted of a juggler, a magician, a clown, and some musical performers" (235). For more on Barnum's time with Aaron Turner, see A. H. Saxon's *P. T. Barnum: The Legend and the Man*, 78–80.

16. As A. H. Saxon explains in *P. T. Barnum: The Legend and the Man*, in 1881 "spectators and reporters were overwhelmed by another

innovation that has since become a distinctive hallmark of the American circus: the three-ring format, often with one or two platforms in between for cycle and other acts requiring a firm surface, augmented by the great hippodrome track surrounding the whole and the rigging for trapeze, high-wire, and other aerial numbers taking place above. Curiously, as was also true for his two-ring circus, Barnum made no claim to being the first to introduce this confusion, possibly because he knew better (the English showman George Sanger insisted he experimented with three rings as early as 1860)" (287).

17. For the first time, these stores created an environment designed to encourage motion. Like Galeries Lafayette, which opened in Paris in 1912 and where the glass-domed ceiling is reminiscent of a circus big top, department stores offered customers the opportunity to browse, to move around a large space while viewing a vast array of items for purchase. Even the arrangement of objects inside became more complex and, in a sense, more three-dimensional.
18. Cummings specifically makes this argument in his essay "Theater II" for *The Dial* in 1926.
19. As Sarah Bey-Chang and Barbara Cole note in *Poets at Play*, "For [Cummings], the theater needed to become a place of revelation, not simply observation. If mainstream theater wanted to make pretense that looked like real life, then Cummings's theater would expose reality as merely pretense" (159).
20. All of the paintings discussed in this chapter can be found in *CIOPW*.
21. Quoted from "The Adult, the Artist and the Circus."
22. Emily Essert, in "'Since Feeling Is First': E. E. Cummings and Modernist Poetic Difficulty," has argued that Cummings' poetry resonates with readers at a "sub-rational level upon first reading...; But... his poems then beg to be re-read in order to be understood, and it is mostly upon rereading that Cummings challenges the reader's intellect" (199). Robert E. Maurer's "E. E. Cummings' *Him*," in *E. E. Cummings: A Collection of Critical Essays*, suggests a similar reading of Cumming's play: "When Cummings wrote *Him* he wanted to arouse within the spectator that feeling of aliveness, an extra-literary quality, that is the peculiar attribute of the drama and that effectively produces its results before intellectual analysis begins" (137).
23. The Weirds investment in social hierarchies and etiquette (they have doubts about Him until he explains that he is "very noble," for example) is reminiscent of Cummings' upper-class Cambridge ladies, who knit for social causes merely because it is fashionable to do so.

24. Months of advance work, which included posting thousands of billposters, went into each stop. As Davis notes, "[T]he advance team transformed gray, weather-beaten barns and dull, brick stores into a colorful frenzy of clowns, tigers, semi-bare women, and elephants... In short, circus billposters marked the landscape, claimed it, and transformed it months before the actual onslaught of crowds, tents, and animals" (45).
25. According to the *Oxford English Dictionary*, the term "freak" first appears in the sixteenth century, but before the 1800s, it means a capricious or whimsical notion, a vagary. Not until the 1840s did "freak" refer to "a monstrosity, an abnormally developed individual of any species; in recent use (especially the United States) a living curiosity exhibited in a show." This distinction suggests that something about these presentations changed significantly at this time, and this change can largely be attributed to Phineas Taylor Barnum's ownership and management of the American Museum. For more on the history of the freak show and dime museums, see Robert Bogdan's *Freak Show: Presenting Human Oddities for Amusement and Profit* and Andrea Stulman Dennett's *Weird & Wonderful: The Dime Museum in America*.
26. For more on the decline of the freak show, see Bogdan, Rosemarie Garland Thomson's "Introduction" to *Freakery*, and Thomas Fahy's *Freak Shows and the Modern American Imagination*.
27. Marc Robinson views these images of body parts in relation to Me's demands on Him. She is asking for "a quality of engagement far stronger than he, in his autonomous creativity and cultural sightseeing, prefers... Throughout *Him,* Cummings writes of faces, hands, whole bodies 'folding,' closing, and opening again, at the same time as the characters note how darkness falls, wraps around them, and enforces an intimacy they might not be capable of on their own. In that hushed dusk, the entire play contracts, and Him's claims for the supremacy of his imagination, and of the fictions it creates, collapses before Me's more palpable reality" (226).
28. Cummings also presents Madame Petite in similar ways. Early in the scene, the barker explains that Madame Petite (the Eighteen Inch Lady) has been married seven times to "famous specimuns uv duh uppercrust" (128) like Tom Thumb, and this type of personal information was integral to the appeal of freak shows. The sexual lives of dwarfs, hermaphrodites, bearded ladies, and Siamese twins tapped into the crowd's curiosity about the sexual practices of freaks. Barnum made Tom Thumb and Livinia Warren's marriage in 1863,

for example, a sensational media event, and over 100,000 onlookers clamored to attend the marriage of Violet Hilton (who was conjoined with her sister Daisy) to James Moore at the Texas Centennial Exposition in 1936.

29. This phrase is quoted in Cohen's *POETandPAINTER: The Aesthetics of E. E. Cummings's Early Work* (46). Of course, numerous artistic styles influenced Cummings' paintings, including the cubism, synchromism, and fauvism. Cohen argues that "Cézanne without a doubt exerted the greatest influence on Cummings's early painting, aesthetics, and even professional identity" (43). Cohen also singles out the importance of the futurism for Cummings, who felt that the dynamism of these works solved some of the problems of Cubism's "cold and frozen grammar" (46). "To convey motion in much of his later painting, Cummings was far more spontaneous, using faster, looser brushwork, rougher textures, and often impastoed strokes" (57). For more on the influence of art on Cummings' poetry, see Rushworth Kidder's "'Twin Obsessions': The Poetry and Painting of E. E Cummings" and "Cummings and Cubism: The Influence of Visual Arts on Cummings' Early Poetry." For some recent discussions on the visual dimensions of his poetry, see Gudrun M. Grabher's "i Paint (My Poems), Therefore I Am: The Visibility of Language and Its Epistemological Implications for the 'I' in e. e. Cummings' Poetry" and Sheeva Azma's "Poem-painter: E. E. Cummings' Artistic Mastery of Words."

30. John Marin (1870–1953) studied at the Pennsylvania Academy of Fine Arts with Thomas Anschutz and William Merritt Chase. His travels to Europe in the early twentieth century exposed him to the avant-garde art scene. Cummings' *New York, 1927* is reminiscent of Marin's paintings and drawings of the city, including *Brooklyn Bridge* (1912) and *Lower Manhattan (Composition Derived from Top of Woolworth Building)* (1922).

31. For more on the Great Migration of African Americans during the twentieth century, see Ann Douglass' *Terrible Honesty* and James Gergory's *The Southern Diaspora: How the Great Migrations of Black and White Southerners Transformed America*. For more on immigration, see Sollors, "Immigrants and Other Americans," 569–570, and John Higham *Strangers in the Land*, 267.

32. The Midway Plaisance at the Chicago World's Columbian Fair in 1893, for example, displayed anthropological exhibits that allowed white spectators to see representations of people and customs from around the world. These displays began with the most primitive

black tribes and ended with the white, middle-class family, a progression designed to present white, middle-class America as the pinnacle of social and cultural achievement. As Robert Rydell explains in *All the World's a Fair*, these exhibits "provided visitors with ethnological, scientific sanction for the American view of the nonwhite world as barbaric and childlike and gave a scientific basis to the racial blueprint for building a utopia" (43). The popularity of these exhibits would heighten their popularity in freak shows and dime museums, and in some cases, ethnological exhibits from World's Fairs subsequently became part of traveling sideshows. This was certainly the fate of the Bontoc Igorots, a Philippine tribe displayed at the 1904 World's Fair in St. Louis. For more on this, see chapter seven in Rydell's *All the World's a Fair* and Christopher A. Vaughan's "Ogling Igorots: The Politics and Commerce of Exhibiting Cultural Otherness, 1898–1913."

33. Bogdan explains in *Freak Show* that African Americans with this condition were often "cast as 'missing links' or as atavistic specimens of an extinct race" (112). For more, see chapter 1 of Thomas Fahy's *Freak Shows and the Modern American Imagination* and James W. Cook's examination of the social and political significance of this exhibit in "Of Men, Missing Links, and Nondescripts: The Strange Career of P. T. Barnum's 'What Is It?' Exhibition."

34. E. E. Cummings may have viewed Zip and other freaks as versions of the delectable mountains in *The Enormous Room*. Zulu, Surplice, and Jean Le Nègre, for example, have powerful ways of communicating without language. Jean Le Nègre is described as using language in a picturesque manner, "[courting] above all the sounds of words" (199). Nevertheless, the historical link between freak shows and institutional racism in the United States cannot be ignored here.

35. Seldes viewed the higher and lower arts as complimentary to each other. As a result, he disliked the false dichotomy created by the terms "highbrow" and "lowbrow." For more on *The 7 Lively Arts*, its critical reception, and context, see chapter three of Michael Kammen's *The Lively Arts: Gilbert Seldes and the Transformation of Cultural Criticism in the United States*.

36. He discusses *Him* and the three mysteries of love, art, and self-transcendence in "I & Now & Him" from *Six Nonlectures* (1962). He also explains this issue in a 1961 letter to Norman Friedman: "Him's deepest wish is to compose a miraculously intense play-of-art—Me's underlying ambition is to be entirely loved by someone through whom she may safely have a child. He loves,not herself,but

the loveliness of his mistress; she loves, not himself,but the possibility of making a husband out of a lover. For him,sexual ecstasy is a form of selftranscendence:for her,it's a means to an end(motherhood)" (qtd. in Norman Friedman *E. E. Cummings: The Growth of a Writer,* 58).

37. In "The Right to Bare: Containing and Encoding American Women in Popular Entertainments of the 1920s," Angela J. Latham notes the lasting impact of Ziegfeld on the ways in which women would be perceived and evaluated in American culture. For Ziegfeld, "[W]omen were, first and foremost, bodies to be assessed on the basis of visual appeal. Ziegfeld's influence in this regard, on his own and successive generations, was profound. Not only did he determine who and what was beautiful, popularizing if not creating certain standards by which beauty is still largely judged in American culture, he also helped to establish beauty itself as an essential feature of female worth" (107).

38. For more on the origins of burlesque in America and the publicity surrounding Lydia Thompson and Pauline Markham, see chapter 1 of Robert Allen's *Horrible Prettiness.*

39. Critic Michael Webster has noted the ambivalent stance of the poem as well: "[I]f Cummings does not seem to condemn or condone the audience's leering fantasies, neither does he seem to lament or applaud the woman's objectification. The scene is re-created without comment or abstract statement" (31). Likewise, Barry A. Marks notes that the poem "presents a close-up of a stripper without Sally Rand's talent and distinguishes sharply between art and the merely obscene" (82), and Alys Rho Yablon argues that the closing lines "represent a descent into objectification leading to an emptiness and negation symbolized by blank parenthesis. Sex without sensual mutuality is meaningless to Cummings, and to those he includes among 'you and i'" (55).

40. Sarah Bey-Chang and Barbara Cole explain that "Cummings was a fan of Bert Savoy despite his strong dislike for homosexuals and claim that 'enthusiastic advocates of any form of totalitarianism are inclined to be nothing-if-not-queer'" (162).

41. As Robert Rydell has argued, "The Midway, with its half-naked 'savages' and hootchy-cootchy dancers, provided white Americans with a grand opportunity for a subliminal journey into the recesses of their own repressed desires" (67).

42. This text, copied from the original program of the Provincetown Playhouse, can be found at the Rare Book and Manuscript Library at Columbia University.

43. Even if much of the play is Me's dream (as many critics have argued), which would make the freak show her vision of where Him should go to find what he's looking for ("If what you're looking for is not here, why don't you go where it is?" [124]), Cummings message remains the same. Him needs to connect with the real world in order to create meaningful art. He needs to recognize the artifice of these popular amusements even as he celebrates their vitality.

3   PLANES, TRAINS, AND AUTOMOBILES

1. This editorial appeared in *American Home* 3 (July 1929), 463.
2. Interestingly, Dos Passos typically played the female lead in school plays. His delicate features and gentle smile enabled him to portray a convincing heroine without makeup or a wig, and his reputation for being "pretty" onstage helped earn him the nickname "Maddie" (a play on his legal surname at the time, Madison; this would not change until his parents married two years later in 1912). Even when Dos Passos' voice deepened and he grew to nearly six feet tall by his senior year, he could not escape his reputation as a scrawny "girlboy" with thick glasses and European mannerisms. For more on his experiences in the theatre at the Choate School, see Townsend Ludington's *John Dos Passos: A Twentieth Century Odyssey*, 26–30, and Virginia Spencer Carr's *Dos Passos: A Life*, 35–36.
3. This quote comes from Dos Passos' introduction to *Three Plays: The Garbage Man, Airways, Inc., and Fortune Heights*, xxi. Dos Passos decided to become a playwright during a trip to Spain in 1916—after witnessing the Spanish public's admiration for their dramatists. For more on Dos Passos' experiences with Spanish theatre, see Virginia Spencer Carr's *Dos Passos: A Life*, 105–107.
4. "Summerresort" is typical of Dos Passos' unusual spellings, but it would be far too cumbersome to mark "[sic]" throughout the text.
5. Dos Passos even spent two-and-a-half months traveling around Moscow and its suburbs during a 1928 trip to the Soviet Union. See Carr, 246.
6. The play, which he began writing in 1918, was completed in 1923, and after its 1925 premiere in Cambridge by the Harvard Dramatic Club, it ran a few days later in Boston. In 1926, it was staged at the Cherry Lane Playhouse in Greenwich Village and published by Harper and Brothers as *The Garbage Man*. See Ludington, *John Dos Passos*, 223–224, 236–237. The original title, *The Moon Is a Gong*, came from one of Dos Passos' early poems, "Memory," which

concludes: "That night from a dingy hotel room/ I saw the moon, like a golden gong,/ Redly loom/ Across the lake; like a golden gong" (36)—from *Eight Harvard Poets* (New York: Laurence J. Gomme, 1917)

7. According to a diary entry in 1922, the image of the garbage man gave Dos Passos the idea for the play: "Here is an idea for the play thing that has thrust itself so obtrusively into my consciousness—the scene in the garden in Greenwich Village with skyscrapers in the background and garbage cans in the foreground—enter the Garbage Man" (qtd. in Carr 193).

8. As Knox notes, "[T]he career of the New Playwrights Theatre closed on the production of Dos Passos' *Airways, Inc.*" (143). The Theatre had been struggling with financial and ideological problems from its inception. As Dos Passos explains in his March 1929 letter of resignation to Lawson, "As I see it the trouble with this organization from the start has been that the men who made it up have not been sure of their aims or honest about them. Half the time we have been trying to found an institution and the rest of the time trying to put over ourselves or each other, and occasionally trying to knife each other in the back. I dont think that this is anybody's fault; it is due to a typically New York confusion of aims. The best thing to do is to dissolve the organization and let the members of it paddle their own canoes" (*The Fourteenth Chronicle* 390).

9. See Knox 75.

10. He attributes his professional woes to an incident years earlier when he lost a prestigious position at Western Electric by accidentally stepping on J. P. Morgan's toes in an office elevator.

11. The play was both a popular and critical failure. As Carr notes, "[M]ost critics attacked the play for its lack of unity, the failure of its two narratives to converge successfully, and for having as many themes 'as flies in a sugar bowl'" (251).

12. The general breakdown of community contributes to Owen's eviction as well. The Depression has left people destitute and desperate, which threaten personal and communal ties. Ike Auerbach, an aspiring writer of clichéd crime stories, for example, works as a freelance detective who earns money by selling out acquaintances and friends to the authorities; Owen's wife, whom he has cheated on previously, begins an affair with Ellery Jones, the local real-estate agent; Ellery's former girlfriend, Fay, tries to extort money from him when he ventures into politics; Owen and Morry become estranged; the College Boy bandits, who benefited from Owen's generosity in the past,

return to the station to rob him, and in the process they kill Rena, whose family had picked them up as hitchhikers years earlier. Even when the community of farmers comes together to prevent Owen's eviction, violence breaks out between them and the police, leading to Morry's death and Owen's homelessness. Their attempt at unity is temporary and ineffectual.

13. See Kenneth T. Jackson's *Crabgrass Frontier: The Suburbanization of America*, 95.
14. For more on the history of elite suburbs, see chapter 5 in Jackson's *Crabgrass Frontier*.
15. "Between 1914 and 1920, almost half a million blacks left the South to take advantage of the new opportunities; another 750,000 flowed by the end of the '20s" (Jacqueline Jones *The Dispossessed: America's Underclasses from the Civil War to the Present* [Basic Books, 1992], 13).
16. See Gerald Leinwand's *1927: High Tide of the 1920s* (New York: Four Walls Eight Windows, 2001), 6.
17. "Often [the working class] built those houses themselves, because they could not pay a builder. Zoning regulations and buildings codes made such choices increasingly difficult. If working-class families found such obstacles in the cities, they existed with more force in the suburbs, where even small houses were hard to find for under $6,000. The average American family had an income of $2,000" (Marsh 133). In "The Geography of North American Cities and Suburbs, 1900–1950: A New Synthesis," Harris and Lewis note: "The unserviced and unregulated suburb offered households the best opportunity to supplement monetary income with unpaid labor. This opportunity appealed to the families of immigrant workers, who were willing to make exceptional sacrifices to acquire a home. In one sense, it was a willingness to undertake extensive unpaid labor that created this type of residential workers' suburbs. At the same time, such a work strategy was necessary for those who wished to move there: it was a 'price' of entry" (278).
18. As Sam Bass Warner, Jr. notes in *Urban Dwellings*, "[A]bundant residential land opened up by streetcars and rapid transit brought light, air, and yards, but atrocious land planning caused by private profit maximization foreclosed the benefits of good low-density design (even room for off-street parking)" (40, n.9). The New Deal Resettlement Administration used photographs like this one of Dezendorf's Delightful Dwellings to illustrate the abuses and problems with such subdivision.

19. As Barbara Foley notes in *Radical Representations*, "Throughout Dos Passos' *U.S.A.*, which purports to represent the totality of American society through its spectrum of typical fictional characters, not a single black (or other non-white) character is featured as a protagonist. Moreover, Dos Passos' few black and latin characters are portrayed through a mutually reinforcing racist and homophobic discourse that presupposes the reader's assent" (193–194).
20. As Dos Passos recalls in *The Best Times: An Informal Memoir*, "While I was trotting around getting stories from the picketers one afternoon, the cops made one of their periodical raids. They pushed me into the paddywaggon with the rest. The cops were quite unmoved when I tried to produce credentials as a reported for *The Daily Worker*... The ride in the paddywaggon was made delightful by the fact that I found myself sitting next to Edna St. Vincent Millay... We had hardly time to choose our places in the cells at the Joy Street station before Eugene Boissevain [Edna's wealthy husband] was bailing us out" (172–173).
21. For more on the Sacco and Vanzetti crime, see Gerald Leinwand *1927: High Tide of the 1920s*.
22. This essay, "The Pit and the Pendulum," first appeared in the *New Masses* in August 1926, and it was based on his interviews with both men. This material was later used for the Sacco-Vanzetti Defense Committee's pamphlet *Facing the Chair: Story of the Americanization of Two Foreignborn Workmen* (1927). My citations and page numbers refer to reprinted essay in *John Dos Passos: The Major Nonfictional Prose*, Ed. Donald Pizer.
23. Quoted in Linda Wagner's *Dos Passos: Artist as American*, 88.
24. See Ludington 257. *The 42nd Parallel* was published in 1930.
25. Linda Wager has noted that "Walter Goldberg's execution (reminiscent in many ways of the Sacco-Vanzetti situation) goes without notice in the largest sense, because the very people who are well off and might support his defense, on strictly idealistic grounds, ignore the case. Rewarded by capitalism, they adopt its morality in return" (77).
26. Beuka begins his study, *SuburbiaNation: Reading Suburban Landscape in Twentieth-Century American Fiction and Film*, with a chapter on the role of suburbia in Fitzgerald's The Great Gatsby. Jurca's *White Diaspora: The Suburb and the Twentieth-Century American Novel* offers insightful readings of Sinclair's work. Her work primarily examines the idea of sentimental dispossession, which "refers to the affective dislocation by which white middle-class suburbanites begin to see themselves as spiritually and culturally impoverished by prosperity" (7).

27. Dos Passos, who admired Lawson's uses of jazz and vaudeville in *Processional: A Jazz Symphony of American Life* (1925), wanted to achieve something similar in *The Garbage Man (The Moon Is a Gong)*. As Ryan Jerving has argued, *Processional* "may be regarded as a kind of demolition work applied to the wall separating the popular from the serious, the market-driven mass product from the subscription-sustained aura-generating art object" (530). In *The Garbage Man*, Suárez likens Dos Passos' use of jazz to the music played during films at the time. "Imitating movie musical accompaniment, it cued the turns of the plot with snatches of popular songs and sound effects" (*Pop Modernism* 82).
28. Women in the 1920s were expected to maintain the domestic ideal being promulgated by magazines, child-rearing guides, and newspapers at the time. As Margaret Marsh explains, "[O]n the one hand,...husbands and wives in the suburban havens of the 1920s expected romance and excitement from their marriages. On the other hand, the pressure was mostly on the wife to stay young, to keep her husband interested, to make sure that her housekeeping met the standards of the neighborhood so as not to disgrace him professionally" (138).
29. This scene takes place eight months after Dad Turner's death.
30. For more on the marketing of suburbia, see Fogelson's *Bourgeois Nightmares: Suburbia, 1870–1930*.
31. The Turner family listens to Sunday morning broadcasts of the Federation of Suburban Churches. The Reverend begins with an opening prayer asking the "members of this great invisible audience gathered together each in our respective home far from each other in actuality but brought near by the wonders of science" (116). This moment highlights the shared religious beliefs of suburbia as well as the disconnectedness of this community. Technology prevents them from forming an actual community.
32. In this way, Mac becomes like the men in the first biography section who betray Eugene V. Debs, labor activist, politician, and founder of the Industrial Workers of the World, for "a house with a porch to putter around and a fat wife to cook for them" (20). When discussing Mac's decision to abandon his socialist principals to be with Maisie, Donald Pizer has argued that "[t]he polarities of American life in the early portion of *The 42nd Parallel* are either a dangerous commitment to independent thought or a safe acceptance of the status quo, with both possibilities paradoxically leading to decline or defeat"

(120). For more on Eugene Debs and the IWW, see chapter 2 ("The Socialist Challenge") from Howard Zinn's *The Twentieth Century: A People's History* (1998).

33. For more on the Florida real-estate boom and collapse in the 1920s, see chapter 6 of William B. Stronge's *The Sunshine Economy: An Economic History of Florida Since the Civil War*. Stronge notes that "Florida's real estate boom began to collapse in 1926—the crowd clamoring to purchase real estate suddenly switched direction and sought to sell rather than buy... Because of the large speculative element in the boom, it was inevitable that when sentiment changed, the reversal in activity would be dramatic" (100).

34. Interestingly, the death of Ma Turner inspired the family to buy a home in the first place, suggesting that they wanted a suburban house to give them a renewed sense of family. Elmer remarks: "[The house] certainly hasn't brought us any luck... Do you remember after Mother died, you and Dad and Claude though it'd be great not to live in a flat any more" (153).

35. The Miami suburb Coral Gables was founded in 1925. Ozone Park is located in Queens, New York. Crystal Meadow is in Illinois, and Joyland probably refers to the amusement park that was an integral part of Sacramento's first working-class suburb, Oak Park. In the context of his plays, Fortune Heights does not have a specific location, making it representative of suburbia more broadly.

36. After the robbery of Owen and murder of Rena, the police find the Bandits' motorcycle: "We found the motorcycle, an Indian painted red you said it was" (241). The violence of the boys gets compared with a stereotype about Native Americans here. This moment also foreshadows an ironic reference to Native Americans in one of Ellery's political speeches at the end of the play: "It's time... to wrest this country from the hands of greedy privilege. If it wasn't for us the Indians ud still be running wild here. It's ordinary men like us, and our wives and children that did the work that built this country up to where it is today" (288). Ellery does not acknowledge the history of violent imperialism that this country was founded on—a violent history in which the "greedy privilege" of whites and a desire for land led to the extermination of Native Americans.

37. As David A. Hounshell notes in *From the American System to Mass Production 1800–1932: The Development of Manufacturing Technology in the United States:* "Although the motives behind the five-dollar day

are rooted in a sort of industrial beneficence on Henry Ford's part and a consciousness on James Courzen's part that such a wage and profit-sharing system would pay for itself in free advertising, the five-dollar day must be seen as the last step or link in the development of mass production. During 1913 the labor turnover rate at the Ford factory had soared to a phenomenal figure. Keith Sward points out that turnover in 1913 reached 380 percent" (257).

38. See Jackson 160–163.
39. "The Federal Road Act of 1916 offered funds to states that organized highway departments; the Federal Road Act of 1921 designated 200,000 miles of road as 'primary' and thus eligible for federal funds on a fifty-fifty matching basis. More importantly, the 1921 legislation also created a Bureau of Public Roads to plan a highway network to connect all cities of 50,000 or more inhabitants... By 1925 the value of highway construction projects exceeded $1 billion for the first time; thereafter, it fell below that figure only during a few years of the Great Depression and World War II. Even during the troubled thirties, however, state and federal funds were made available for road because they employed many workers and could be planned quickly" (Jackson 167).
40. Dos Passos incorporates a similar theme throughout the *U.S.A* trilogy as well. Charley Anderson's life is framed by car accidents, suggesting the dangerous and often self-destructive aspect of this technology. In *The 42nd Parallel,* Charley's first job at Vogel's Garage involves basic car maintenance, washing cars, draining transmissions, and relining brakes. He loses the job, however, when he crashes the garage truck while drinking and joyriding with a friend. This moment foreshadows Charley's death in *The Big Money*. After drinking heavily at a bar, Charley tries to cross in front of an oncoming train (with someone in the passenger seat), but his car stalls. The accident sends him to the hospital where he dies soon afterwards.
41. As John L. Grigsby points out, "[T]he more personally corrupt Charley Anderson and other characters become, the larger and more expensive their automobiles" (38).
42. For more on the role of airplanes in popular entertainment, see Dominick A. Pisano's "The Greatest Show Not on Earth: The Confrontation Between Utility and Entertainment in Aviation."
43. Lindbergh became an overnight celebrity, and he was bombarded with business opportunities after his 1927 flight across the Atlantic—to

star in films, endorse products, et cetera. He refused most of these, not wanting to capitalize on his success, and this quality garnered even more accolades from the public. Soon the media began using his image to condemn commercialism and to celebrate traditional values. Charles L. Ponce de Leon argues that "he was transformed into a symbol of modesty, dignity, and youthful idealism—values that were antithetical to the avarice, ballyhoo, and cynicism of the 'jazz age'" (83).

44. Film was also a significant part of the popularization of aviation in the 1930s. "After the barnstorming era of the 1920s, aviation as entertainment emerged in two primary forms during the 1930s: feature-length films produced in Hollywood and air racing... Barnstorming and aerial exhibitions had their limitations in terms of satisfying audiences—airplanes could only be seen from a distance, and after the Aeronautics Branch enforced restrictions on the height at which aerial maneuvers could take place, that distance increased. Movies, by contrast, had the opposite effect. Improved film technology and the advent of aerial cameras also helped to provide an intimacy that live production could not approximate...Aviation for amusement was thus channeled into another medium that was potentially more profitable and capable of reaching afar wider audience than other pervious forms had been" (Pisano 59).

45. "America's first coast-to-coast air service was introduced in 1929. With numerous stops along the way, the trip took forty-eight hours to complete. By 1934 propeller driven aircraft could ferry passengers from New York to Los Angeles in a mere thirteen hours, with three or four stops. Only a quarter of a century later, in 1959, did regularly scheduled jet passenger service begin between those two cities, reducing the time involved by nine hours and eliminating all stops in between. The age of jet travel had arrived" (Lubin 137).

46. This reference to bombers also alludes to the Professor Raskolny's, one of Dad Turner's friends, memories of World War I earlier in the play: "After the collapse of the shining socialist dream, I came to America...I wanted to escape the world tortured by airraids and radio. I wanted to escape a warshattered world without hope. I wanted to go far away. Nowhere is far any more. Distance has snapped back in my face like a broken elastic" (93).

47. Donald Pizer reads Bill's death in terms of Charley's deterioration. "Bill's death, in an accident as they take off for New York, is thus one

48. For more on the New Playwrights Theatre, see George Knox's *Dos Passos and "The Revolting Playwrights."* According to Knox, the group wanted to produce works that emphasized "some value, some human element in man that was being destroyed by an overmechanized, selfish, industrial system" (17).
49. See Dos Passos' production notes for *The Garbage Man* in *Three Plays*, 75.
50. As Dos Passos explains in his March 1929 letter of resignation to Lawson, "As I see it the trouble with this organization from the start has been that the men who made it up have not been sure of their aims or honest about them. Half the time we have been trying to found an institution and the rest of the time trying to put over ourselves or each other, and occasionally trying to knife each other in the back. I dont think that this is anybody's fault; it is due to a typically New York confusion of aims. The best thing to do is to dissolve the organization and let the members of it paddle their own canoes" (*The Fourteenth Chronicle* 390).
51. In *Dialogues in American Drama*, Cohn even concludes her discussion of his plays by saying that "he had the wisdom not to attempt drama again" (182).

Conclusion

1. It should also be noted that no African Americans were cast in the play.
2. As historian Lynn Dumenil has argued, Americans turned toward leisure culture in the early twentieth century as a response to "the degradation of work and the erosion of individual autonomy in mass corporate culture" (57). Modern machine production for blue-collar laborers and bureaucracy for white-collar employees created working environments that demanded routine tasks over individual autonomy. Henry Ford's assembly-line technology at Highland Park epitomized some these changes, creating a workplace defined by backbreaking speed and mind-numbing repetition. At the same time, this type of innovation (which became increasingly widespread) helped give laborers time to enjoy popular culture. Although "the nine-hour day and fifty-four hour week continued to be the legal standard in New

York well into the 1920s" (Peiss 43), labor unions were successfully reducing this time. By 1923 many working-class women worked forty-eight hours or less per week. Salaried workers also began to receive a paid, two-week vacation by the middle of the decade, and this trend reflected the growing interest among white-collar workers for commercial entertainment as well.

Bibliography

Adams, Rachel. *Sideshow U.S.A: Freaks and the American Cultural Imagination.* Chicago: University of Chicago Press, 2002.

Allen, Robert C. *Horrible Prettiness: Burlesque and American Culture.* Chapel Hill: University Press of North Carolina, 1991.

Anderson, E. N. *Everyone Eats: Understanding Food and Culture.* New York: New York University Press, 2005.

Azma, Sheeva. "Poem-painter: E. E. Cummings' Artistic Mastery of Words." *Spring: The Journal of the E. E. Cummings Society* 11 (October 2002): 79–88.

Bach, Gerhard. "Susan Glaspell: Provincetown Playwright." *The Great Lakes Review* 4.1 (1978): 31–43.

Bakhtin, Makhail. *Rabelais and His World.* Trans. Hélène Iswolsky. Bloomington: Indiana Unviersity Press, 1984.

Bay-Cheng, Sarah and Barbara Cole. "Modernist Poetic Drama: A Critical Introduction." *Poets at Play: An Anthology of Modernist Drama.* Eds. Sarah Bay-Cheng and Barbara Cole. Selingsgrove: Susquehanna University Press, 2010.

Beuka, Robert. *SuburbiaNation: Reading Suburban Landscape in Twentieth-Century American Fiction and Film.* New York: Palgrave MacMillan, 2004.

Bilstein, Roger. "The Airplane and the American Experience." *The Airplane in American Culture.* Ed. Dominick A. Pisano. Ann Arbor: University of Michigan Press, 2003.

Bogdan, Robert. *Freak Show: Presenting Human Oddities for Amusement and Profit.* Chicago: University of Chicago Press, 1988.

Bradley, Mark Jonathan. *E. E. Cummings "Him": An Annotation with Analysis and Production History.* Dissertation. University of Minnesota. June 1984.

Britten, Norman A. *Edna St. Vincent Millay.* Revised edition. Boston: Twayne Publishers, 1982.

Butsch, Richard. *The Making of American Audiences: From Stage to Television, 1750–1990*. Cambridge: Cambridge University Press, 2000.

Calder, Lendol. *Financing the American Dream: A Cultural History of Consumer Credit*. Princeton, NJ: Princeton University Press, 1999.

Capozzola, Christoper. *Uncle Sam Wants You: World War I and the Making of the Modern American Citizen*. Oxford: Oxford University Press, 2008.

Carr, Virginia Spencer. *Dos Passos: A Life*. Evanston: Northwestern University Press, 1984.

Chauncey, George. *Gay New York: Gender, Urban Culture, and the Making of the Gay Male World, 1890–1940*. New York: Basic Books, 1994.

Cheney, Anne. *Millay in Greenwich Village*. Alabama: University of Alabama Press, 1975.

Clark, Suzanne. *Sentimental Modernism: Women Writer and the Revolution of the Word*. Bloomington: Indiana University Press, 1991.

Cohen, Milton A. *POETandPAINTER: The Aesthetics of E. E. Cummings's Early Work*. Detroit: Wayne State University Press, 1987.

Cohn, Ruby. *Dialogue in American Drama*. Bloomington: Indiana University Press, 1971.

Cook, Jr., James W. "Of Men, Missing Links, and Nondescripts: The Strange Career of P. T. Barnum's 'What Is It?' Exhibition." *Freakery: Cultural Spectacles of the Extraordinary Body*. Ed. Rosemarie Garland Thomson. New York: New York University Press, 1996: 139–157.

Cummings, Edward Estlin. *Complete Poems*. Ed. George J. Firmage. New York: Liveright, 1991.

———. *i:Six Nonlectures*. Cambridge: Harvard University Press, 1953.

———. *CIOPW*. New York: Covici-Friede, 1931.

———. *Him*. New York: Liveright, 1927.

———. "The Theater II" (1926). *E. E. Cummings: A Miscellany* (1958). Revised edition. Ed. George J. Firmage. New York: Liveright, 1978.

———. "You Aren't Mad, Am I?" (1925). *E. E. Cummings: A Miscellany* (1958). Revised edition. Ed. George J. Firmage. New York: Liveright, 1978.

———. "The Adult, the Artist and the Circus" (1925). *E. E. Cummings: A Miscellany* (1958). Revised edition. Ed. George J. Firmage. New York: Liveright, 1978.

———. *The Enormous Room* (1922). Ed. George J. Firmage. New York: Liveright, 1978.

Davis, Janet M. *The Circus Age: Culture and Society Under the American Big Top*. Chapel Hill: University of North Carolina Press, 2002.

Dennett, Andrea Stulman. *Weird and Wonderful: The Dime Museum in America*. New York: New York University Press, 1997.

Dos Passos, John. *The Best Times: An Informal Memoir*. New York: New American Library, 1966.
———. *The Big Money (1936)*. New York: Mariner Books, 2000.
———. *Three Plays: The Garbage Man, Airways, Inc. and Fortune Heights*. New York: Harcourt, Brace, and Company, 1934.
———. *1919* (1932). New York: Mariner Books, 2000.
———. *The 42nd Parallel* (1930). New York: Mariner Books, 2000.
———. "Did the New Playwrights Theatre Fail?" (1929). *John Dos Passos: The Major Nonfictional Prose*. Ed. Donald Pizer. Detroit: Wayne State University Press, 1988: 118–120.
———. "Toward a Revolutionary Theatre" (1927). *John Dos Passos: The Major Nonfictional Prose*. Ed. Donald Pizer. Detroit: Wayne State University Press, 1988: 101–103.
———. "The Pit and the Pendulum" (1926). *John Dos Passos: The Major Nonfictional Prose*. Ed. Donald Pizer. Detroit: Wayne State University Press, 1988: 85–91.
———. "Is the 'Realistic' Theatre Obsolete?" (1925). *John Dos Passos: The Major Nonfictional Prose*. Ed. Donald Pizer. Detroit: Wayne State University Press, 1988: 75–78.
Douglas, Ann. *Terrible Honesty: Mongrel Manhattan in the 1920s*. New York: Farrar, Straus, and Giroux, 1996.
Dumenil, Lynn. *The Modern Temper: American Culture and Society in the 1920s*. New York: Hill and Wang, 1995.
English, Mary. C. "Aristophanic Comedy in E. E. Cummings' Him." Classical and Modern Literature. 24.2 (2004): 79–99
Erenberg, Lewis A. *Steppin' Out: New York Nightlife and the Transformation of American Culture, 1890–1930*. Westport, CT: Greenwood Press, 1981.
Essert, Emily. "'Since Feeling Is First': E. E. Cummings and Modernist Poetic Difficulty." *Spring: The Journal of the E. E. Cummings Society*. 14–15 (Fall 2006): 197–210.
Fahy, Thomas. *Freak Shows and the Modern American Imagination: Constructing the Damaged Body from Willa Cather to Truman Capote*. New York: Palgrave Macmillan, 2006.
Fava, Antonio. *The Comic Mask in the Commedia Dell'Arte: Actor Training, Improvisation, and the Poetics of Survival*. Evanston, IL: Northwestern University Press, 2007.
Fearnow, Mark. "Theater Groups and Their Playwrights." *The Cambridge History of American Theatre, Volume Two: 1870–1945*. Eds. Don B. Wilmeth and Christopher Bigsby. Cambridge University Press, 1999: 343–377.

Finn, Meghan. "Director's Book Based on the Production of Him by E. E. Cummings." MFA Thesis. Brooklyn College, 2008.
Fishbein, Leslie. *Rebels in Bohemia: The Radicals of the Masses, 1911–1917.* Chapel Hill: University of North Carolina Press, 1982.
Fogelson, Robert M. *Bourgeois Nightmares: Suburbia, 1870–1930.* New Haven: Yale University Press, 2005.
Foley, Barbara. *Radical Representations: Politics and Form in U.S. Proletarian Fiction, 1929–1941.* Durham: Duke University Press, 1993.
Foucault, Michel. "Of Other Spaces." *Diacritics* 16.1 (Spring 1986): 22–27.
Friedman, Norman. *(Re) Valuing Cummings: Further Essays on the Poet, 1962–1993.* Gainesville: University Press of Florida, 1996.
———. *E. E. Cummings: The Growth of a Writer.* Carbondale: Southern Illinois University Press, 1964.
Goldberg, David J. *Discontented America: The United States in the 1920s.* Baltimore: John Hopkins University Press, 1999.
Gordon, Marsha. "Onward Kitchen Soldiers: Mobilizing the Domestic During World War I." *Canadian Review of American Studies* 29.2 (November 1999): 61–87.
Gordon, Sarah H. *Passage to Union: How the Railroads Transformed American Life, 1829–1929.* Chicago: Ivan R. Dee, 1996.
Grabher, Gundrun M. "i Paint (My Poems), Therefore I Am: The Visibility of Language and Its Epistemological Implications for the 'I' In E. E. Cummings' Poetry." *Spring: The Journal of the E. E. Cummings Society* 10 (October 2001): 48–57.
Graziano, John. "Images of African Americans: African-American Musical Theatre, Show Boat and Porgy and Bess." *The Cambridge Companion to the Musical.* Second edition. Eds. William A. Everett and Paul R. Laird. Cambridge: Cambridge University Press, 2008.
Gregory, James N. *The Southern Diaspora: How the Great Migrations of Black and White Southerners Transformed America.* Chapel Hill: University of North Carolina Press, 2007.
Grigsby, John L. "The Automobile as Technological Reality and Central Symbol in John Dos Passos's the Big Money." *Kansas Quarterly* : 35–41.
Grimm, Jacob and Wilhelm. "Cinderella." *The Annotated Brothers Grimm.* Ed. Maria Tatar. New York: W. W. Norton and Co., 2004.
Harris, Neil. *Cultural Excursions: Marketing Appetites and Cultural Tastes in Modern America.* Chicago: University of Chicago Press, 1990.
———. *Humbug: The Art of P. T. Barnum.* Chicago: University of Chicago Press, 1973.

Harris, Richard and Robert Lewis. "The Geography of North American Cities and Suburbs, 1900–1950: A New Synthesis." *Journal of Urban History* 27.3 (March 2001): 262–292.

Higham, John. *Strangers in the Land: Patterns of American Nativism 1860–1925.* New York: Atheneum, 1975.

Hounshell, David A. *From the American System to Mass Production 1800–1932: The Development of Manufacturing Technology in the United States.* Baltimore: John Hopkins University Press, 1984.

Huyssen, Andreas. *After the Great Divide: Modernism, Mass Culture, Postmodernism.* Bloomington: Indiana University Press, 1986.

Jackson, Kenneth T. *Crabgrass Frontier: The Suburbanization of the United States.* New York: Oxford University Press, 1985.

Jerving, Ryan. "An Experiment in Modern Vaudeville: Archiving the Wretched Refuse in John Howard Lawson's Processional." *Modern Drama* 51.4 (Winter 2008): 528–551.

Jones, Jacqueline. *The Dispossessed: America's Underclasses from the Civil War to the Present.* New York: Basic Books, 1992.

Jurca, Catherine. *White Diaspora: The Suburb and the Twentieth-Century American Novel.* Princeton: Princeton University Press, 2001.

Kaiser, Jo Ellen Green. "Feeding the Hungry Heart: Gender, Food, and War in the Poetry of Edna St. Vincent Millay." *Food and Foodways* 6.2 (1996): 81–92.

Kammen, Michael. *American Culture, American Tastes: Social Change and the 20th Century.* New York: Knopf, 2000.

———. *The Seven Lively Arts: Gilbert Seldes and the Transformation of Cultural Criticism in the United States.* Oxford: Oxford University Press, 1996.

Kasson, John F. *Amusing the Million: Coney Island at the Turn of the Century.* New York: Hill and Wang, 1978.

———. *Rudeness and Civility: Manners in Nineteenth-Century Urban America.* New York: Hill and Wang, 1990.

Kennedy, David. *Over Here: The First World War and American Society.* Oxford: Oxford University Press, 1980.

Kennedy, Richard S. *Dreams in the Mirror: A Biography of E. E. Cummings.* Second edition 1994. New York: Liveright, 1980.

Kidder, Rushworth M. "Cummings and Cubism: The Influence on the Visual Arts on Cummings' Early Poetry." *Journal of Modern Literature* 7 (1979): 255–291.

———. "'Twin Obsessions': The Poetry and Paintings of E. E. Cummings." Reprinted in *Critical Essays on e. e. Cummings.* Ed. Guy Rotella. Boston: G.K. Hall & Co, 1984.

Knox, George, and Herbert M. Stahl. *Dos Passos and "The Revolting Playwrights."* Uppsala: Uppsala University Press, 1964.

Kyvig, David E. *Daily Life in the United States, 1920–1940: How Americans Lived through the "Roaring Twenties" and the Great Depression.* New York: Ivan R. Dee, 2004.

Latham, Angela J. *Posing a Threat: Flappers, Chorus Girls, and Other Brazen Performers of the American 1920s.* Hanover: Wesleyan University Press, 2000.

Lears, Jackson. *Fables of Abundance: A Cultural History of Advertising in America.* New York: Basic Books, 1994.

Leinwand, Gerald. *1927: The High Tide of the Twenties.* New York: Four Walls Eight Windows, 2001.

Lerner, Michael A. *Dry Manhattan: Prohibition in New York City.* Cambridge, MA: Harvard University Press, 2007.

Levenstein, Harvey A. *Revolution at the Table: The Transformation of the American Diet.* Oxford: Oxford University Press, 1988.

Levine, Lawrence W. "Jazz and American Culture." *The Jazz Cadence of American Culture.* Ed. Robert G. O'Meally. New York: Columbia University Press, 1998.

———. *Highbrow/Lowbrow: The Emergence of Cultural Hierarchy in America.* Cambridge, MA: Harvard University Press, 1988.

Lévi-Strauss, Claude. *The Raw and the Cooked: Introduction to a Science of Mythology, Volume 1* (first published in France in 1964 as *Le Cru et le Cuit*). Trans. John and Doreen Weightman. Chicago: University of Chicago Press, 1983.

Lott, Eric. *Love and Theft: Blackface Minstrelsy and the American Working Class.* Oxford: Oxford University Press, 1993.

Lowry. E. D. "The Lively Art of Manhattan Transfer." *PMLA* 84 (1969): 1628–1638.

Lubin, David M. *Shooting Kennedy: JFK and the Culture of Images.* Berkeley: University of California Press, 2003.

Ludington, Townsend. John Dos Passos: A Twentieth-Century Odyssey. New York: Dutton, 1980.

———. Ed. *The Fourteenth Chronicle: The Letters and Diaries of John Dos Passos.* Boston: Gambit, 1973.

Maik, Thomas A. The Masses Magazine (1911–1917): Odyssey of An Era. New York: Garland, 1994.

Marks, Barry A. *E. E. Cummings.* New York: Twayne Publishers, 1964.

Marsh, Margaret. *Suburban Lives.* New Brunswick: Rutgers University Press, 1990.

Maurer, Robert. E. "E. E. Cummings' Him." *E. E. Cummings: A Collection of Critical Essays.* Ed. Norman Friedman. Englewood Cliffs, NJ: Prentice-Hall, 1972.

May, Henry F. *The End of American Innocence: The First Years of Our Own Time, 1912–1917.* Oxford: Oxford University Press, 1959.

McCarthy, Tom. *Auto Mania: Cars, Consumers, and the Environment.* New Haven: Yale University Press, 2007.

McEntee, Ann Marie. "Feathers, Finials, and Frou-Frou: Florenz Ziegfeld's Exoticized Follies Girls." *Art, Glitter, and Glitz: Mainstream Playwrights and Popular Theatre in 1920s America.* Eds. Arthur Gewirtz and James J. Kolb. Westport, CT: Praeger, 2004: 177–188.

Merwin, Ted. *In Their Own Image: New York Jews in Jazz Age Popular Culture.* Newark: Rutgers University Press, 2006.

Milford, Nancy. *Savage Beauty: The Life of Edna St. Vincent Millay.* New York: Random House, 2001.

Millay, Edna St. Vincent. *The Murder of Lidice.* New York: Harper and Brothers, 1942.

———. *The Princess Marries the Page.* New York: Harper and Brothers, 1932.

———. *The Harp-Weaver and Other Poems.* New York: Harper and Brothers, 1923.

———. "'Say Shibboleth': a Dialogue between a Sentimental Citizen and An Advertising Expert." *Vanity Fair* (April 1923): 40.

———. *A Few Figs from Thistles: Poems and Sonnets.* New York: Harper and Brothers, 1922.

———. *Two Slatterns and a King: A Moral Interlude.* Cincinnati: Stewart Kidd Publishers, 1921.

———. *Aria da Capo.* New York: Mitchell Kennerley, 1920.

Moi, Toril. *Henrik Ibsen and the Birth of Modernism: Art, Theater, Philosophy.* Oxford: Oxford University Press, 2006.

Mullen, Patrick B. "E. E. Cummings and Popular Culture." *Journal of Popular Culture* 5 (1971): 503–520.

Murphy, Brenda. *The Provincetown Players and the Culture of Modernity.* New York: Cambridge University Press, 2005.

———. "Plays and Playwrights: 1915–1945." *The Cambridge History of American Theatre, Volume Two: 1870–1945.* Eds. Don B. Wilmeth and Christopher Bigsby. Cambridge University Press, 1999: 289–342.

Nasaw, David. *Going Out: The Rise and Fall of Public Amusements.* New York: Basic Books, 1993.

Nicolaides, Becky M. and Andrew Wiese. "Introduction." *The Suburb Reader.* New York: Routledge, 2006.

Nicoll, Allardyce. *The World of Harlequin: A Critical Study of the Commedia dell'Arte.* Cambridge, MA: Cambridge University Press, 1963.

Ozieblo, Barbara. "Avant-Garde and Modernist. Women Dramatists of the Provincetown Players: Bryant, Davies, and Millay." *Journal of Drama and Theatre* 16.2 (Spring 2004): 1–16.

Patinkin, Sheldon. *"No Legs, No Jokes, No Chance": A History of American Musical Theater.* Evanston, IL: Northwester University Press, 2008.

Patton, John Joseph. *Edna St. Vincent Millay as Verse Dramatist.* Dissertation. University of Colorado, 1962.

Peiss, Kathy. *Cheap Amusements: Working Women and Leisure in Turn-of-the Century New York.* Philadelphia: Temple University Press, 1986.

Pisano, Dominick A. "The Greatest Show Not on Earth: The Confrontation between Utility and Entertainment in Aviation." *The Airplane in American Culture.* Ed. Dominick A. Pisano. Ann Arbor: University of Michigan Press, 2003.

Pizer, Donald. *Dos Passos' U.S.A.: A Critical Study.* Carlottesville, VA: University Press of Virginia, 1988.

Poggi, Jack. *Theater in America: The Impact of Economic Forces, 1870–1967.* Ithaca: Cornell University Press, 1968.

Ponce de Leon, Charles L. "The Man Nobody Knows: Charles A. Lindberg and the Culture of Celebrity." *The Airplane in American Culture.* Ed. Dominick A. Pisano. Ann Arbor: University of Michigan Press, 2003.

Raico, Ralph. "World War I: The Turning Point." *The Costs of War: America's Pyrrhic Victories.* Ed. John V. Denson. New Brunswick: Transaction Publishing, 2001: 203–247.

Riis, Thomas. "Musical Theatre." *The Cambridge History of American Theatre, Volume Two: 1870–1945.* Eds. Don B. Wilmeth and Christopher Bigsby. Cambridge University Press, 1999: 411–445.

Roberts, Helen Lefferts. *Putnam's Handbook of Etiquette: A Cyclopedia of Social Usage, Giving Manners and Customs of the Twentieth Century.* New York: G. P. Putnam's Sons, 1913.

Robinson, Marc. *The American Play, 1787–2000.* New Haven: Yale University Press, 2009.

———. *The Other American Drama.* Cambridge: Cambridge University Press, 1994.

Rydell, Robert W. *All the World's a Fair: Visions of Empire at American International Expositions, 1876–1916.* Chicago: University of Chicago Press, 1984.

Sayville, Deborah. "Freud, Flappers, and Bohemians: The Influence of Modern Psychological Thought and Social Ideology on Dress, 1910–1923." *Dress* 30 (2003): 63–79.

Saxon, A. H. *P. T. Barnum: The Legend and the Man.* New York: Columbia University Press, 1989.

Seldes, Gilbert. *The 7 Lively Arts.* New York: Sagamore Press, 1924, 1957.

———. "Introduction." *Him and the Critics.* New York: Provincetown Playhouse, 1928.

Shteir, Rachel. *Striptease: The Untold History of the Girlie Show*. New York: Oxford University Press, 2004.
Silverman, Kenneth. *Houdini!!!: The Career of Ehrich Weiss*. New York: HarperCollins, 1996.
Sklar, Robert. *Movie-Made America: A Cultural History of American Movies*. 1975. New York: Vintage, 1994.
Sollors, Werner. "Immigrants and Other Americans." *Columbia Literary History of the United States*. Ed. Emory Elliott. New York: Columbia University Press, 1988. 568–588.
Stansell, Christine. *American Moderns: Bohemian New York and the Creation of a New Century*. New York: Metropolitan Books, 2000.
Stearns, Peter N. *Fat History: Bodies and Beauty in the Modern West*. New York: New York University Press, 1997.
Stronge, William B. *The Sunshine Economy: An Economic History of Florida Since the Civil War*. Gainesville: University Press of Florida, 2008.
Suárez, Juan A. *Pop Modernism: Noise and the Reinvention of the Everyday*. Urbana: University of Illinois Press, 2007.
———. "John Dos Passos's *USA* and Left Documentary Film in the 1930s: The Cultural Politics of 'Newsreel' and 'The Camera Eye.'" *American Studies in Scandinavia* 33 (1999): 43–65.
Thomson, Rosemarie Garland. *Extraordinary Bodies: Figuring Physical Disability in American Culture and Literature*. New York: Columbia University Press, 1997.
———. "Introduction: From Wonder to Error—A Genealogy of Freak Discourse in Modernity." *Freakery: Cultural Spectacles of the Extraordinary Body*. Ed. Rosemarie Garland Thomson. New York: New York University Press, 1996: 1–19.
Toll, Robert. *Blacking Up: The Minstrel Show in Nineteenth-Century America*. Oxford: Oxford University Press, 1975.
Tomes, Robert. *The Bazar Book of Decorum: The Care of the Person, Manners, Etiquette, and Ceremonials*. New York: Harper and Brothers, 1873.
Trachtenberg, Alan. *The Incorporation of America: Culture and Society in the Gilded Age*. New York: Hill and Wang, 1982.
Vaughan, Christopher A. "Ogling Igorots: The Politics and Commerce of Exhibiting Cultural Otherness, 1890–1913." *Freakery: Cultural Spectacles of the Extraordinary Body*. Ed. Rosemarie Garland Thomson. New York: New York University Press, 1996: 219–233.
Vogel, Shane. *The Scene of Harlem Cabaret: Race, Sexuality, Performance*. Chicago: University of Chicago Press, 2009.
Wagner, Linda W. *Dos Passos: Artist as American*. Austin: University of Texas Press, 1979.

Wagner-Martin, Linda. "Cummings' *Him*—And Me." *Spring: The Journal of the E. E. Cummings Society* 1.1 (October 1992): 28–36.

Wainscott, Ronald H. *The Emergence of the Modern American Theater, 1914–1929.* New Haven: Yale University Press, 1997.

Walker, Cheryl. "The Female Body as Icon: Edna Millay Wears a Plaid Dress." *Millay at 100: A Critical Reappraisal.* Ed. Diane P. Reedman. Carbondale, IL: Southern Illinois University Press, 1995: 85–99.

Walker, Julia A. *Expressionism and Modernism in the American Theatre: Bodies, Voices, Words.* Cambridge: Cambridge University Press, 2005.

Warner, Jr., Sam Bass. *The Urban Wilderness: A History of the American City.* New York: Harper, 1972.

Warren, Louis S. *Buffalo Bill's America: William Cody and the Wild West Show.* New York: Knopf, 2005.

Webster, Michael. "Poemgroups in No Thanks." *Spring: The Journal of the E. E. Cummings Society* 11 (2002): 10–40.

Woollcott, Alexander. "Second Thoughts on First Nights: There Are War Plays and War Plays." Reprinted in *Critical Essays on Edna St. Vincent Millay.* Ed. William B. Thesing. New York: G. K. Hall, 1993: 39–43.

Yablon, Alys Rho. " 'Myself Is Sculptor of / Your Body's Idiom': Representations of Women in Cummings' Love Poetry." *Spring: The Journal of the E. E. Cummings Society* 7 (1998): 39–67.

Zinn, Howard. *The Twentieth Century: A People's History.* New York: HarperPerennial, 1998.

Žižek, Slavoj. *The Plague of Fantasies.* New York: Verso, 1997.

Index

activism, *see* sociopolitical engagement
Adams, Rachel, 66
advertising, 27, 28, 55, 57, 62–3, 68, 79, 89, 98, 102, 108, 121–2, 135, 143 n.7, 150 n.24
African Americans, 9–10, 13, 16, 19, 56, 58, 64, 69–70, 71–2, 83, 92, 101, 109, 121, 139 n.15, 140 n.16, 151 n.31, 152 n.33, 156 n.15, 162 n.1
   and music, 9–10
   and racial caricatures, 19, 56, 69–70, 71, 83
   as racial freaks, 64, 71–2, 152 n.33
   and theatre, 139 n. 15, 140 n.16
airplanes, *see* aviation
alcohol, 3–4, 45, 125
Allen, Robert, 74, 80, 153 n.38
ambivalence, 18–19, 23, 51, 56, 72–3, 75, 134, 153 n.39
American Home, 85, 98, 154 n.1
American Museum, 64, 148 n.15, 150 n.25
amusements, popular, 2, 10, 16, 19, 53–4, 135, 140 n.17, 154 n.43
Anderson, Charley (*The Big Money*), 105, 118, 119, 124, 128, 130, 160 n.40–1, 161 n.47
Anderson, E.N., 25, 40
apathy, 2, 24, 33, 135, 136,
   see also sociopolitical disengagement
appetite, *see* hunger

assembly line, 77, 116, 118, 122, 140 n. 17, 162 n.2
audience involvement, 3, 6, 17, 24, 55, 58–9, 60–1, 65, 67, 72–3, 75–6, 149 n.18–19
authenticity, 6, 10, 12, 43–4, 60, 66, 70
   see also superficiality
automobiles, 7, 16–17, 91, 93, 97, 114–20, 128, 160 n.39–41
avant-garde, 15,22–3, 151 n.30
aviation, 88, 91, 120–9, 130, 160–1 n.42–3, 161 n.45–6
   commodification of, 124–5, 160–1 n.43
   entertainment, 121, 160 n.42, 161 n.44

Bach, Gerhard, 142 n.4
Bailey, James A., 53, 57
Bakhtin, Mikhail, 41
Barnum, Phineas Taylor, 53, 57, 64, 72, 121, 148–9 n.15–16, 150 n.25, 150 n.28, 152 n.33
Basshe, Em Jo, 129
Bay-Cheng, Sarah, 20, 145 n.17, 149 n.19, 153 n.40
Berlin, Irving, 9, 138 n.7, 139 n.15
Beuka, Robert, 98, 157 n. 26
Bilstein, Roger, 122
bodies, 16, 17, 19, 22, 28, 41, 46–7, 48, 49, 50, 56, 61–2, 63–5, 67–8,

69–70, 71–3, 74–5, 79–80, 83,
    151–2 n.32, 153 n.37, 153 n.39
  African American, 16, 69–70, 71
  female, 28, 56, 67–8, 74–5, 79–80,
    83, 153 n.37, n.39
  freak, 63–5, 72–3
  non-white, 71–3, 151–2 n.32
Bogdan, Robert, 150 n.25–6, 152 n.33
bohemian culture, 10, 15, 16, 22–3,
  30–1, 32–3, 39, 45, 50, 78,
  142 n.3, 143 n.8
Boissevain, Eugene, 15, 157 n.20
Bolton, Guy, 9
Bonaparte, Napoleon, 79
Brennan, Jay, 78
Broadway Theatre, 8–10, 12, 14,
  138 n.12, 139 n.15, 140 n.16
burlesque, 6, 15, 16, 18, 54, 55, 59, 63,
  69, 70, 73–81, 83, 134, 135,
  148 n. 12, 153 n.38
  audience involvement, 75, 76
  movement, 75–6
  see also strippers, striptease
Burns, Tom (*The Garbage Man*), 86–8,
  98–101, 117, 130
Bustanoby's, 2, 39
Butsch, Richard, 8, 138 n.9
Byeta (The *Murder of Lidice*), 48

cabarets, 2–3, 6, 10, 137 n.1–2
Caesar (*Him*), 78–9
Calder, Lendol, 117
capitalism, 23, 89, 94, 102, 103, 105–6,
  110, 113, 114, 118, 124–7,
  129–30, 157 n.25
Caroll, Jane (The *Garbage Man*), 86–8,
  98–101, 114, 117–18, 130
Carr, Virginia Spencer, 129, 154 n.2–3,
  154 n.5, 155 n.7, 155 n.11
cars, *see* automobiles
Castello, Dan, 57, 148 n.15
celebrity, 6, 28, 49, 124–5, 128,
  160–1 n.43

Chauncey, George, 77–8
Cheney, Anne, 23
chorus girls, 4–6, 39, 79, 135
Churchill's, 2, 39
circus, 53–6, 56–63, 72–3, 148 n.12–14,
  148–9 n.16, 149 n.17–19
  audience involvement, 60–1, 65, 67,
    72–3, 149 n.18–19
  movement, 58–9, 61, 149 n.17
  perfect acrobat, image of, 61–2, 63
  risk, 59–60, 61
class, 1–10, 14, 15, 19–20, 24, 38–41,
  42–3, 44–5, 50, 57, 66, 91–2,
  93–4, 98–101, 102, 109, 110–11,
  115, 118–19, 126–8, 140 n.17,
  149 n.23
Cohen, Milton A., 68, 71, 146 n.8,
  151 n.29
Cohn, Ruby, 129, 162 n.51
Cole, Barbara, 20, 145 n.17, 149 n.19,
  153 n.40
College Boy Bandits (*Fortune Heights*),
  90, 109, 110, 113, 119, 155 n.12
colonialism, *see* imperialism
Columbian World Exposition, 4, 80,
  151–2 n.32
Columbine (*Aria da Capo*), 22, 24,
  33–4, 37, 39, 44–7, 50–1
commedia dell'arte, 22, 44–6,
  145 n.17–18
community, *see* solidarity
complacency, 2, 30, 47, 100, 136
Coney Island, 15, 72, 78
conformity, 79, 87, 95, 100, 101–2,
  104
consumerism, 24, 34, 46, 50, 63, 77,
  97, 98, 104–6, 112, 115–17, 135,
  140 n.17
Cook, George Cram, 12–13, 77
Cook, James W., 152 n.33
Cook, Will Marion, 9, 139 n.15
Corydon (*Aria da Capo*), 34, 36,
  37–8, 46

Cothurnus (*Aria da Capo*), 22, 35–6, 38, 46–7, 51
Cotton Club, The, 10, 14
Coup, W.C., 57, 148 n.15
critical engagement, 16, 19, 27, 41, 45–6, 49, 55, 56, 62–3, 79, 135, 149 n.2
cubism, 22, 23, 56, 63, 67, 80, 148 n.12, 151 n.29
Cummings, E.E., 1, 2, 14–20, 53–84, 133–6, 146 n.1–2, 146 n.6, 146 n.8
&, 54, 146 n.3
XLI Poems, 54, 146 n. 3
Acrobats, 61, 68
"Adult, the Child, and the Circus, The," 55, 58, 61–2, 65, 72, 148 n.11, 149 n.21,
"Buffalo Bill's," 54, 146 n.5
CIOPW (Charcoal, Ink, Oil, Pencil, and Watercolor), 149 n.20
Complete Poems, 54, 62
Danseuse "Égyptienne", 80
Enormous Room, The, 54, 146 n. 4, 152 n. 34
Him (1927), 16–20, 53–84, 146 n.7–8, 147 n.9–10, 150 n.27, 152–3 n.36, 154 n.43
"sh estiffl," 75–6
Small's, 17
Tulips & Chimneys, 54, 146 n.3–4
"You Aren't Mad, Am I?", 55
Curtiss, Glenn, 121, 124

dance craze, 3
dancers, cootch, 4, 65, 80
Davis, Janet M., 58, 60, 72, 148 n.14, 150 n.24
Death (*The Garbage Man*), 87–8
debt, 16, 90, 104, 105, 109, 111, 116–17, 130, 135
dehumanization, 86, 87, 89, 109, 110, 126, 128, 129

Dell, Floyd, 12, 22–3, 50
Angel Interludes, The, 22
Dennett, Andrea Strulman, 150 n.25
Dial, 54, 81, 149 n.18
dime museums, 64, 148 n.15, 150 n.25, 152 n.32
Dos Passos, John, 1, 2, 85–131, 135–6, 154 n.2, 154 n.5, 157 n.20, 162 n.50
42nd Parallel, The, 97, 104–5, 130, 157 n.24, 158 n.32, 160 n.40
1919, 115
Airways, Inc., 86, 88–9, 94, 96, 97, 101–8, 117, 120, 124–8, 129–30, 155 n.8–11, 158 n.29, 158 n.31, 159 n.34
Big Money, The, 96–7, 118, 119, 124, 127–8, 160 n.40
"Facing the Chair: Story of the Americanization of Two Foreignborn Workmen," 96, 157 n.22
Fortune Heights, 16, 86, 89–90, 94, 108–14, 115, 117, 118, 119–20, 128, 129–31, 155–6 n.12, 159 n.35–6
Garbage Man, The (Or The Moon is a Gong), 16–17, 86–8, 94, 98–101, 117–18, 129, 130, 155 n.7, 158 n.27, 162 n.49
"Pit and the Pendulum, The," 95, 97, 157 n.22
Suburb, The, see *Airways, Inc.*
Three Plays, 15, 129, 154 n.3, 162 n.49
U.S.A. trilogy, 94, 96–7, 105, 108, 118–19, 127–8, 130, 157 n.19, 160 n.40
Douglas, Ann, 121, 124, 151 n.13
Dumenil, Lynn, 162–3 n.2
Dunbar, Laurence, 9, 139 n.15

Eastman, Max, 22
Ellis, Charles, 22

English, Mary C., 147 n.9
entertainment culture, 8, 15, 24, 38, 47, 51, 111, 137–8 n.6, 140 n.17, 162 n.2
Erenberg, Lewis A., 3, 4, 39, 137, n.1
eroticization, 19, 28, 56, 67–8, 80, 83
escapism, 1, 3, 7–8, 16–18, 22, 25, 33, 39, 49, 51, 105, 114, 134, 135, 140 n.17
Essert, Emily, 149 n.22
etiquette, 24, 38–50, 66, 149 n.23
  and class, 38–41, 42–3, 44–5, 66
  and fine dining, 38–9
  and sociopolitical engagement, 41, 45–7
  and superficiality, 43–4
eugenics, 9, 93
excess, 4, 18, 22, 25, 31–4, 41, 43–4, 87, 100
exoticization, 1, 4, 9, 64, 67, 80, 137–8 n.6, 151–2 n.32
expressionism, 17, 141 n.23

Fahy, Thomas, 150 n.26, 152 n.33
fashion, 4, 24, 69, 135, 142 n.3
Fava, Antonio, 44–5, 47
Fearnow, Mark, 12, 140 n.18
film, 6–8, 79, 138 n. 9–11, 161 n. 44
Fogelson, Robert M., 92, 93, 100, 110, 158 n.30
Foley, Barbara, 97, 157 n.19
Folies Bergère, 2, 137–8 n. 6
Follies, 4, 6, 15, 59, 69, 74–5, 137 n.5, 138 n.6
food, 24–8, 30–8, 49, 143 n.6–7
  and conservation, 25–7, 33–4
  and dieting, 28, 143 n.7
  and imperialism, 37–8, 49
  and over indulgence, 31–2, 33–4
  and propaganda, 27–8, 34–7, 143 n.6
  and sexual desire, 30, 31
  and social liberation, 30, 31
  and sociopolitical disengagement, 32–3

Food Administration, 18, 25, 26–8, 33–4, 39, 51, 143 n. 7
Ford, Henry, 115–16, 118, 140 n.17, 159–60 n.37, 162–3 n. 2
freak shows, 64–73, 150 n.25–6, 150–1 n.8, 154 n.43
  audience involvement, 65
  performers, 72–3, 150 n.25
free love, 28, 30, 147 n.8
French, Mary (*The Big Money*), 96–7
Friedman, Norman, 59–60,146 n.8, 152–3 n.36
futurism, 151 n.29

gaze, 60, 64, 69
gender, 2, 20, 28, 30–1, 42–3, 77–9, 91, 98, 99–100, 101, 106–8, 112–14, 130, 144 n.16, 158 n.28
Gershwin, George, 9, 139 n.15
Gilpin, Charles, 13
Ginsberg, Allen (*Howl*), 30
Glaspell, Susan, 12, 22, 77
  Trifles, 12
  Suppressed Desires, 12, 77
Goldberg, Walter (*Airways, Inc.*), 89, 97, 103–4, 107–8, 126–7, 157 n.25
Gordon, Marsha, 143 n.6
Grabher, Gudrun M., 151 n.29
Graziano, John, 139 n.15
greed, 22, 35–6, 38, 50, 51, 79, 109, 110–11, 113, 118, 125
Greenwich Village, 11, 12, 14, 15, 22–4, 25, 31, 32–3, 38–9, 42, 45, 48, 54, 78, 88
Gregory, James N., 151 n. 31
Griffith, W. D. (*The Birth of a Nation*), 7–8
Grigsby, John L. 160 n. 41

Hammerstein, Oscar, 9–10
Harlem, 10, 15, 78, 121
Harlem Renaissance, 71
Harris, Neil, 141 n.20, 148 n.15

Index

Harris, Richard, 93, 156 n.17
Hemingway, Ernest, 59, 60
  Sun Also Rises, The, 59
Heydrich the Hangman (*The Murder of Lidice*), 48
Him (*Him*) 54–6, 60–3, 65–70, 79, 83, 150 n.27, 154 n.43
home ownership, 85, 88, 89, 90–1, 93, 94, 98, 104–5, 107–8, 108–9, 110–11, 112, 114, 120, 127–8, 130–1, 135, 136, 159 n.34
homosexuals, 77–9, 136, 153 n.40
Hoover, Herbert, 26, 27
Hounshell, David A., 116, 159–60 n.37
hunger, 30–2, 34, 38, 41, 47–8
Hunter, Owen (*Fortune Heights*), 89, 90, 108, 109, 110–11, 112, 114, 118, 119, 120
Hutchinson, A.S.M. (*If Winter Comes*), 78–9
Hutchinson, James L., 57
Huyssen, Andreas, 16, 141 n.22

Ibsen, Henrik, 44, 144–5 n.16
immigrants, 7, 58, 71, 95–6, 101, 103, 156 n.17
imperialism, 35–8, 49, 129, 135, 195 n.36
industrialization, 86–7, 88, 92–3, 98–9, 104, 125–6
industry, 27, 48, 55, 77, 99, 125–6
isolation, 54, 61, 102, 108, 114

Jackson, Kenneth, 92, 93, 97, 108, 116, 156 n.13, 156 n.1, 160 n.38–9
jazz, 3, 9–10, 15, 17, 19, 71, 73, 87, 98–9, 139 n.14
Jazz Singer, The, 8, 138 n.11
Jerving, Ryan, 158 n.27
Jewishness, 103–4, 109
Johnson, William Henry, 65, 72–3, 152 n.34
Jolson, Al, 8, 138 n.11

Jones, Ellery (*Fortune Heights*), 90, 110–11, 112, 113, 119, 120
Jones, Jacqueline, 156 n.15
Jones, Robert Edmond, 12, 140–1 n.19
Jurca, Catherine, 98, 157 n.26

Kaiser, Jo Ellen, 47–8
Kammen, Michael, 141 n.20, 142 n.24, 152 n.35
Kasson, John, 40, 80
Kennedy, Richard S., 53, 146 n.1–2, 146 n.4, 146 n.6–8
Kern, Jerome, 9–10, 139 n.15
Kidder, Rushworth M., 63, 68, 151 n.29
Knox, George, 155 n.8–9, 162 n.48

Langner, Lawrence, 140 n.18
Latham, Angela J., 153 n.37
Lawson, John, 17, 129, 147 n.10, 155 n.8, 158 n.27, 162 n.50
Lawyer, James, 50
Leinwald, Gerald, 117, 124, 156 n.16, 157 n.21
Leisure culture, 140 n.17, 141 n.20, 162–3 n.2
  see also entertainment culture
Lerner, Michael A., 4, 137 n.3–4
Lévi-Strauss, Claude, 40
Levine, Lawrence W., 139 n.14, 141 n.20
Levinstein, Harvey A., 26, 39
Lewis, Robert, 93, 156 n.17
Lewisohn, Alice and Irene, 11
Liberal Club, The, 11
Lindbergh, Charles, 88, 122–4, 124, 130, 160 n.43
Little Egypt, 4, 80
Little Theater Movement, 1, 2, 11–17
Lott, Eric, 70
Lubin, David M., 161 n.45
Ludington, Towsend, 86, 154 n.2, 154 n.6, 157 n.24

macaroons, 33, 44, 144 n.16
Maik, Thomas A., 23

mainstream culture, *see* popular culture
manners, *see* etiquette
Marin, John, 68, 151 n.30
Markham, Pauline, 75, 153 n.38
Marks, Barry A., 153 n.39
Marsh, Margaret, 92, 93, 156 n.17, 158 n.28
mass culture, *see* popular culture
Masses, The, 15, 22, 23
materialism, 1, 2, 7, 16–18, 30, 86, 90, 111, 115, 119–20, 127, 130, 136
Maurer, Robert E., 149 n.22
May, Henry F., 137 n.2, 142 n.2
McCarthy, Tom, 115, 116
McCreary, Mac (Fainy), 104–5, 130
McEntee, Ann Marie, 137–8 n.6
Me (*Him*), 54–6, 60–1, 65, 67, 69–70, 79–81, 83, 150 n.27, 154 n.43
melodrama, 7, 8
Merwin, Ted, 139 n.13
Milford, Nancy, 21, 22, 23, 33, 41, 50, 144 n.14, 145 n.19–20
Millay, Edna St. Vincent, 1, 2, 14–20, 21–51, 83, 95, 135–6, 142 n.3–4, 143–4 n.9–11, 145 n.19, 157 n.20
 Aria da Capo, 16, 18, 22, 21–5, 27, 32–8, 39, 44–51, 142 n.4, 144, n.10–11
 Feast, 30
 Few Figs from Thistles, 30
 Food, 42
 Hardigut, 41
 Harp-Weaver and Other Poems, The, 30
 "Macdougal Street," 42
 Murder of Lidice, The, 47–9
 Princess Marries the Page, The, 31–2, 50
 "Recuerdo," 30, 32, 33, 51
 "'Say Shibboleth': a Dialogue between a Sentimental Citizen and An Advertising Expert," 27, 35
 Two Slatterns and a King, 42–3

Minksy Brothers, 70, 75
minstrelsy, 10, 16, 59, 60, 69–71, 73–4, 133, 134, 135, 139 n.15
misogyny, 106–8, 109, 112–13
 see also gender
Model T, 115–16, 119
 see also automobiles
modern life, 54, 58, 73, 83, 87, 92
modernism, 16, 53
modernist art, 15, 18, 23–5, 33, 50, 53, 55, 58
modernist drama, 16–17
Moi, Toril, 144–5 n.16
moving pictures, *see* film
Murphy, Brenda, 8, 12–13, 33, 144 n.12
Murray's Roman Gardens, 2, 3
Mussolini, Benito, 79, 133

Nasaw, David, 6, 139 n.15, 140 n.16, 141 n.21,
Neighborhood Players, 11–12
New Masses, The, 88
New Playwrights Theatre, 88, 89, 129, 162 n.48
New Woman, 23, 30, 103
New York, 1–10, 86, 87, 94, 116, 121, 122, 126
Nichols, Ann, (*Abie's Irish Rose*), 8–9, 139 n.13
nickelodeons, 6, 7, 8, 138 n.8
Nicolaides, Becky M., 91
Nicoll, Allardyce, 145 n.18
Norton, Morry (*Fortune Heights*), 89, 90, 109, 112–13, 118, 120
nudity, 74–5

O.Him (*Him*), 55, 70, 71, 77
O'Neill, Eugene, 12, 13, 17, 22, 59, 86, 140–141 n. 19
 Beyond the Horizon, 13
 Bound East for Cardiff, 12
 Emperor Jones, The, 13

Great God Brown, 59
Hairy Ape, The, 13, 86
Other Players, 42, 144 n. 15

Palace Theater, 138 n.7
Patinkin, Sheldon, 137 n.5
patriotism, 27, 39, 79, 85, 98, 126, 128
Patton, John Joseph, 143–4, n.9–11
Peiss, Kathy, 140 n.17, 141 n.20, 162–3 n.2
picture palaces, 1, 7–8, 138 n.11
Pierrot (*Aria da Capo*), 22, 24, 33–5, 37, 39, 44–7, 50–1
Pisano, Dominick A., 121, 160 n.42, 161 n.44
Pizer, Donald, 158 n. 32, 161–2 n.47
Players, The, *see* Provincetown Players
Poggi, Jack, 8, 11, 13, 14, 138 n.12, 141 n.19
Ponce de Leon, Charles L., 160–1 n. 43
popular culture, 2–10, 22–5, 32–3, 43–5, 47, 49–50, 51, 53,54, 55, 56, 61, 111–112, 142 n. 24
  elite popular culture, 16, 18, 25
popular entertainment, *see* amusements, popular
Post, Emily (*Etiquette in Society, in Business, in Politics and Home*), 66
power, 4, 7, 17, 18, 23, 25, 27, 28, 30, 37–8, 39, 71, 73, 79, 80, 84, 101, 112, 127
Princess Anankay (*Him*), 67–8, 79–81
Prohibition, 3, 137 n.3–4
propaganda, 27–8, 34–8, 48, 51, 79, 85, 98, 145 n.21
prosperity myth, suburban, 1, 19–20, 86, 89, 90–1, 94, 104–6, 108–14, 120, 129, 130, 136
Provincetown Players, 2, 11–14, 22, 24, 31, 32, 33, 54, 81, 82, 133, 140–1 n.19, 144 n.11–13

Provincetown Playhouse, 15, 82, 140 n.18, 153 n.42
psychoanalysis, 55, 77

racial homogeneity, 9, 80, 92–3, 98, 101, 102–4, 114
racism, 7, 20, 58, 66–7, 69–73, 89, 92–3, 95–7, 99, 100–1, 103, 109–10, 130, 135
ragtime, 9–10, 53, 73, 98, 139 n.15
Raico, Ralph, 142–3 n.5
realism, 1, 10
Rector's, 2
Reed, John, 22–3
repetition, 18, 25, 36, 63, 140 n.17, 162 n.2
restaurant culture, 2, 5, 15, 16, 18, 25, 38–9, 40, 44, 135
restrictive covenants, 92–3, 100–1
Ringling Brothers, 53
Roberts, Helen Lefferts, 44
Robinson, Marc, 20, 150 n.27
Rydell, Robert, 151–2 n.32, 153 n.41

St. Clare, June, 75
Sacco and Vanzetti, 15, 88, 89, 94–7, 157 n.21
satire, 22, 24, 26, 27, 33–5, 41, 42, 45, 55, 66, 71, 72, 77, 79, 147 n.9
Savoy, Burt, 78, 153 n.40
science, scientists, 55, 64, 66, 72
Seldes, Gilbert (*The Seven Lively Arts*), 73, 152 n.35
self/other dynamic, 67, 81
selftranscendence, 73, 152–3 n.36
Showboat, 9–10
Shteir, Rachel, 6, 70, 74, 78
Shubert, Lee, 11
Sklar, Robert, 7, 138 n.8, 138 n.11
Sloan, Joan, 22
Slut (*Two Slatterns and a King*), 42–3
social conventions, 23, 30, 41, 43

social hierarchies, 56, 66, 67, 91, 101, 102, 135, 149 n.23
social mobility, 39–40, 91, 119
social status, 1, 19, 39, 46, 91, 104, 114, 119, 120
socialist philosophy, 22, 103, 104, 129, 158 n.32
sociopolitical disengagement, 2, 24, 33, 103, 120, 135
sociopolitical engagement, 16, 23, 24–5, 30–1, 41, 45–7, 48, 49, 88, 89, 90, 96–7, 103, 107–8, 110, 114, 120, 130, 158 n.32
Solidarity, 25, 48, 61–2, 66,110, 111, 119, 130, 155–6 n.12, 158 n.31
speakeasies, 3–4, 137 n.3–4
spectacle, 10, 19, 28, 45, 47, 55, 56–8, 60, 63, 66, 73, 77, 79, 83
speculation, real-estate, 90, 92, 101, 103, 105–6, 108–9, 110–12, 113, 117, 119, 126, 130, 159 n.33
Spirit of St. Louis, The, 122, 123
Stansell, Christine, 143 n.8
Stearns, Peter N., 143 n.7
strippers, striptease, 6, 54, 68, 75–6, 77–8, 80, 83
Stronge, William B., 159 n.33
suburbanization, 86, 88, 89, 91–7, 97–8, 102, 103, 104, 106, 108, 110, 113, 114, 116–17, 120–1, 125–6, 127, 129–30, 156 n.17, 159 n.35
suburbia, 16, 19–20, 89–91, 91–130, 156 n.14, 157 n.26, 158 n.30
and socialist theatre, 129–131
suburbs, industrial, 93, 98, 99
suicide, 78, 88, 102
superficiality, 43–4, 62–3, 66, 77, 78–9, 82, 99, 102, 135
Sward, Keith, 159–60 n.37

technology, 16–17, 19, 88, 91–3, 97, 114–20, 120–9, 130, 140 n.17, 142 n.24, 148 n.14, 156 n.18, 158 n. 31, 162–3 n.2
dehumanizing aspects of, 118–19, 128–9
theatre, hybrid (popular and formal), 17–18, 18–20, 50, 54, 55, 56, 61, 63, 68, 82–4, 147–8 n.10
theatre, noncommercial, 11–17, 129
Theatre Guild, The, 12, 140 n. 18
thirst, 30, 37–8, 45–6, 50
Thompson, Lydia, 75, 153 n.38
Thomson, Rosemarie Garland, 66–7, 150 n.26
Thyrsis (*Aria da Capo*), 35–6, 38, 46
Tidy (*Two Slatterns and a King*), 42–3
Times Square, 2
Tin Lizzie, 115
see also automobiles
Toll, Robert, 69, 74
Tomes, Robert, 41, 43
Trains, 17, 57, 87, 91–3, 117–18, 127, 128, 160 n.40
Transportation, 16–19, 91–3, 117, 124, 126, 127, 129, 142 n.24, 142 n.24, 156 n.18
see also automobiles and aviation
Turner, Claude (*Airways, Inc.*), 88, 101, 102–3, 104, 106–7, 126–7
Turner, Dad (*Airways, Inc.*), 88, 101–2, 104, 105, 106, 108, 126
Turner, Eddy (*Airways, Inc.*), 88, 101, 104
Turner, Elmer (*Airways, Inc.*), 88, 89, 104, 105–6, 124–6, 127, 128
Turner, Martha (*Airways, Inc.*), 88, 102–3, 104, 105, 106–7, 114, 126, 128

unconscious, 17, 77
urban life, 56, 58, 68–9, 83, 88, 91–3, 106, 112, 124, 130, 139 n.14, 156 n.18

Vanity Fair, 26, 27, 28
Vaudeville, 6
Vaughan, Christopher A. 151–2 n.32
violence, 22, 26, 37, 38, 44, 48–9, 68, 88, 89, 91, 102, 104, 112–14, 115, 135
Virgil (*Ecologues*), 30
Vogel, Shane, 10

Wagner, Linda, 101, 157 n.23
Walker, Cheryl, 28, 145 n.21
Walker, Julia A., 17, 141 n.23
war, 21, 22, 24, 25–7, 33–5, 37–9, 44, 47–9, 50–1
Warner, Sam Bass, Jr., 156 n. 18
Washington Square Players, 11–12, 140 n. 18
wealth, 1, 6–7, 18, 25, 30, 37, 39–41, 88, 100, 109, 110–12, 114, 128
Webster, Michael, 153 n.39
Weirds (*Him*), 62–3, 66, 67, 149 n.23
Weise, Andrew, 91
Wilson, Edmund, 33, 50
Wilson, Woodrow, 26, 51

Wodehouse, P.G., 9
Women, 4–6, 23, 24, 28, 30–1, 41–3, 56, 62, 67–9, 70, 74–6, 78, 79–81, 83, 99–100, 106–8, 112–14, 130, 134–6, 150 n.27, 153 n.37, 153 n.39, 158 n.28
   as sexual objects, 16, 19, 28, 56, 67–9, 74–6, 79–81, 83, 134, 136, 150 n.27, 153 n.37, 153 n.39
World War I, 23, 26, 50, 54, 92, 114, 121, 142 n.5, 143 n.6, 161 n.46, 142–3 n.5
World War II, 38, 160 n.39
Wright, Orville and Wilbur, 121
Writer's War Board, 38, 48

Yablon, A.ys Rho, 153 n.39

Ziegfeld, Florenz, 4–6, 59, 69–70, 74, 137–8 n.6, 153 n.37
   see also Follies
Zinn, Howard, 158–9 n.32
Zip, the What-Is-It?, *see* Johnson, William Henry

GPSR Compliance

The European Union's (EU) General Product Safety Regulation (GPSR) is a set of rules that requires consumer products to be safe and our obligations to ensure this.

If you have any concerns about our products, you can contact us on

ProductSafety@springernature.com

In case Publisher is established outside the EU, the EU authorized representative is:

Springer Nature Customer Service Center GmbH
Europaplatz 3
69115 Heidelberg, Germany

www.ingramcontent.com/pod-product-compliance
Lightning Source LLC
LaVergne TN
LVHW011827060526
838200LV00053B/3933